BLACK AMERICA SERIES

KINLOCH

MISSOURI'S FIRST BLACK CITY

GRAND DOUBLE

FREE. ALL ARE W

TO

Kinloch Park

ON LOCUST ST. ELECTRIC AND DOUBLE TRACK WABASH RAILWAYS.

ONLY FEW MINUTES RIDE FROM ST. LOUIS.

KINLOCH PARK

Points to Consider

At Kinloch Park you see an Electric Road in operation.

No proposed road.

No taffy to sell lots.

You actually see with your own eyes cars running all day long, 365 days in the year. They go to 6th and Locust Streets (Hare's Store).

You also have the Wabash Railway, which is noted for its splendid suburban service.

KINLOCH PARK

The Queen of Suburban Towns!

Where $70.00 Buys a Whole Lot.

on a BEAUTIFUL GRADED STREET, within a few hundred feet of Suburban Electric Railway.

$5.00 CASH. BALANCE 50c. PER WEEK.

NO INTEREST OR TAXES FOR TWO YEARS.

KINLOCH PARK

KINLOCH PARK

WATER IN THE STREETS! WATER IN THE STREETS!

KINLOCH PARK

PIPED FROM KINLOCH WATER WORKS.

Will have Electric Light in the near future, plant now being built.

Post Office, Express Office, Telegraph and Telephone Office, etc., at Kinloch Park.

You can buy anything you need in Kinloch Park.

SPECIAL OFFER.—To those building good Houses of five Rooms or more, I w... Head of Family free transportation daily for one year from Kinloch Park ... Houses to be erected within four months.

Many Fine Lots right on the Suburban Electric and on Beautiful Graded Streets and ... yard, for $70.00, $80.00, $90.00, $100.00 and upwards. Cars run all day long. **1000 Lots sold in the past five weeks. Follow the crowd. The great majority don't go wrong.** The Train Service is not surpassed by ... St. L...

KINLOCH PARK

OUR FREE SPECIAL TRAIN Leaves Union Station,

SUNDAY, JULY 14, 9:30 A. M., Returning at 12 M.
2:15 P. M., Returning at 6 P. M.

Via the Wabash Railway, Stopping at Ewing Avenue, Grand Avenue and Forsythe Junction for Passengers. ALL ARE WELCOME. No Children without Parents allowed.

The Great Kinloch Quartette and Jubilee Singers.

PHIL CHEW, 9 North ...

BLACK AMERICA SERIES

KINLOCH

MISSOURI'S FIRST BLACK CITY

John A. Wright Sr.

ARCADIA PUBLISHING

ISBN 978-0-7385-0777-4

Published by Arcadia Publishing
Charleston, South Carolina

Printed in the United States of America

Library of Congress Catalog Card Number: 00-107781

For all general information contact Arcadia Publishing at:
Telephone 843-853-2070
Fax 843-853-0044
E-mail sales@arcadiapublishing.com
For customer service and orders:
Toll-Free 1-888-313-2665

Visit us on the Internet at www.arcadiapublishing.com

DEDICATION

This book is dedicated to those who came to Kinloch seeking better lives and stayed despite almost insurmountable odds, to create a community of homes, businesses, places of worship, and education. It is a place of nurturing and friendship. Additionally, it is dedicated to the late Samella Woodson and Harriet Dezell, who helped the author gain insight and knowledge about the Kinloch Community. Also to Victoria Cothran, who willingly gave her time and unlimited access to the archives she has collected to the author for the publication of this book.

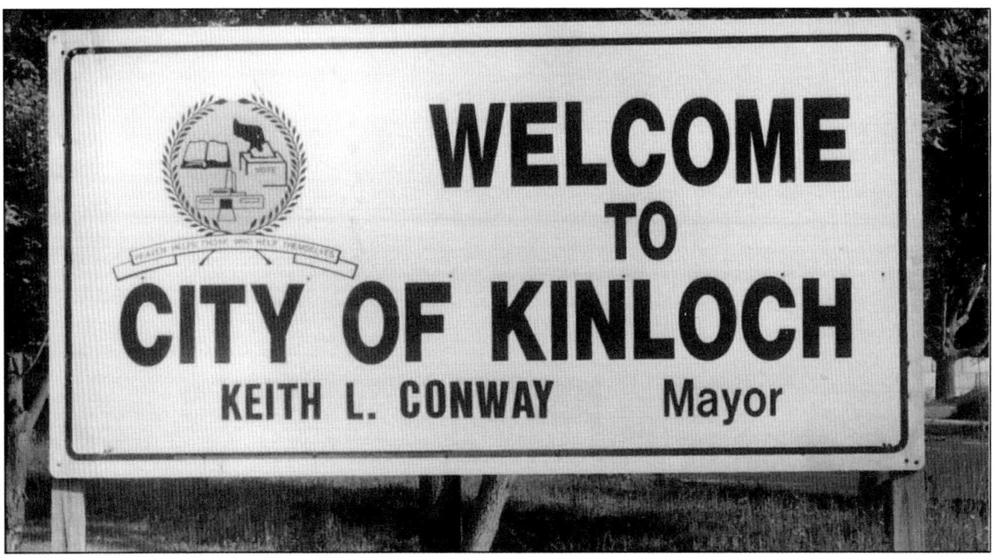

CONTENTS

ACKNOWLEDGMENTS

I would like to express a special thanks to Sylvester Smith, William Arnett, Hattie Stevenson, Dorothy Lewis, Yvonne Samuels of the *St. Louis Post-Dispatch*, Duane Sneddeker with the Missouri Historical Society, and Nancy Merz with the Midwest Jesuit Archives for their invaluable assistance and for being available for never-ending calls for assistance.

Thanks also goes to the following individuals and institutions for their help and support in making this book possible. The individuals are: Rev. James W. Atkins, Ann Boyd, Samuel and Bernice Boyd, Charlene Brown, Joy Burns, Audrey Clemmons, Yvonne Chatwell, Margarite Clay, Harriet Coleman, Wetona Coleman, Mayor Keith Conway, John Cothran Jr., Geneva Dalton, Charlene Earhart, Jean Ellis, Harold Gaskin, Kevin Kinder, Leola Henderson, Ruby Herndon, Sara Irons, Marion Holbrook, Rev. Ann MacDonald, Rev. Dr. Earl Miller, Rev. and Mrs. John Mitchell Sr., Vernon Mitchell, Peggy Murry, Lesie Oliver, Marquita Patton-Miles, Wiley Price, Elizabeth Rucks, Carol Scott, Alberta Squires, Edmond and Dorothy Squires, Lucille Walton, Betty Walls, Ernest and Verna Wells, Joseph Wells, Evelyn White, Charles Whitener, Howard Whitener, Pat Whitener, Frances ("Cookie") Whitfield, Claude Wilson, Nellie Batt Williams, and Sylvia A. Wright. The institutions are: Archdiocesan Pastoral Center, Berkeley City Hall, Ferguson-Florissant School District, Kinloch City Hall, Midwest Jesuit Archives, Missouri Historical Society, *St. Louis Post-Dispatch*, St. Louis Public Library, and the Urban League and YWCA of Metropolitan St. Louis. To those whose names should be included in this list but are not, please forgive me for the oversight. You know who you are, and I thank you, too.

INTRODUCTION

Kinloch, Missouri's first all-black city, which is located approximately five miles northwest of the city of St. Louis, was settled over one hundred years ago. The word "Kinloch" is a Scottish place-name derived from "kind a 'loch" meaning "at the head of the lake." One source indicates that the naming of the community was influenced by Major Henry Smith Turner who, prior to the Civil War, lived a short distance southeast of the area in Normandy. Turner was a descendant of a family named Kinloch that resided in his home state of Virginia.

Kinloch has a rich history and is credited for many firsts, such as: the first International Air Meet in America was held here, the first airmail letter was sent from here, and for the first time, a president of the United States (Theodore Roosevelt) flew in an airplane.

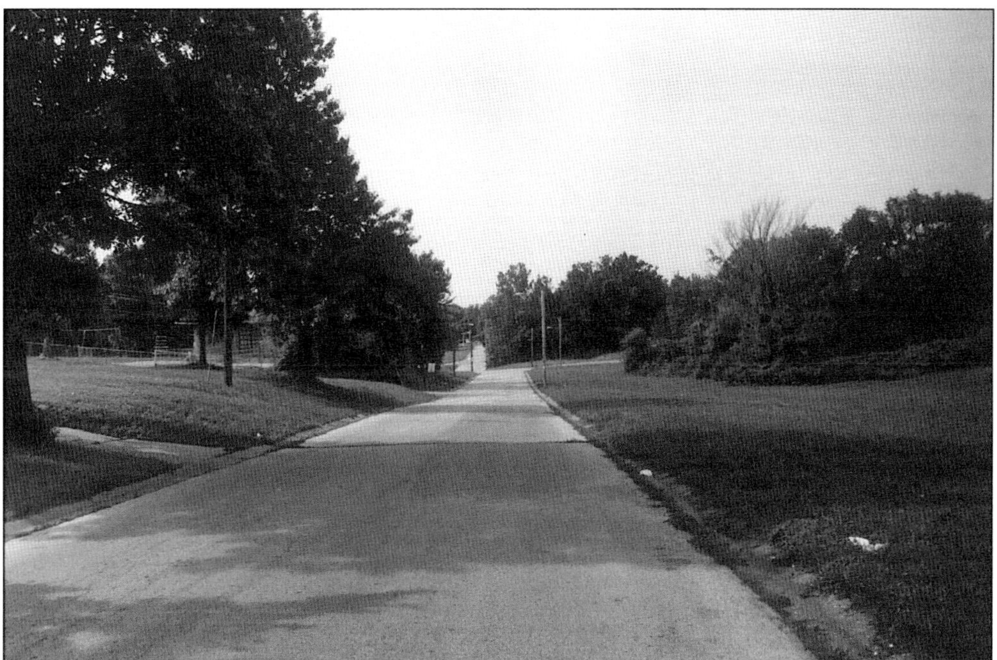

It was also at Kinloch Field where the first parachute jump was performed, a control tower was erected, an aerial photo was taken from a plane, meals served on a plane, and an animal (a cow) was airlifted. It was Kinloch that produced Missouri's first six black superintendents of schools and first black boards of education and Missouri's first black school board member. Kinloch is also credited with naming the first known school in America for President John F. Kennedy and being the site of the first black Catholic laymen's retreat center in the world. The community was also the home of the longest operating school for black students in St. Louis County, Dunbar Elementary School (1914–1975), the oldest continuing black parish in the St. Louis Archdiocese, Holy Angels (1924–present), and involvement in the first desegregation in America of three school districts through a court order.

In 1939 after several attempts, white residents were not allowed to establish a separate school district, so they established the separate community of Berkeley. The first order of business after incorporation of the new town was the establishment of a new school district. The newly-established community surrounded the black residents on three sides. On one side was a creek, another was a major thoroughfare, and the other a man-made barrier. The fourth side was bordered by Ferguson, Missouri. The black residents at that point were restricted from growth and confined to approximately 1 square mile, without a tax base. It eventually became one of the poorest communities in America. In 1965, the United States Congress added the Kinloch Amendment to a Senate Housing Act to enable the city to qualify for a sewer system.

This book documents Kinloch's history through pictures. It is the story of Kinloch's struggle and its fight for survival and attempts to provide a decent environment for its citizens, in spite of what some might call insurmountable odds. This is the story of a community where neighbors once all knew each other and looked after each other, where children grew up knowing they could be a business owner or an elected official, because they saw those role models every day. It is a place where doors once could be left open and crime was nearly non-existent.

The story of Kinloch is the story of a place in time that may never be repeated or found. The courts have made it possible for all citizens to purchase homes in almost any community their money will allow them. Schools are no longer segregated. This is not to say race and skin color is still not a factor in many aspects of life and business in St. Louis or America. These factors will play a role in the treatment of people of color for a long time to come.

The City of St. Louis is buying land and homes in the Kinloch community to make way for the expansion of nearby Lambert International Airport. Today, most of Kinloch looks as it must have looked one hundred years ago with fields of green grass and trees. This book will, hopefully, capture some of the community's rich history before it is gone forever.

One

The Beginning

Kinloch Park was developed in the 1890s as a commuter suburb for whites, though a small portion of land was reserved for blacks who came to work as servants. This early community boasted of having a golf and country club, an air field, and a horse racing track to serve its residents and visitors. Its developers also touted the fact that the area was served by both the Narrow Gauge Streetcar and the Wabash Railroad. Just how the black migration started is not clear, but it is reported that a Mrs. "B" and her husband purchased a piece of property through their friendship with the white owner. When neighbors discovered that the new owners were black, they immediately sold their lots and moved. Other white families would not move in. The lots were then opened to blacks. Within a few years, 30 or more black families came to occupy five or six blocks in the extreme southeast portion of the area, later to be called South Kinloch Park.

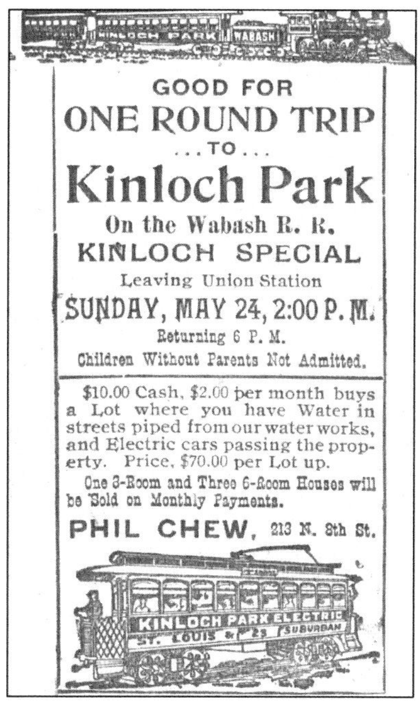

This railroad pass was *"Good for one round trip to Kinloch on the Wabash R.R. Kinloch Special, Sunday, May 24, 2:00 p.m., 1896, sponsored by Phil Chew."* (Copy Courtesy Missouri Historical Society.)

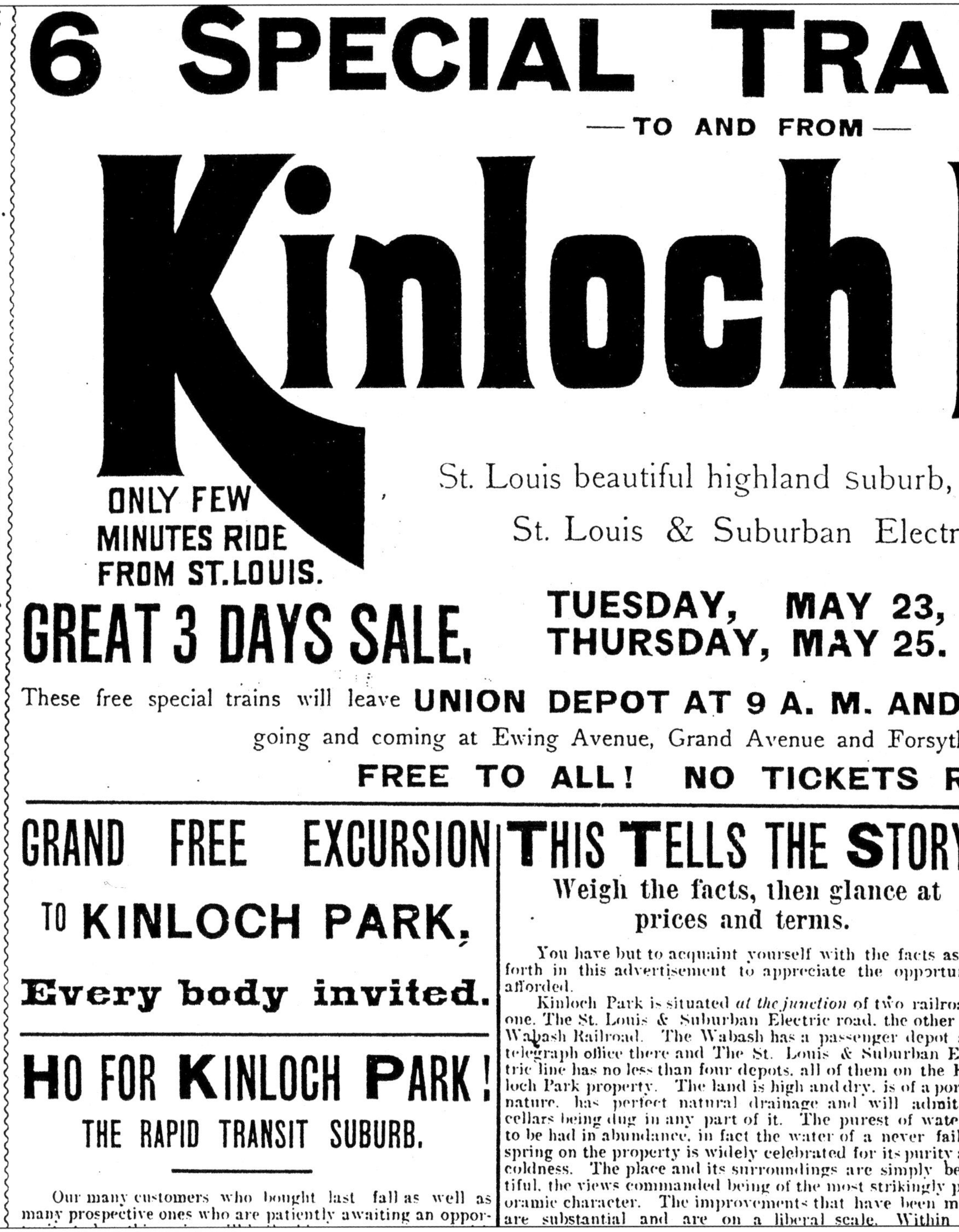

This advertisement is from an 1895 issue of the *St. Louis Suburban Journal* by the St. Louis Suburban Improvement Company to attract prospective white buyers. Phil Chew, the realtor for the area, promised: "To those building good houses of five

S FREE

ark

d at the Junction of the

way and Wabash R. R.

SPECIAL TRAINS EACH DAY FREE ON THE WABASH RAILROAD.

M. on above dates, and will stop both

n for passengers.

RED !

PRICES

FOR WHOLE LOTS,

$45, $50, $55, $60, $65, $70 EACH,

AND UPWARDS, ACCORDING TO LOCATION.

ink of it! whole lots at such prices in a place having such advantages.

TERMS:

)0 per lot at the time the property selected.

)0 more per lot on or before 9 o'clock n the evening of the next business day.

A RICH, PALATABLE PUDDING

Composed of "Absolutely Pure" Facts.

KINLOCH PARK has electric cars.
KINLOCH PARK has steam railway trains.
KINLOCH PARK has the advantages of two lines, it being situated at the junction of the St. Louis Suburban Electric and Wabash Railroads.
KINLOCH PARK has not only frequent, but also rapid transit car service by electric and steam railways to and from St. Louis.
KINLOCH PARK is the most easily and certainly reached of any of St. Louis' suburbs, and does not depend on only one line of railway.
KINLOCH PARK has the advantage of cheap car fares.
KINLOCH PARK has no less than four depots on the Suburban Electric line; and one on the Wabash Railroad.
KINLOCH PARK has rapid transit at all hours on lines that touch great manufacturing districts, and land passengers at the St. Louis post-office, the Union Depot and Franklin Avenue.
KINLOCH PARK is the merchant's, the clerk's and the workingman's suburb.
KINLOCH PARK, justly entitled "the rapid transit suburb," has solved the problem of cheap yet pleasantly situated healthful homes.
KINLOCH PARK has by far the best lots for investment for yourself or your children.
KINLOCH PARK affords the delicious quiet of the country, at the same time has electric and other cars at its doors.
KINLOCH PARK lots are offered at prices that defy competion in such high class, gilt edge property.
KINLOCH PARK has not only electric and steam railways, but also has post-office and telegraph office.
KINLOCH PARK has as many as six public parks within it.
KINLOCH PARK has a wide, central boulevard, with serpentine drive.
KINLOCH PARK has all its streets and avenues nicely graded.
KINLOCH PARK has a most charming and healthful situation.
KINLOCH PARK has as fine spring water as there is in the world.
KINLOCH PARK has perfect natural drainage.
KINLOCH PARK can never have a flood; is all high and dry, and is entirely free from mud at all seasons.
KINLOCH PARK has a title without flaw or blemish, certified to by August Gehner and Company.
KINLOCH PARK has lots at only $40 each, $45 each, $50 each, $55 each, $60 each, $65 each, $70 each and upwards according to location.

These facts all speak for themselves, proclaim its desirability as a place for residence and give positive assurance of the rapid growth of St. Louis' finest suburb.

HOUSES BUILT

AND PLANS FOR MANY.

Building has already begun and two houses have been completed by parties who used their own money. Many others who will build in the same way have had their plans drawn and are receiving bids from contractors, so within a few weeks the sound of the saw, the hammer and the trowel will be heard in all directions. We will lend you money to build with or build for you on very favorable terms.

rooms or more, I will furnish the head of the family free transportation daily for one year from Kinloch Park to the city and return." (Copy Courtesy of the 1983 Kinloch History Committee.)

ST. LOUIS POST-DISPATCH WEDNESDAY EVENING, JANUARY 24, 1917.

LOTS WHITE MEN BUY DOUBLED IN PRICE TO NEGROES

Realty Company Engages to Re-sell Sites in New South Kinloch Park Subdvision.

WANTS NEGOTIABLE NOTES

Unable to Use Negro Purchasers' Paper as Collateral—Company Officers Explain Plan.

While segregation of negroes in St. Louis is restrained by a temporary injunction in the United States District Court and the question is pending in the United States Supreme Court, it is being exploited in St. Louis County by a real estate company which is selling lots to negroes in South Kinloch Park at double the price quoted to white investors.

The Olive Street Terrace Realty Co. is selling 25-foot lots in the subdivision at an average of $150 to white persons and reselling them at an average of $300 to negroes, and is doing so well it has just moved from the Merchants-Laclede Building to larger quarters in the Boatmen's Bank Building.

Negro Subdivision Laid Out.

The company first placed on the market the Kinloch Park subdivision. Negroes applied for lots there, but the restrictions prevented sales being made to them. That suggested, officers of the company say, the plan of laying out a subdivision exclusively for negroes. Property adjoining the Kinloch Park subdivision, restricted to whites, was purchased, and South Kinloch Park subdivision, restricted to negroes, was put on the market.

Negroes bought readily on the terms of $5 down and $5 a month, but difficulty was encountered when the company wished to use the negroes' notes as collateral for bank loans. To get around that difficulty the plan of selling to whites and reselling to negroes was adopted.

This plan, as explained by officers of the company, is to sell a lot or group of lots to a white person, who makes a small cash payment and gives a note to cover deferred payments at $2.50 per month on each lot.

White Men's Notes as Collateral.

The notes of the white purchasers are accepted as collateral at the bank and are discounted by the company, which then undertakes to resell the lots at double the price, charging 10 per cent for its services. If a resale is made the white investor receives monthly payments from the negroes in double the amount of the white person's payments.

After a ... of the company had

Map Showing Kinloch Park's New Negro Subdivision and Its Relation to St. Louis

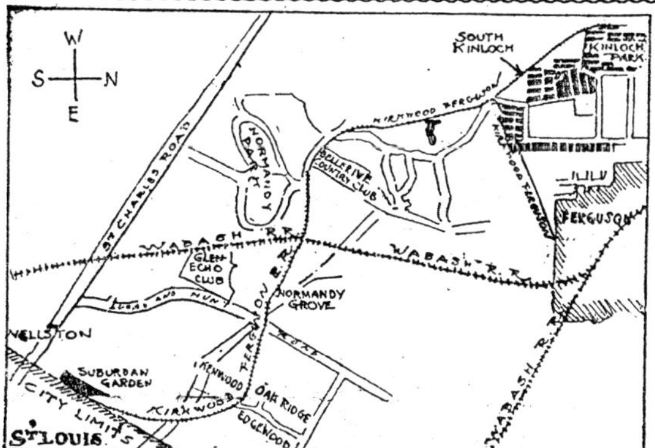

The lots to be sold to negroes are in South Kinloch Park, designated on the map by an arrow.

From *THE ARGUS*

This announcement has been running in St. Louis' principal negro newspaper.

White people who have bought more than one thousand lots in old Kinloch Park have been paying the same prices on the same terms as the colored people who have bought in South Kinloch Park. If there is any difference, the colored people have been getting the best of it, because South Kinloch Park is nearer the city and has better street car service.

The good colored people of South Kinloch Park have built themselves a little city of which they have a right to be proud.

More than a hundred homes, three churches, and a splendid public school have been built in the last few years.

And now we have something new that is going to mean a bigger and better South Kinloch Park.

We have been able to induce a number of white people of good standing to come in with us and co-operate with us—to help with their money, their influence and their good will to make South Kinloch Park a bigger and better place for the self-respecting negro to live and make his home.

We have given these people a big share of our profits in order to get their help because we believe it is for the benefit of everybody concerned.

We have always been ready to give land to the churches at a nominal price—because we believe they would help South Kinloch Park.

We have always been ready to give land to schools and public institutions at a nominal price—because we believed they would help South Kinloch Park.

And now we are giving land to a certain number of white people of good standing at a nominal price because we believe their money, their influence and their good will are going to help South Kinloch Park.

If you have any friends who have been thinking of buying, urge them to come out now, because there are bigger and better things in store for South Kinloch Park.

Olive Street Terrace Realty Company

This flyer, with articles from an African-American and white newspaper, was used by the Olive Street Terrace Realty Company to attract white investors. (Copy Courtesy of the 1983 Kinloch History Committee.)

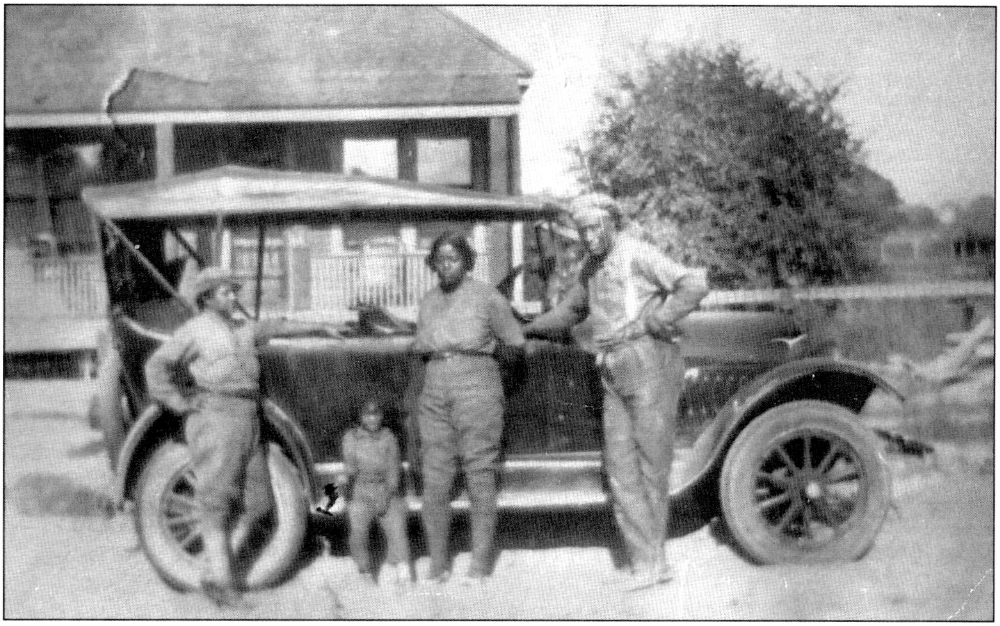

The Dezell family, early Kinloch residents, are pictured here outside of their home in South Kinloch Park. (Photo Courtesy of Harriet Dezell.)

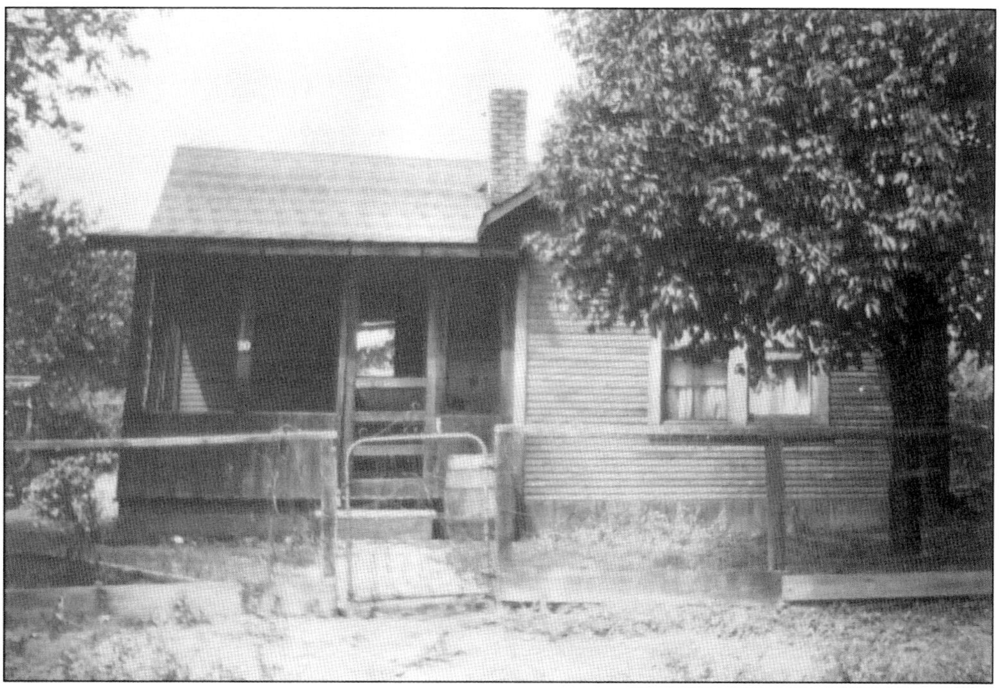

Pictured here is one of the 15 homes built by the Olive Street Terrace Realty Company on King Street. (Photo Courtesy of Carlson Oliver.)

ACTUAL EXPERIENCES

February 23, 1917.

Olive Street Terrace Realty Co.,
1403 Boatmen's Bank Bldg.,
City.

Gentlemen:

I have just received check for the first payment made to me by the negro who bought two of my lots. These lots cost me $325.00 and were sold inside of ninety days at a price that will net me over $600.00.

I am well pleased with the investment.

Yours truly,

(Signed) W. B. CRAWFORD,
1601 Locust St

February 19, 1917.

Olive Street Terrace Realty Co.,
Boatmen's Bank Bldg.,
City.

Dear Sirs:

I am very glad that you advised me to purchase lots in your South Kinloch Park Subdivision. Since making this investment a little over sixty days ago, two of my lots have been sold for just double what they cost me.

Your proposition is conservative and safe, as I consider these lots at one-half the market price, ample security. Sincerely,

(Signed) MRS. IDA E. GLADDING,
6012 Waterman Ave.

February 23rd, 1917.

TO WHOM IT MAY CONCERN:

Fortunately for me, I was given the opportunity to buy some lots in the negro subdivision of South Kinloch Park. Looked like would surely make money, if I had to hold them indefinitely.

Two of my lots were sold for me last week at double the price I paid.

Very truly,

(Signed) M. M. SEUFERT,
810 N. Fourth St.

February 19, 1917

To Whom it May Concern:

On December 6th, 1916, I bought lots six, seven, eight and nine (6, 7, 8 and 9) block two (2) of South Kinloch Park.

These lots cost me $550.00, and were sold for me by the Olive Street Terrace Realty Co. on Feb. 17th, 1917, for $1100.00, or just double what I paid.

The Company has made good their promises and I appreciate their service.

Yours truly,

(Signed) LURA M. GOCHENOUR
1715 Pierce Bldg.

WE HAVE MANY SUCH LETTERS

Miss Lura Gochenour felt like she wanted a larger income - there are so many additional comforts, pleasures and luxuries one can buy with a little extra money.

She heard of several people who had been making a great deal of money in something quite unusual in the way of a very profitable land deal.

So she tried it herself.

She paid $50.00 cash - giving her note for a small amount additional.

In less than 90 days she made a profit of $550.00 on a cash investment of $50.00

Read her letter on the back of this sheet - read the letters from others who had the same experience read the article from the Post-Dispatch.

Let us show you how it is possible to invest $50.00 cash and make a legitimate profit of $500.00 or $1,000.00 in a few months and at the same time help these people to get homes who need them and want them.

Give our representative a few minutes to explain the details of this unique plan.

Just sign and mail the card.

Yours very truly,

W C Ferris

President.

This document was issued by the Olive Street Terrace Realty Company to attract white investors to purchase land to sell back to black buyers, with a promise of making huge gains on their investment. (Copy Courtesy of the 1983 Kinloch History Committee.)

Pictured here are the owners of the Live and Let Live store, Ann Pollett-Smith and Leallie Smith. They came to Kinloch in 1916. Their son, Sylvester, was a graduate of the Kinloch School System who later became superintendent of the Kinloch School District. (Photo Courtesy of Dorothy Lewis.)

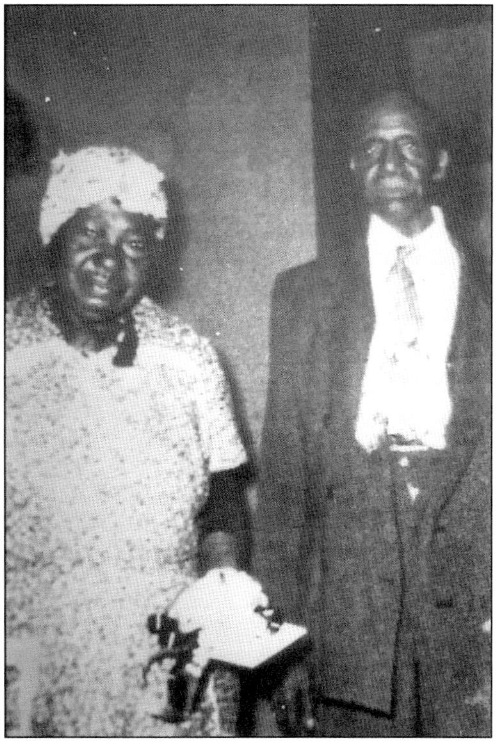

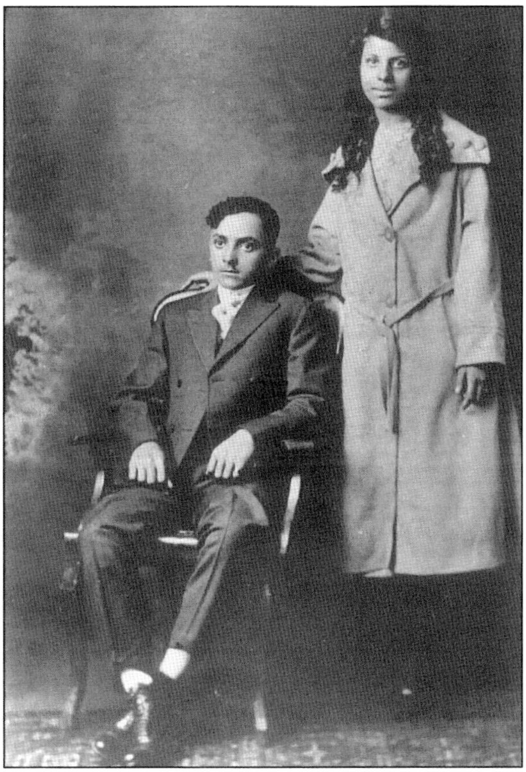

Theodore and Geneva Reed-Cothran, pictured here, came to Kinloch in 1915. Their children graduated from Holy Angels School. One daughter, Victoria, after graduating from college, returned to become the school's first lay principal. Another daughter, Delores, returned to teach at the school for over 39 years. Geneva was one of the pillars of Holy Angels Church, and an active community and civic leader. Theodore operated the Kinloch Market on Lix Street from the 1930s to the 1940s. (Photo Courtesy of Victoria Cothran.)

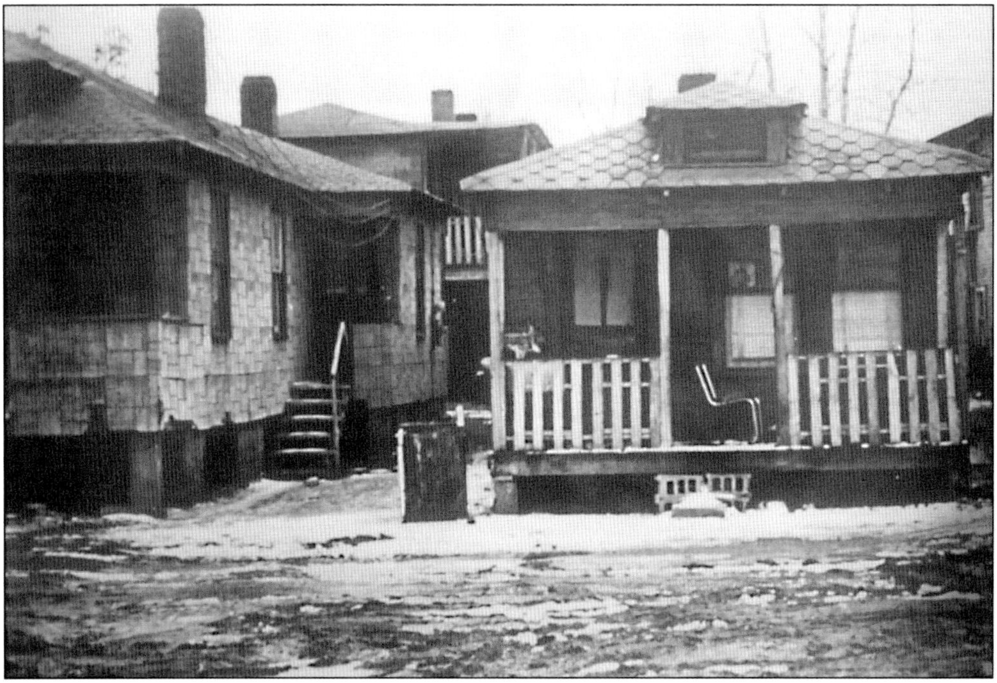

Pictured here is one of the early homes constructed in South Kinloch Park. (Photo Courtesy of Kinloch City Hall.)

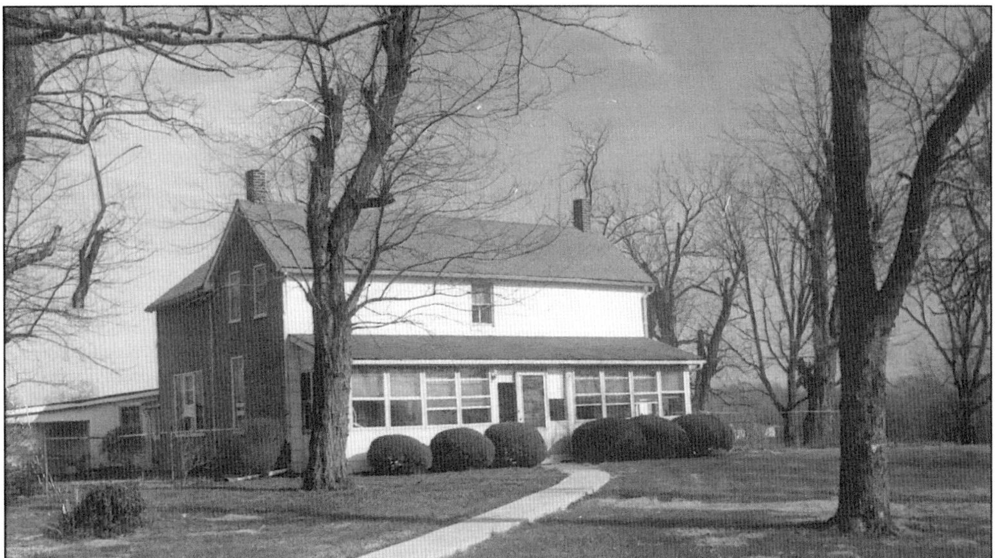

This home was built by the Behle family in the 1860s, and was later sold to John and Fannie O'Guinn. John was a very active member of the community and served on the land redevelopment committee. His son John Jr., a Kinloch High School graduate, served on Kinloch's Board of Education and was later the first black member to serve on the consolidated board of the merged school districts of Kinloch, Ferguson-Florissant, and Berkeley. (Photo by John A. Wright.)

Pictured here in 1924 are Theodore and Pearl Whitener with their first child, Howard. In 1935, they purchased a home located on North Evergreen in Kinloch for $5,000. Mr. and Mrs. Whitener remained in the community for over 50 years. The Whiteners were active members of Holy Angels Church. Their son, Charles, became Kinloch's first formerly trained police chief. (Photo Courtesy of Patricia Whitener.)

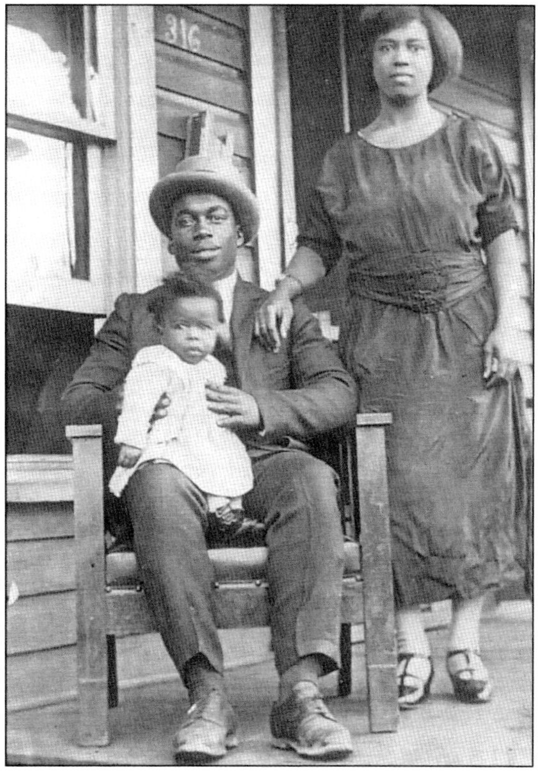

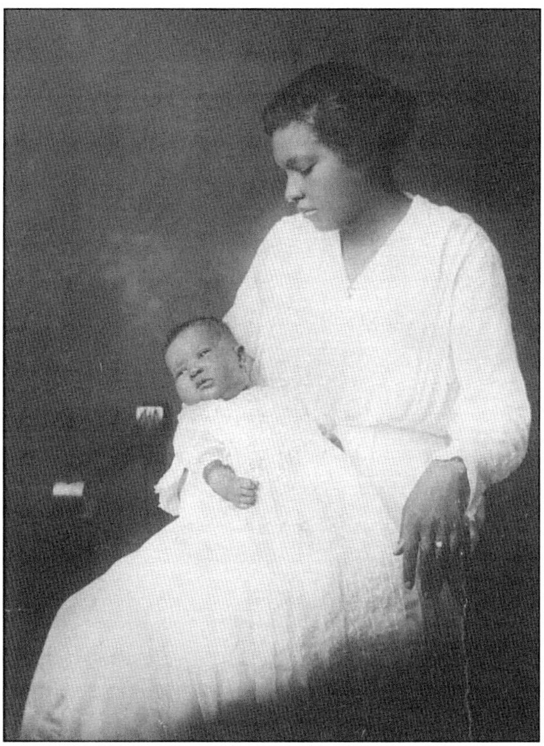

Lucy Simms with her daughter Margarite, pictured here, came to Kinloch in 1919 with her husband, Lawrence. Margarite became the first postmistress of the Kinloch Post Office under Civil Service. (Photo Courtesy of Margarite Clay.)

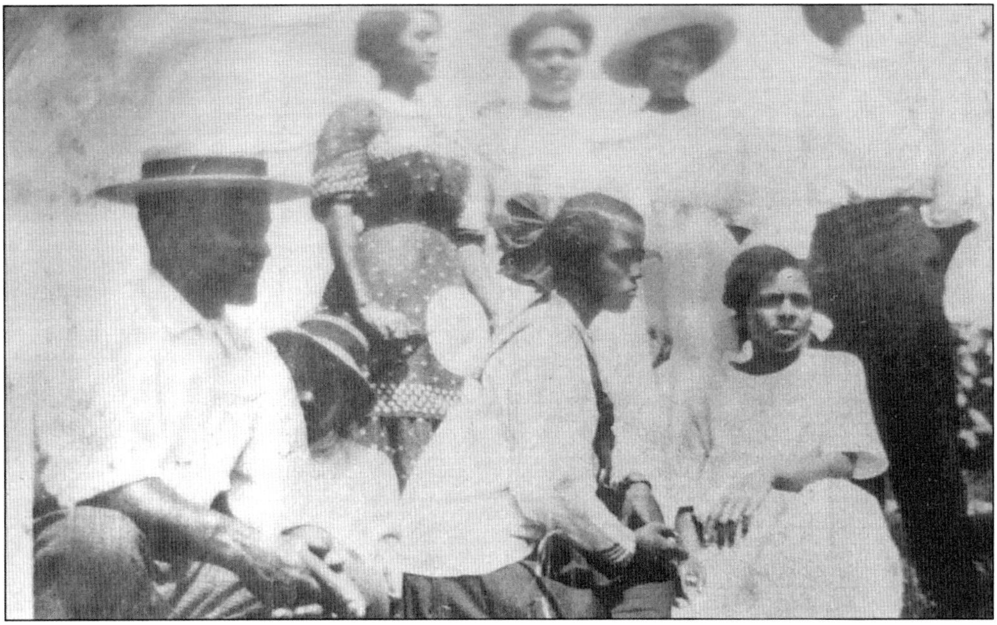

These early Kinloch residents were captured on film while enjoying an afternoon at Drake Park, which was located on Scudder Avenue between Evergreen and Jackson Avenues. The lot was called Drake Park because the side was next to the home of Willis Drake. (Photo Courtesy of Harriet Dezell.)

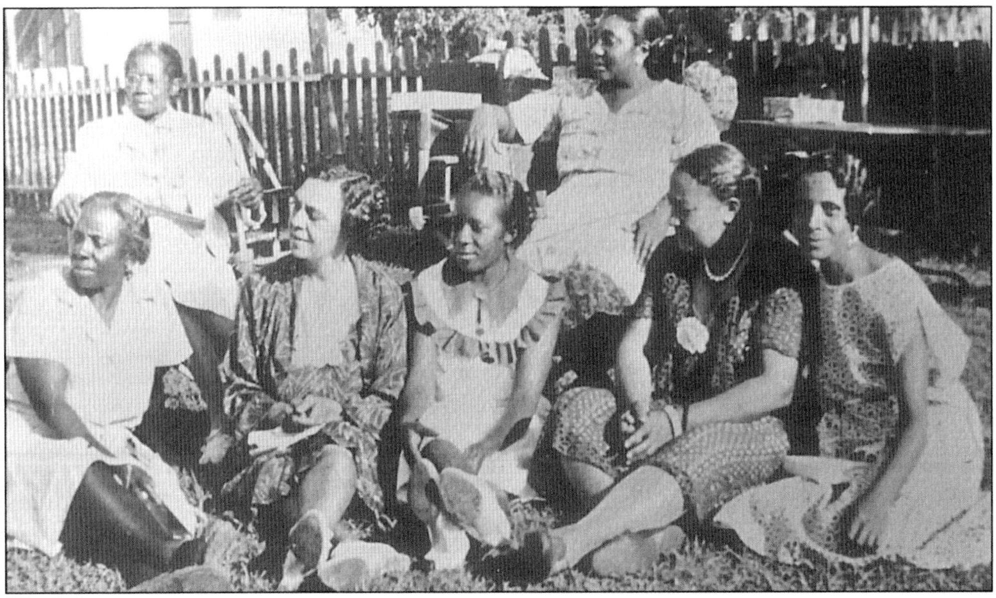

Pictured here are the ladies of the Casino Matrons Club, established in 1918. Its membership was limited to 12 who were considered "upper class" and engaged in business of some type, or had some kind of semi-professional afflictions. When asked if there was a vacancy among the membership to be filled, a member once explained "We may let you go around with us, see how you fit in (and) then we take you in." (Photo Courtesy of Victoria Cothran.)

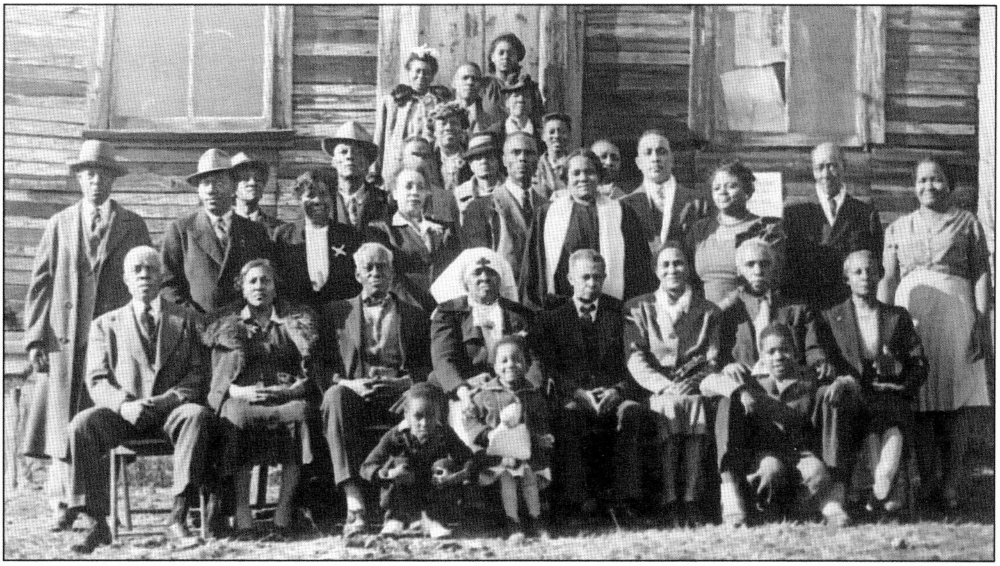

The members of Division 198 of the Universal Negro Improvement Association are shown here outside their headquarters on Warwick Street. This branch of the UNIA was established in the late 1920s with Elijah Woodson as chairman. The organization described itself as a "social-friendly, humanitarian, charitable, educational, instructional, constructive and expansive society." (Photo Courtesy of Samella Woodson.)

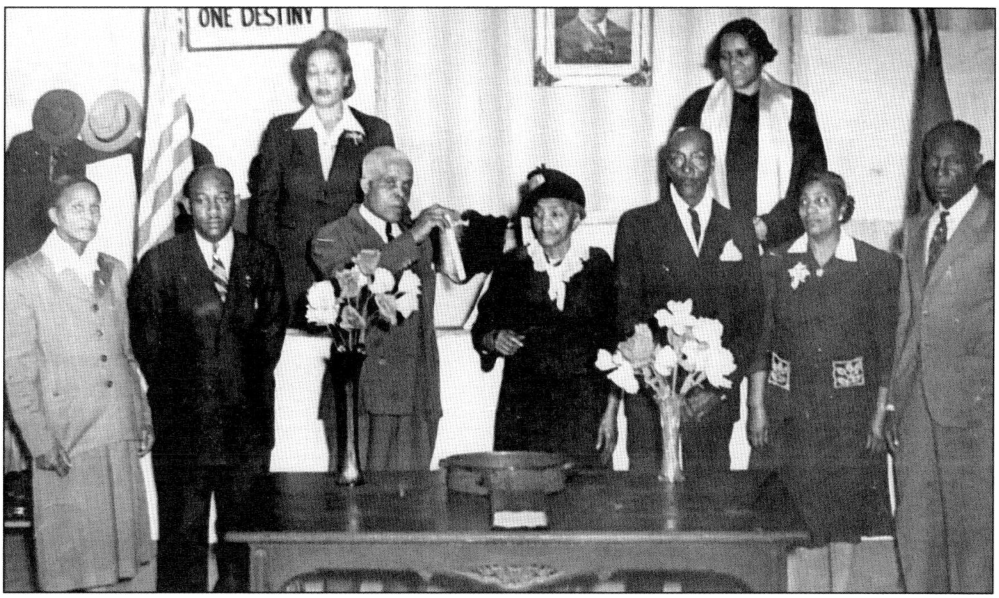

This picture was taken inside of the Universal Negro Improvement Association Headquarters, where members planned and worked to carry out the organization's objectives of promoting racial pride and love, support for an independent Africa, and the fostering of black-owned business. Early members included Octia Moss, Salmon Barrow, John Gray, Will Mullen, Jan Mullen, and Elijah Woodson, chairman. (Photo Courtesy of Samella Woodson.)

RACING at Kinloch

Opens August 17th.

Five or more races each day, rain or shine. The best horses in the West will compete

Stewards—Jas. H. Rees, chairman; Wilson P. Hunt, Chas. J. McLaran. Judges—Jos. A. Murphy, E. C. Hopper. Starters—Richard Dwyer, Jacob Holtman. Clerk of the Course—Jno. B. Dillon. The betting ring open to all reputable bookmakers. Wabash trains leave Union Station at 1 o'clock, 1:30, 2:00 and 2:45. From the foot of Olive street, 1:30 and 1:55. Returning trains 4 o'clock to Forsythe Junction and to the city immediately after the last race. Suburban cars run direct to grand stand.

ADMISSION, $1.00.

This admission ticket is for Kinloch Track. It was one of the locations for the popular sport of horse racing in the early part of the 1900s. An area magazine stated the following in a 1901 story: "It is conceded by everyone that the Kinloch Track is the fastest in the world, on account of its peculiar construction. Records were broken on it last season, and it was new. Since that time it has been roned, and this year it will be even faster than it was...." (Photo Courtesy of Berkeley City Hall.)

AERO CLUB OF ST. LOUIS

AVIATION GROUNDS
KINLOCH, MO.

ADMISSION TICKET A 10303

In case of no flights a black flag will be hoisted at the main gate and this ticket will be good for the next day

RETAIN THIS STUB

This admission ticket is for Kinloch Airfield, which took over Kinloch Track after horse racing was made illegal in the state. The first International Air Meet held in the United States took place at Kinloch Field in October 1910, and attracted many famous persons. Orville and Wilbur Wright brought their company's entire fleet of six planes to the meet. (Photo Courtesy of the 1983 Kinloch History Committee.)

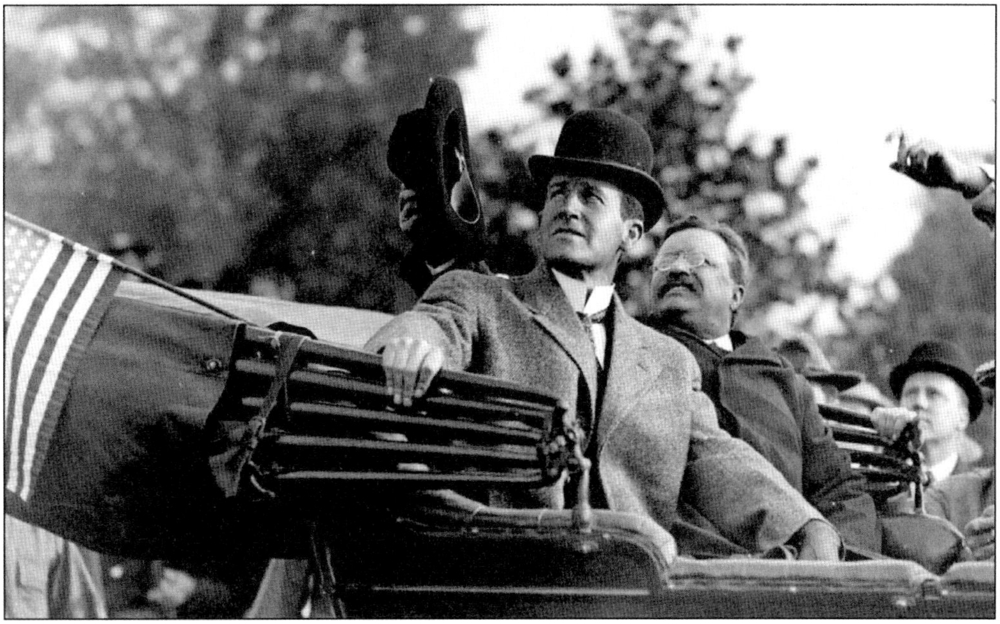

President Theodore Roosevelt was *en route* to St. Louis when he received the Aero Club's telegraphed invitation to visit the field and make a flight. He replied, "Will visit the field, but under no circumstances will I make a flight." This picture shows the president and Governor Herbert Hadley of Missouri looking at the planes flying upon his arrival at the field, October 1910. (Photo Courtesy of Missouri Historical Society.)

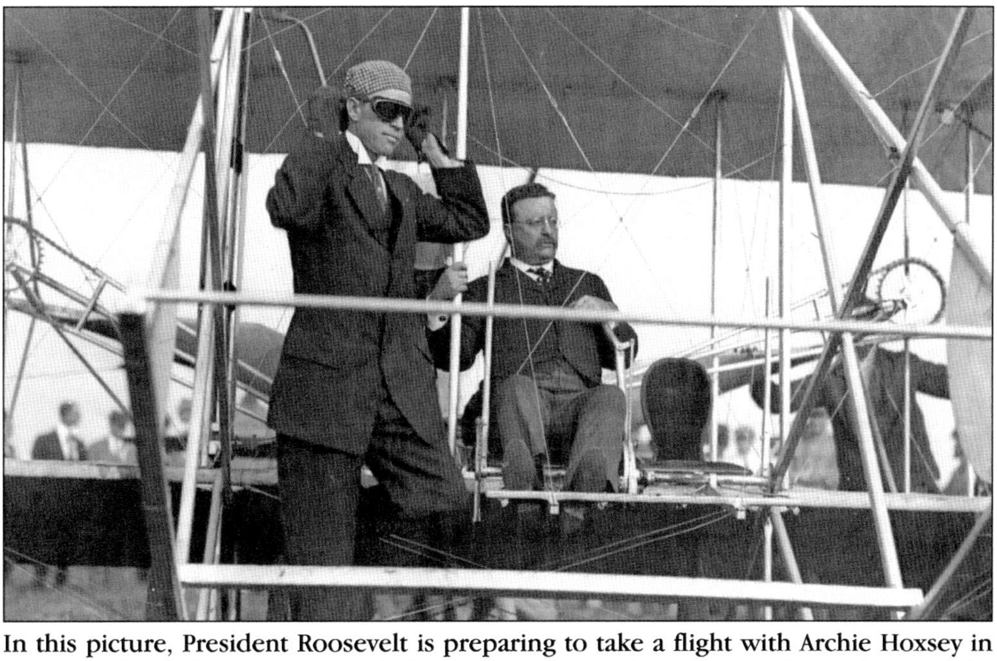

In this picture, President Roosevelt is preparing to take a flight with Archie Hoxsey in October 1910. He was taken aloft for three and a half minutes, and thus became the first president to fly in an airplane. News of the event made headlines around the world. (Photo Courtesy of Missouri Historical Society.)

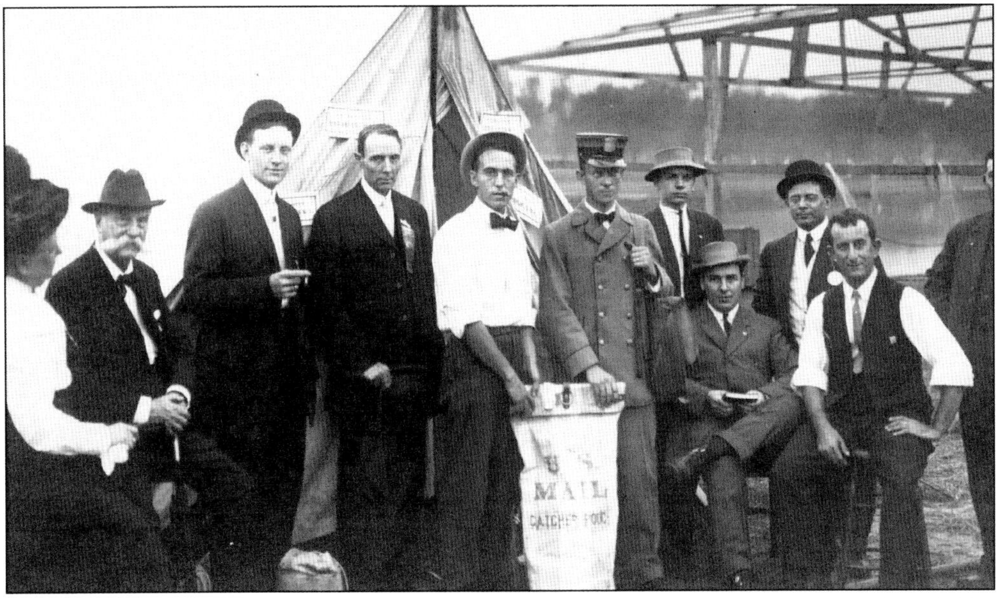

Shown here is a group at the U.S. Post Office's Aeroplane Station #1, at Kinloch Field in October 1911. Fourth from left is Walter Brookins, pilot; F.W. Hagemeyer, letter carrier; Harry J. Maher, superintendent of mails; and others who are unidentified. The mail, taken from Kinloch Field to Fairground Park, carried the official cancellation "Aero Plane Station No. 1...St. Louis." From Fairground Park the mail was taken to the St. Louis Post Office for sorting and distribution. (Photo Courtesy of Missouri Historical Society.)

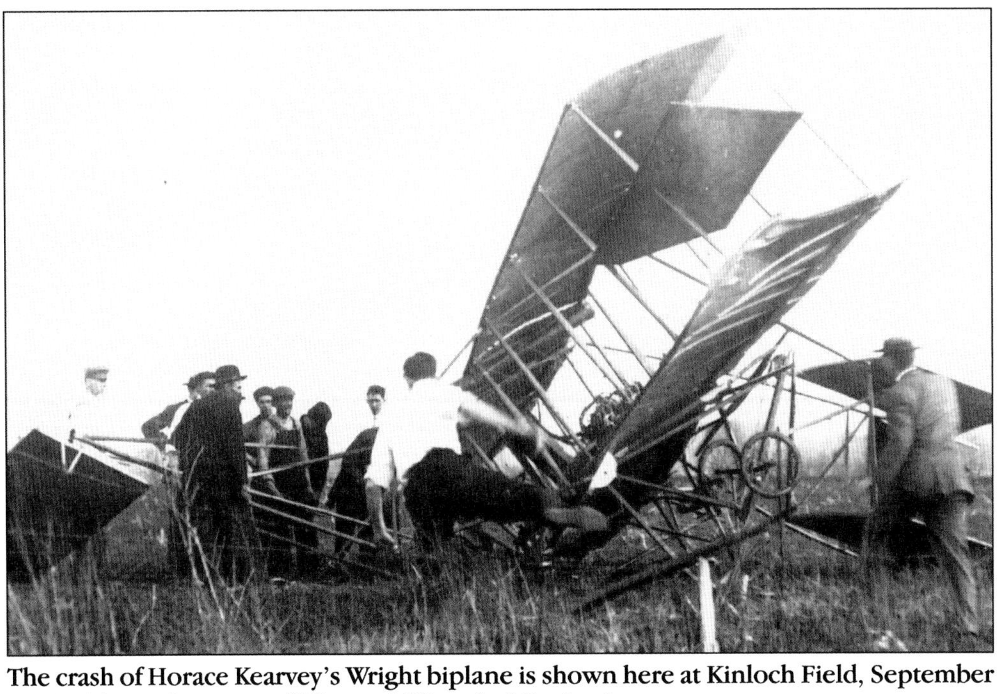

The crash of Horace Kearvey's Wright biplane is shown here at Kinloch Field, September 1911. (Photo Courtesy of Missouri Historical Society.)

Two

EDUCATION IN SPITE OF THE ODDS

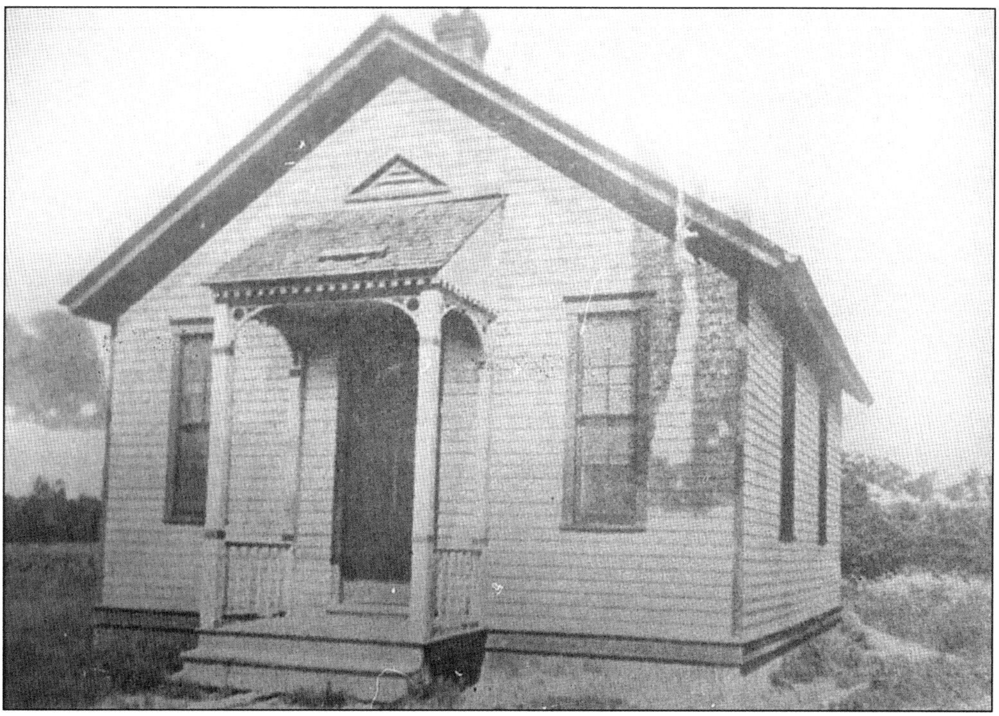

This one-room frame structure, known as Vernon School, was constructed in 1885 to serve the black students of the area. It was located on the east side of Florissant Road, approximately 100 yards south of Maline Creek. The school was closed after a few months when attendance dropped below the legally required number of ten students. (Photo Courtesy of Ferguson-Florissant School District.)

OFFICE OF
BOARD OF DIRECTORS OF
PUBLIC SCHOOL,
DISTRICT 3, ST. FERDINAND TOWNSHIP,
ST. LOUIS CO.

Copy

Ferguson, Mo., May 21, 1900.

Mrs Katie Rector
Teacher Colored School.
Ferguson Mo.

The Board in considering the last Months Reports respecting the attendance of the Colored school of this District find that the daily attendance is less than eight scholars. and under the circumstances must be closed in accordance with Sec. 9775 School Laws State of Mo. 1899. you will please turn over the Keys and Record Books to Prof W. D. Gro[illegible] Principal of the schools of this District.

Very respectfully
P. R. Wagner
Dist. Clerk.

Mrs. Katie Rector received this letter when the school's enrollment dropped below eight students. The correspondence was sent to request that she turn over keys to the building and her record book. Each time the school closed, the students would need to travel to the neighboring communities of Normandy, Carsonville, or as far away as Bridgeton. The location changed frequently, because these schools would also have low enrollment due to the sparse black population in the area. (Letter Courtesy of Ferguson-Florissant School District.)

Hillside, Mo.
Aug. 23, 1902.

Mr. P. R. Wagner:

Dear Sir:

I found the following children whose parents promised to send them regularly:

Frank Edwards ✓
Almeda Edwards ✓ (Virginia)
Edith Edwards ✓
Estella Hall see
Laura Edwards see
Mary Smith ✓
Mattie Wheeler ✓
Jessie Wheeler ✓
John Griffin ✓
Scott Thomas see
Ophelia Thomas see
Walter Clay ✓
Cornelia Clay ✓
Willie Clay see
Susie Simpson ✓

Several parents were not at home; those names I did not take.

Respectfully
Katie Rector

To insure a teaching position for the upcoming school year, Mrs. Katie Rector, writer of this letter, tries to assure the district clerk that there will be enough students for school to open. (Letter Courtesy of Ferguson-Florissant School District.)

This copy of the Ferguson School Board's official minutes, shown here, is from the board's 1902 annual spring meeting. At that meeting, white residents of the Kinloch area voted to split from the district and establish their own. Because of the inconclusiveness of the vote, a Board of Arbitration was appointed by the county superintendent of schools, which ruled the division a necessity. (Minutes Courtesy of Ferguson-Florissant School District.)

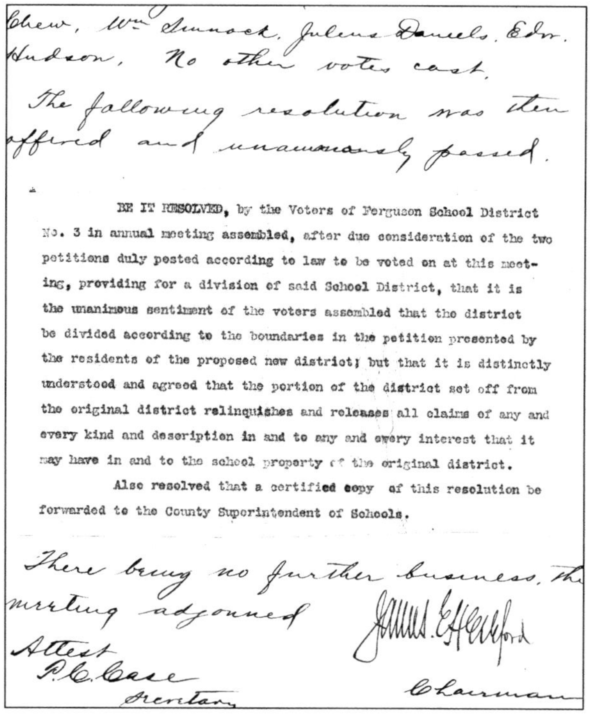

Chew, Wm Annock, Julius Daniels, Edw. Hudson, No other votes cast.

The following resolution was then offered and unanimously passed.

BE IT RESOLVED, by the Voters of Ferguson School District No. 3 in annual meeting assembled, after due consideration of the two petitions duly posted according to law to be voted on at this meeting, providing for a division of said School District, that it is the unanimous sentiment of the voters assembled that the district be divided according to the boundaries in the petition presented by the residents of the proposed new district; but that it is distinctly understood and agreed that the portion of the district set off from the original district relinquishes and releases all claims of any and every kind and description in and to any and every interest that it may have in and to the school property of the original district.

Also resolved that a certified copy of this resolution be forwarded to the County Superintendent of Schools.

There being no further business, the meeting adjourned

[illegible]
Chairman

Attest
P.C. Case
Secretary

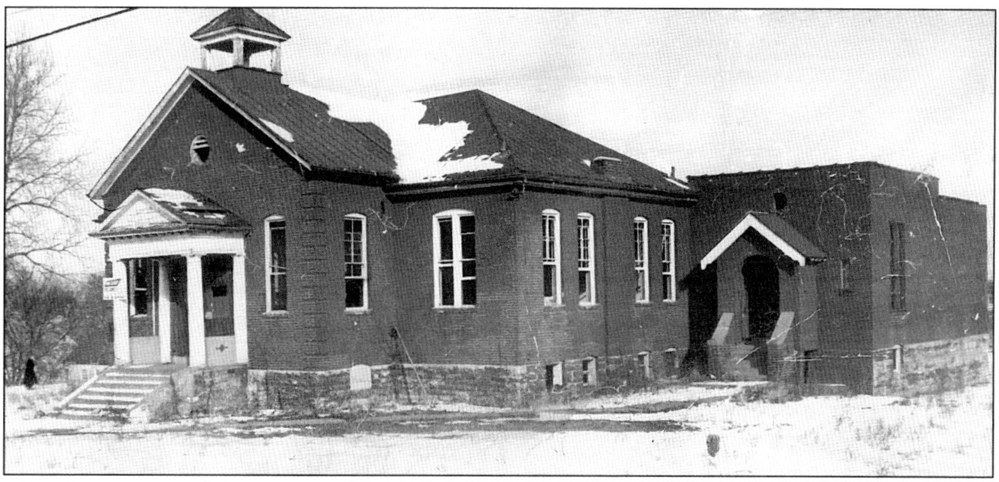

After formation of the new Kinloch District, the Nuroad School, (later named Hancock), shown here, was constructed for white students. Black students continued to attend Vernon School on Florissant Road in the Ferguson District until Nuroad School was completed. The students were then transferred to the former two-room school for white students on Scudder and Brown Road. (Photo Courtesy of the 1983 Kinloch History Committee.)

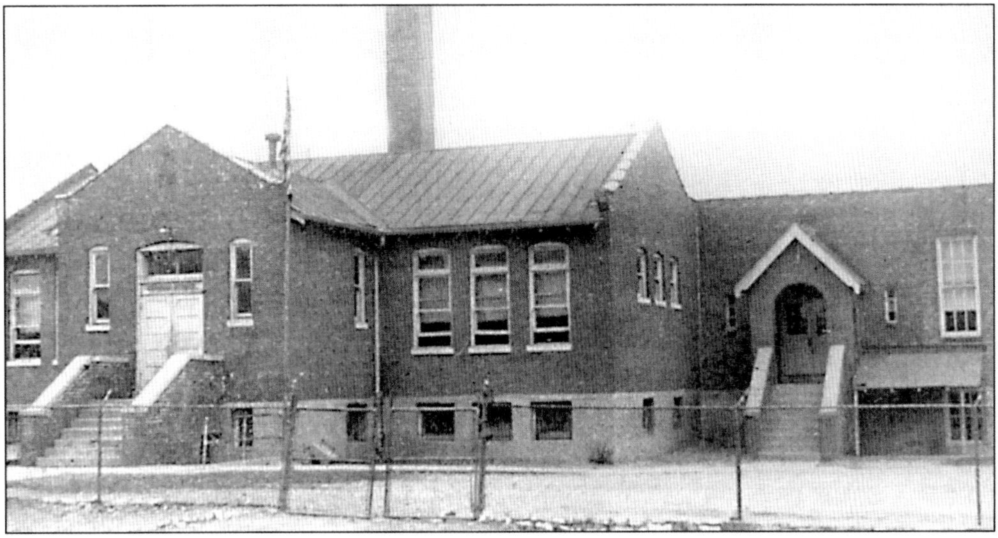

Shown here is the Kinloch School District's second new school, Dunbar Elementary, named in honor of the famous black poet Paul Lawrence Dunbar. The school was constructed in 1913, and dedicated the following year by Frank L. Williams, a former principal of Sumner High School in St. Louis. When the building opened in September 1914, children paraded from their Scudder Avenue School to the new facility to celebrate the event. (Photo Courtesy of the 1983 Kinloch History Committee.)

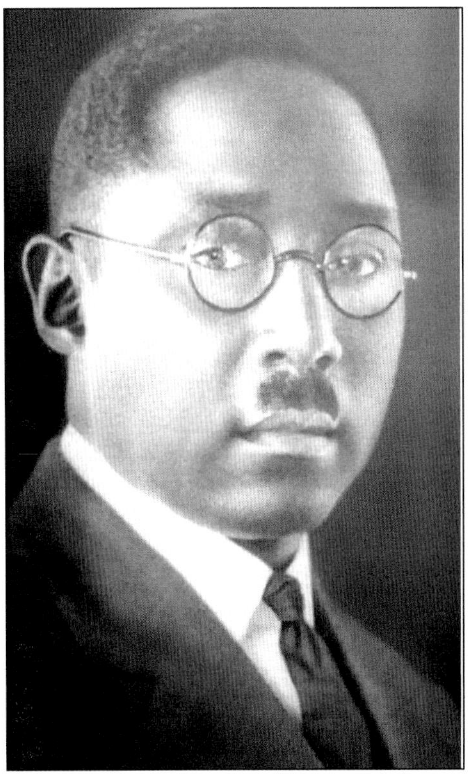

Rev. Walter Johnson, shown here, was elected to the three-member Kinloch School Board in 1924. Johnson soon became an outspoken critic of the treatment of black students and the district's refusal to build a high school for black students. (Photo Courtesy of First Baptist Church.)

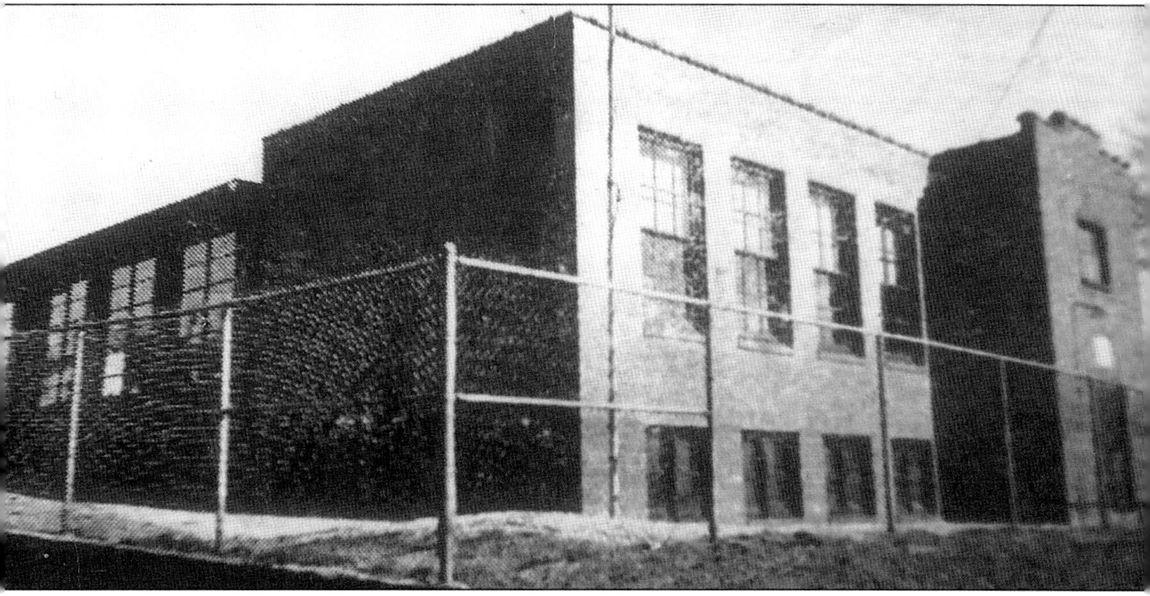

This photograph depicts Vernon School, located at 5764 Carson Road (now Mable Avenue). The building opened in 1927 to serve the black students who lived on two blocks in Kinloch and other black students who resided in the Ferguson School District. After the original two-room school was constructed, the 43-year-old one-room school on Florissant Road was closed. Eventually the new facility became overcrowded and a two-room addition was built during the 1952–53 school year.

Although the U.S. Supreme Court outlawed racial segregation in public schools in 1954, Vernon Elementary School remained all-black until it closed in 1967. During the intervening years, Ferguson-Florissant School officials attempted to persuade Kinloch to assume operation of the school and the education of its students, but the Kinloch School Board declined. When the school closed, the black students were reassigned according to grade level, and many parents were upset for a period of time, since children in the same family attended different schools. (Photo Courtesy of the Ferguson-Florissant School District.)

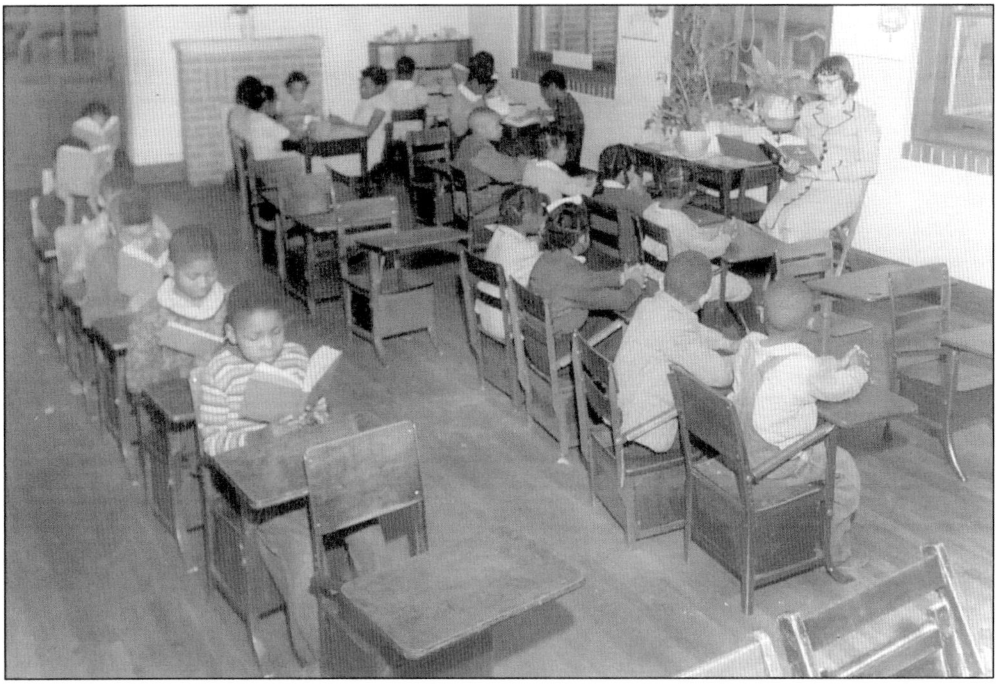

In this photograph, Mrs. Viola Clay Clift is shown working with two groups of four students. The other students, which comprised the balance of the four grades she taught, appear to be occupied with reading and studying. Mrs. Clift began her employment with the Ferguson District in January 1928, and taught at Vernon School for 41 years. (Photo Courtesy of Ferguson-Florissant School District.)

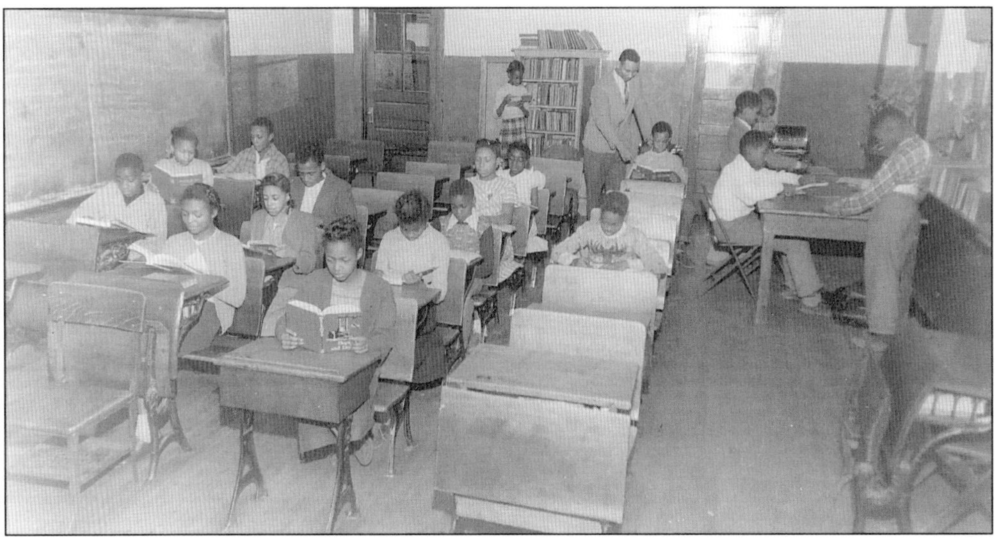

Upper grade teacher George Elliot Jr. is shown here providing individualized instruction to a student. Because of the small black population in the district, the school's enrollment remained rather low throughout its existence. Today, former students and parents of Vernon School fondly remember the warmth and closeness of the small school. (Photo Courtesy of Ferguson-Florissant School District.)

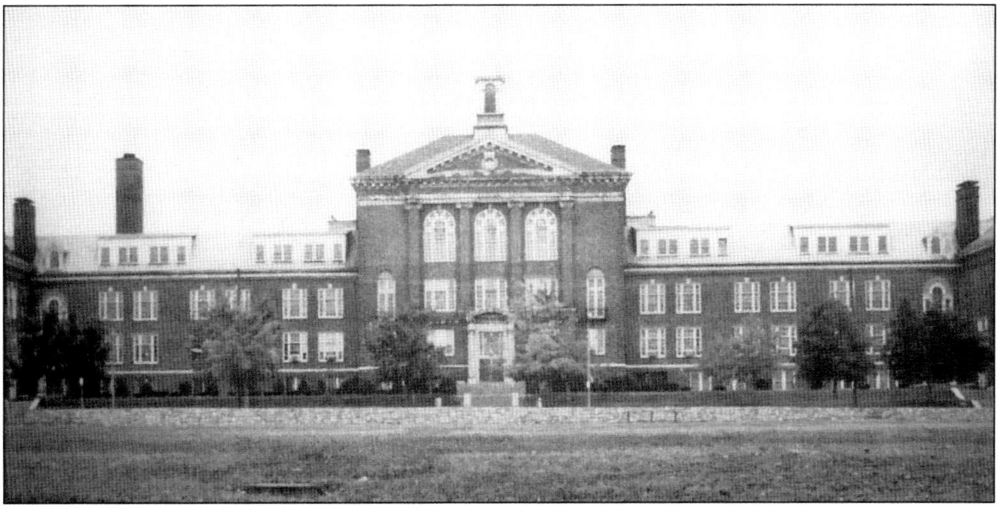

Sumner High School in the City of St. Louis, shown here, is where black students furthered their education after completing elementary school. Many students, however, went without secondary education because the Kinloch District failed to make tuition payments. The district's white students attended high school in Ferguson, Normandy, and Ritenour on a tuition basis until 1937, when the Kinloch High School for white students was constructed at 6033 Caroline Avenue. (Photo by John A. Wright.)

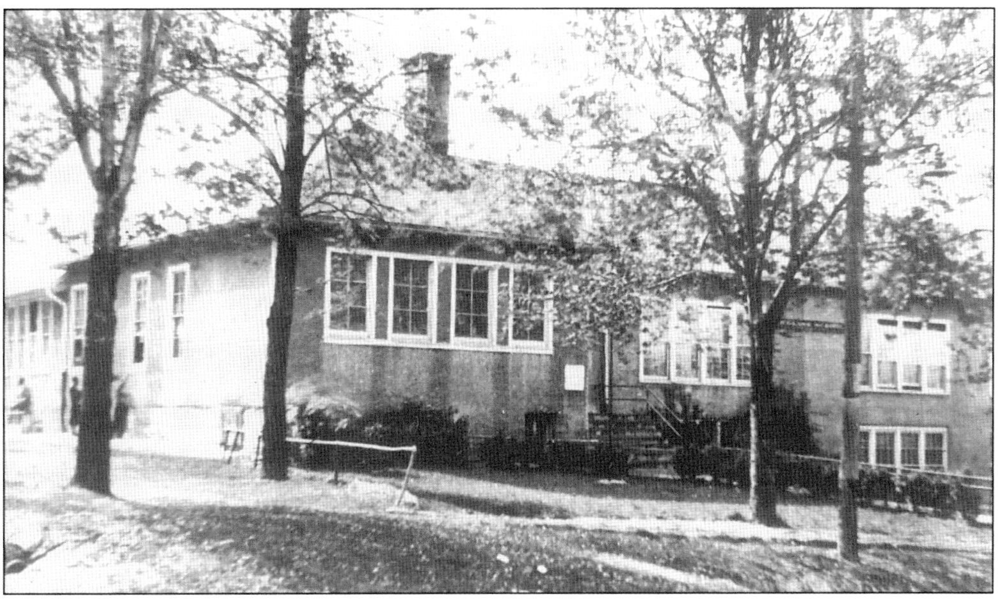

Black students of the Ferguson District attended Douglass High School, shown here, in Webster Groves, Missouri, on a tuition basis until 1954, when the United States Supreme Court ruled segregated schools based on race were unconstitutional. (Photo Courtesy of John A. Wright.)

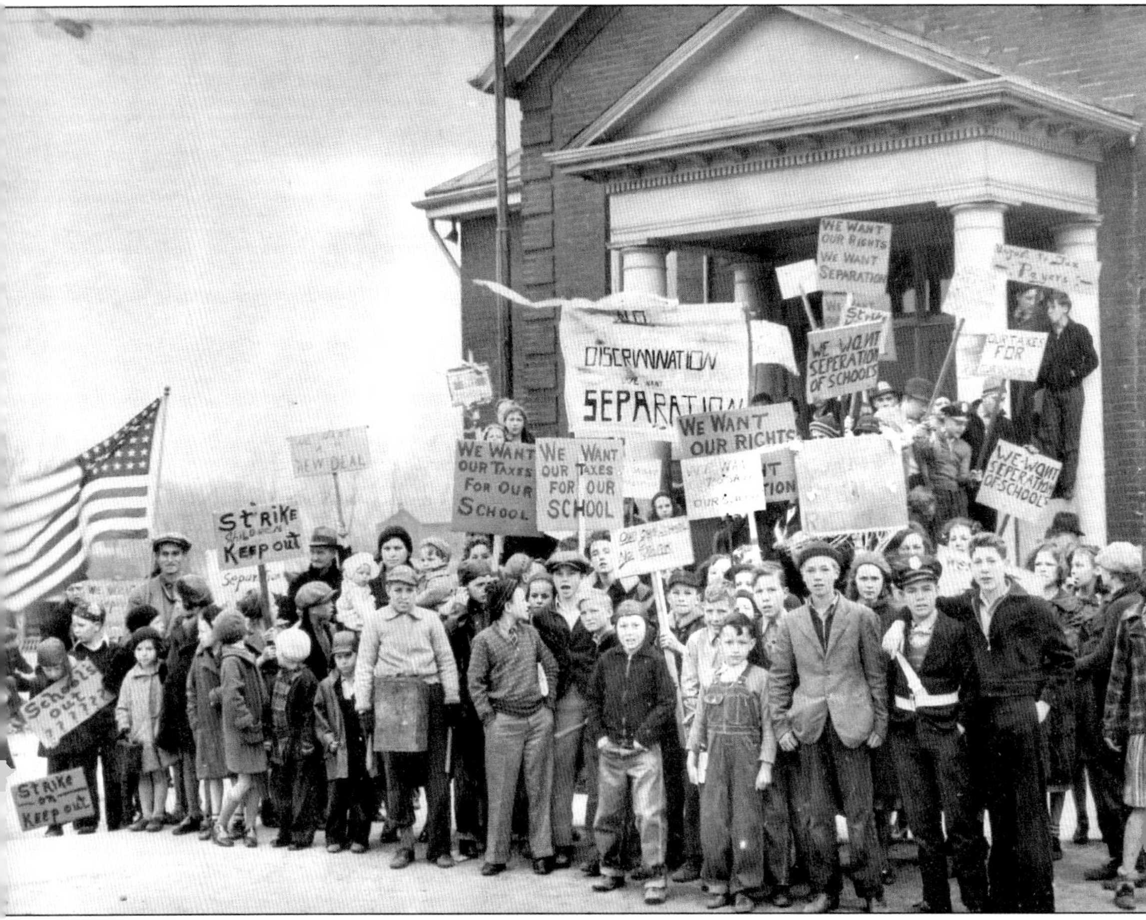

On April 12, 1937, approximately 350 students, accompanied by approximately 25 parents, were photographed as they gathered in front of Nuroad School to protest against what they considered unfair treatment and to demand that they be separated from the predominately black Kinloch District. The district's enrollment for the 1936–37 school year was 543 black students and 349 white students.

The following year, when black Kinlochians threatened to elect a second black member to the school board, whites made their third attempt to divide the district. On election day, the vote was 415 to 0 *against the division*, while those who lived in North Kinloch in the white area voted 234 to 0 *in favor of the split*. The Board of Arbitration met three days later and decided the division was not a necessity. (Photo Courtesy of the *St. Louis Post Dispatch*.)

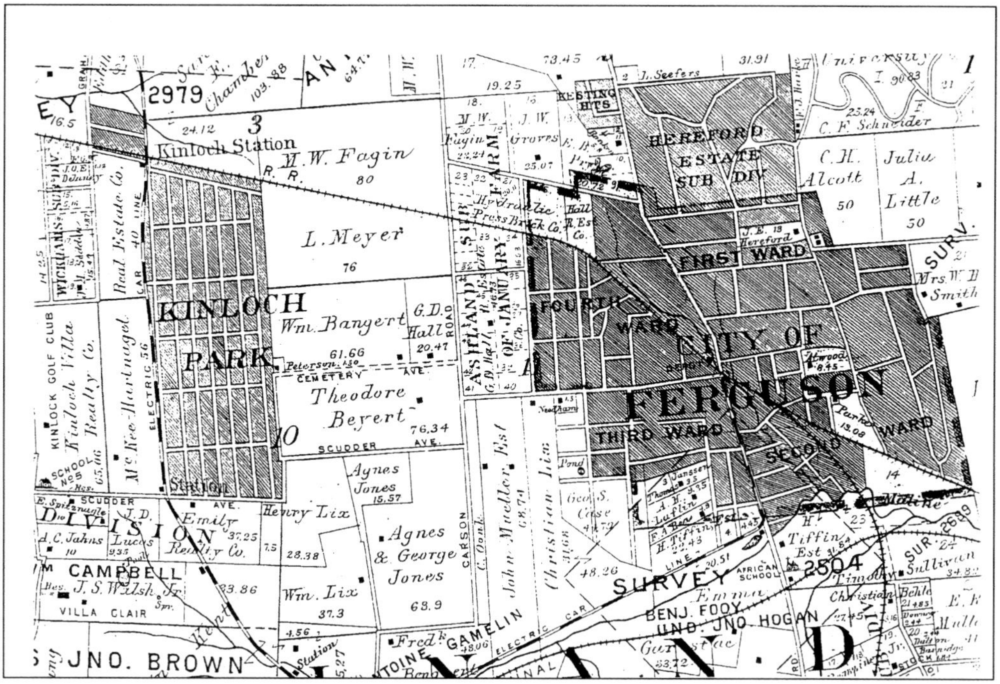

This 1905 map of the Kinloch area shows Kinloch Park, the white residential section. School #5 on Scudder Road, where white district students attended after the district's separation from the Ferguson District, can be seen on the left side of the map and the African School on Florissant Road on the right side. (Map Courtesy of the 1983 Kinloch History Committee.)

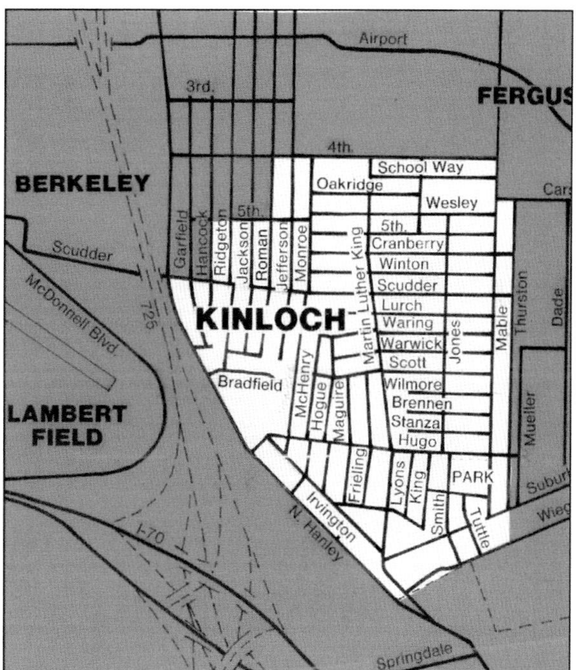

Shortly after receiving notice of the Board of Arbitration's decision not to allow white citizens to form their own school district, a group of citizens met in the Pfitzinger home on Airport Road and agreed to form a separate political subdivision. Permission was granted, and the boundaries of the new City of Berkeley were then drawn in such a way as to exclude the black residential area and confine them to the area on this map. (Map Courtesy of *St. Louis Post-Dispatch*.)

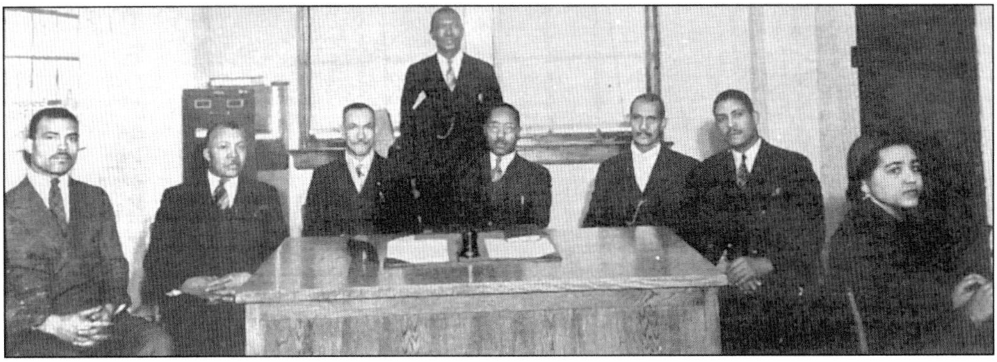

After the separation of the white residential area, the early school boards of the black school district had to deal with continuous financial problems. At that time the district had an assessed valuation of $639,715, with an enrollment of 625 students, compared to the new Berkeley District with an assessed valuation of $1,225,995, and an enrollment of 380 students. The Kinloch School Board members, shown here from left, are: Atkis Boyd, Dr. J.S. Dorsey, Willie Head, President Walter Johnson, Harvey Williams, and F.H. McCollins. Superintendent York Lenoir is standing. (Photo Courtesy of the 1983 Kinloch History Committee.)

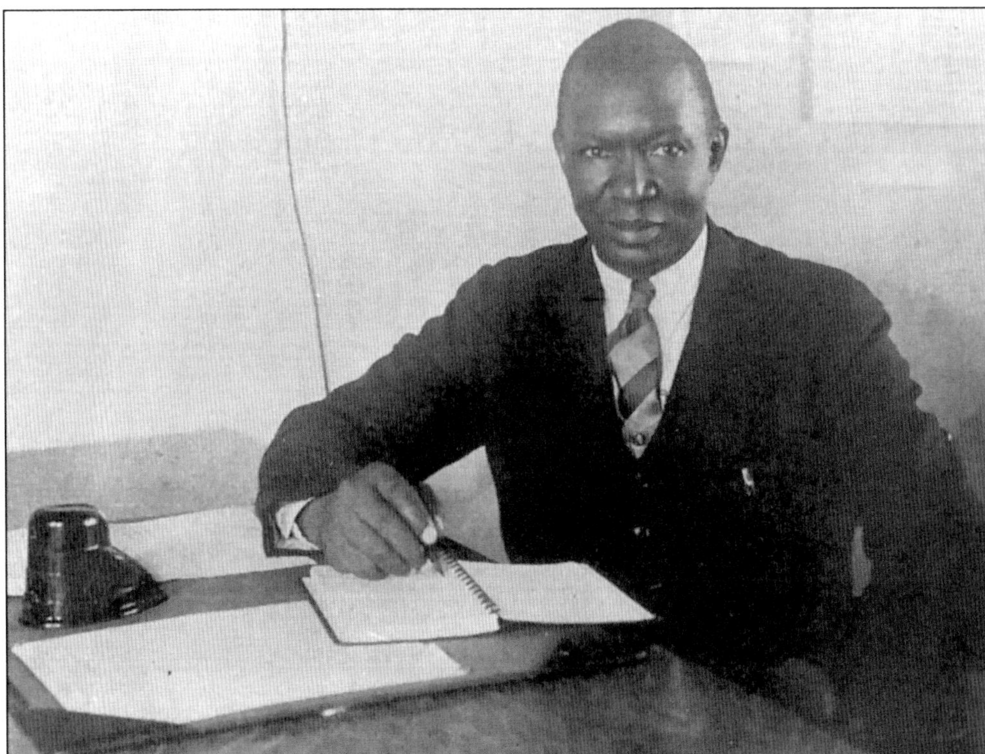

In 1940, the Kinloch Board of Education appointed York Lenoir, pictured here, as its second superintendent. Lenoir, who followed Linnear Bryant, served as superintendent for three years. (Photo Courtesy of the 1983 Kinloch History Committee.)

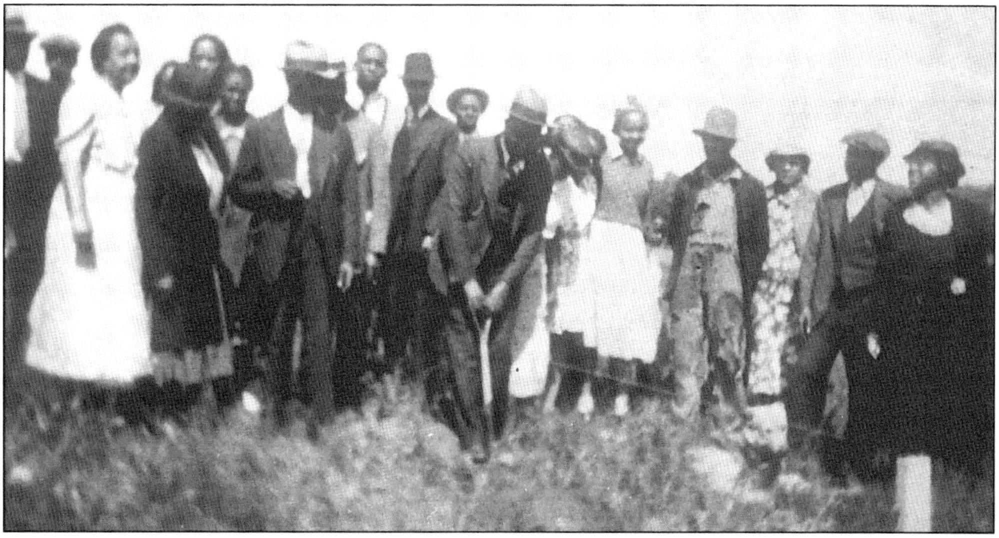

Community members are shown here at a groundbreaking for Kinloch High School. One of the first items on the agenda of the new Kinloch School Board was to prepare for the construction of a new high school. Plans for the school had been delayed by a dispute over its location within the white community. Many whites felt the proposed location was too close to their residential area. (Photo Courtesy of Sylvester Smith.)

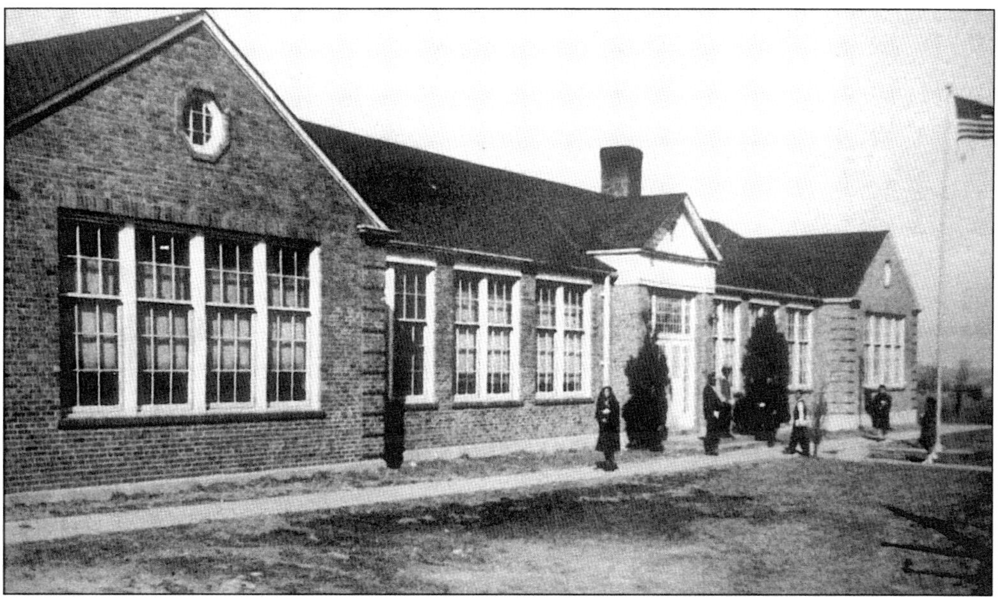

Under the leadership of Superintendent York A. Lenoir, Kinloch High School, shown here, opened in 1938. Lenoir oversaw the construction of the high school's gymnasium. He was also instrumental in the establishment of the Mother's Club and served as the club's first chairman. (Photo Courtesy of the 1983 Kinloch History Committee.)

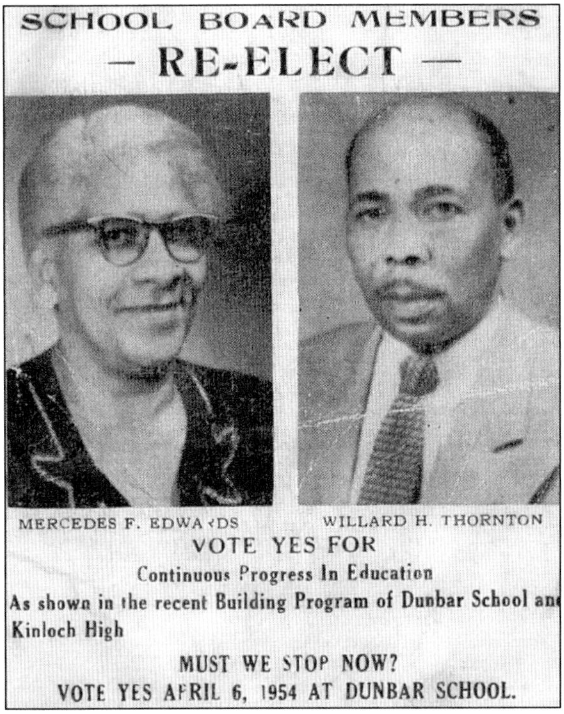

Community members such as Mercedes F. Edwards and Willard H. Thornton, shown here on their school board campaign literature, volunteered many hours to the school system. Their campaign flyer noted the building program at Kinloch High and Dunbar Elementary Schools in which they had been actively involved. (Photo Courtesy of the 1983 History Committee.)

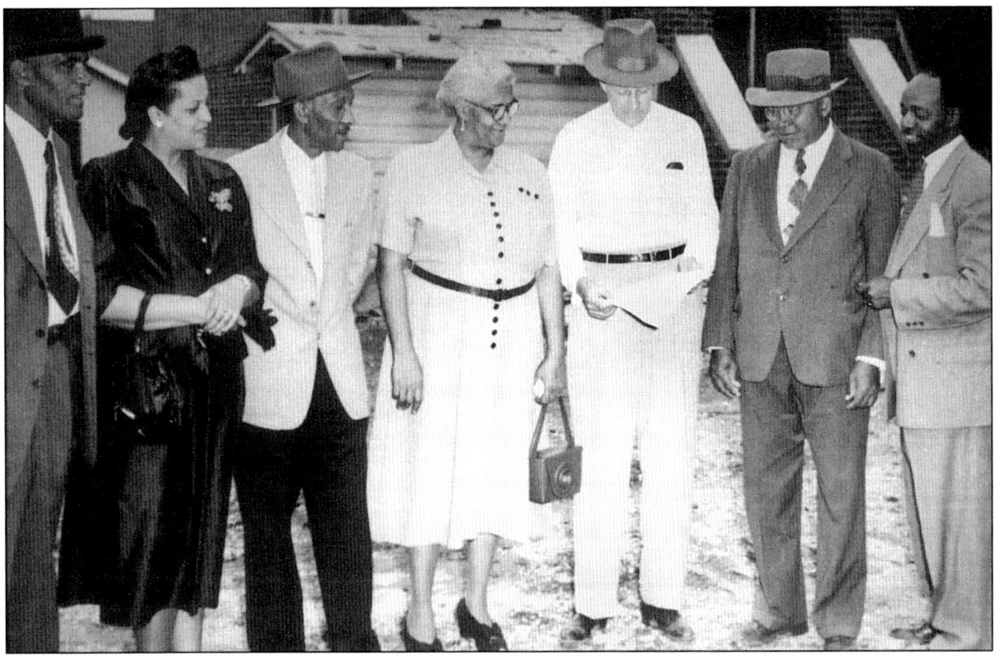

School board members, along with Superintendent of Schools Sylvester Smith, are shown here inspecting the Dunbar School expansion project with two construction managers. From left to right are: Atkis Boyd, Mr. and Mrs. Victor Burton, Mercedes Edwards, and construction managers Dr. J.S. Dorsey and Sylvester Smith. (Photo Courtesy of Ann Boyd.)

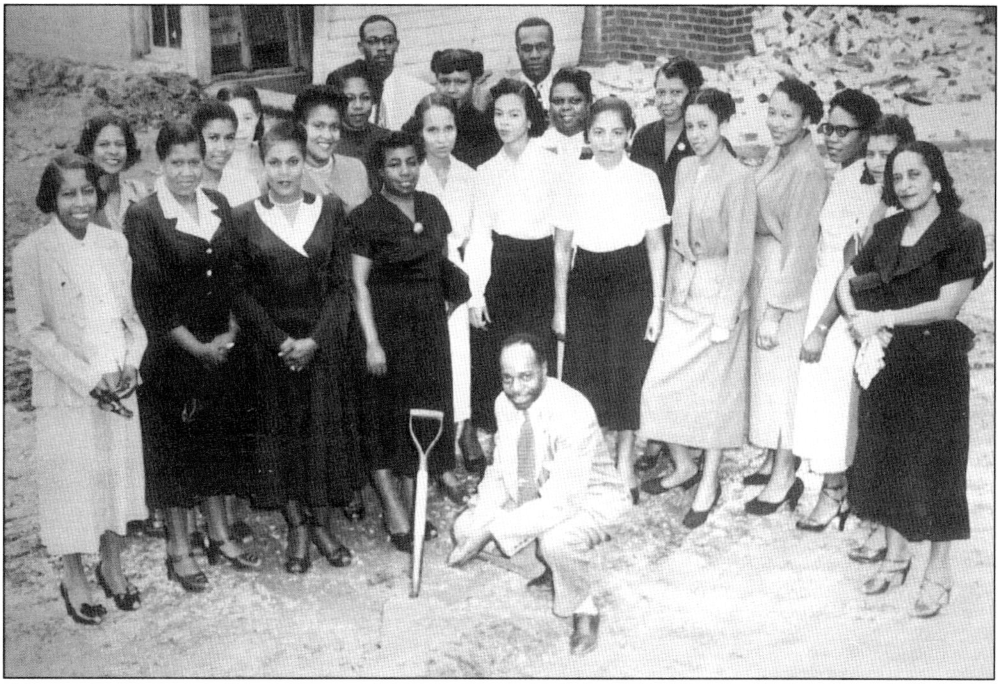

Dunbar Elementary School's teachers are shown here with Superintendent Sylvester Smith during a groundbreaking ceremony for the expansion of the school. From left to right are: (front row, front center) Sylvester Smith, (front row) Emma McNovel, Willie Tyler, Rolla Jean Thompson, Osea Hill Crumes, LaGloria Hunter-Waters, Emma Myers-Dillon, Ollie Dowsing, Juanita Carter, Ida Wiley, Etta B. Hill; (second row) Marie Offett, Doris Kelley, Corine Moore-Thompson, Frances Washington, Addie B. Clay Reed, Anna Thompson; (third row) Maggie Watson, Mike Hoskins, Reuben Fairfax, and Ollie Mack. (Photo Courtesy of Ann Boyd.)

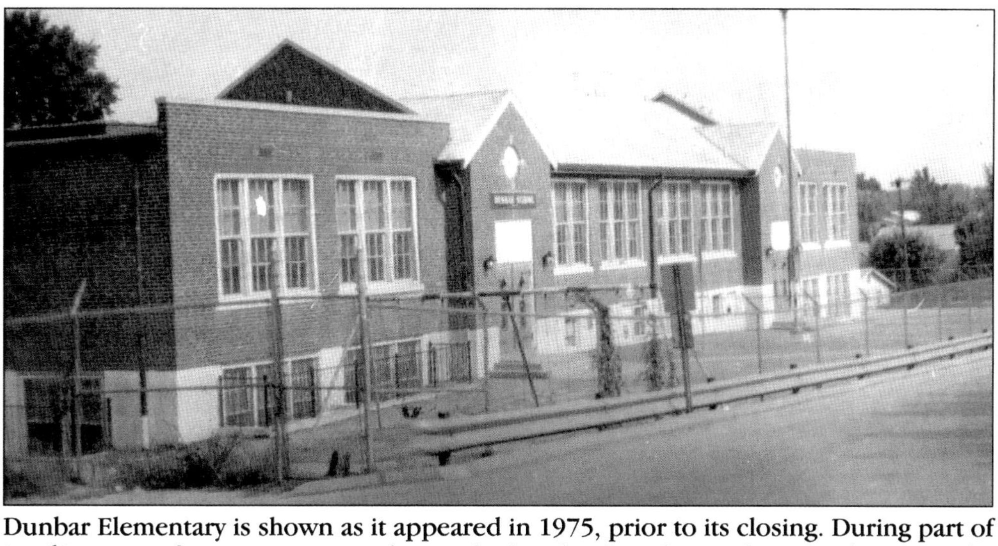

Dunbar Elementary is shown as it appeared in 1975, prior to its closing. During part of its 62 years of service, it served as a high school and a night school. (Photo by John A. Wright.)

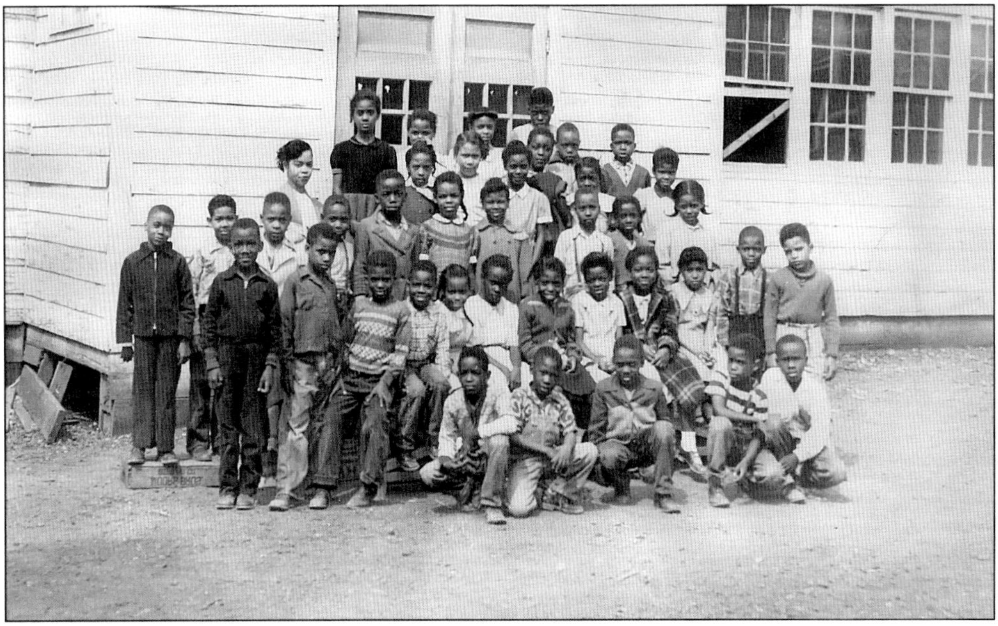

Dunbar Elementary teacher LaGloria Hunter and her second grade class are pictured here in the late 1940s. In this photograph, they were posed in front of one of the school's portable classrooms. (Photo Courtesy of John A. Wright.)

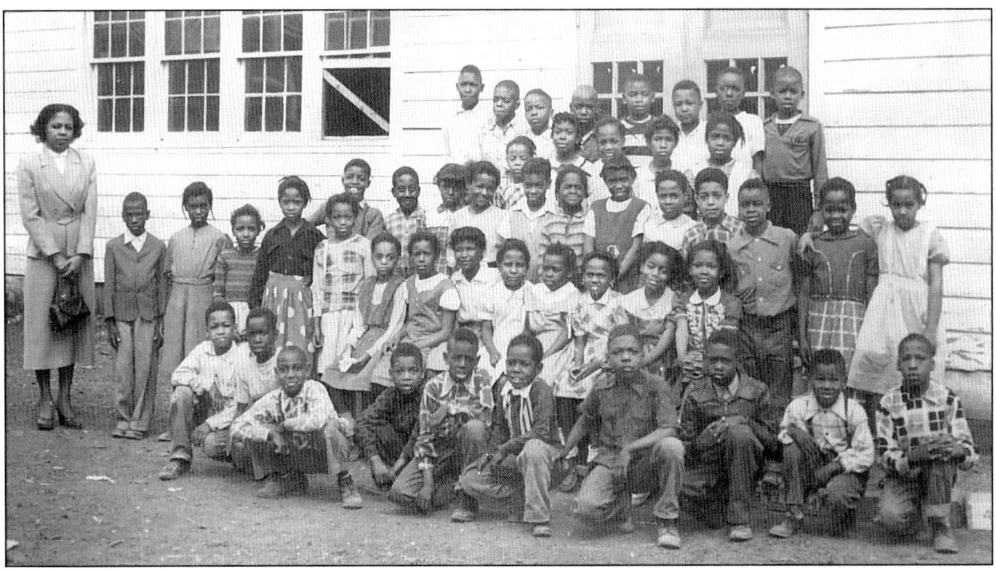

This 1940s photograph shows Dunbar Elementary teacher Maggie Watson and her second grade class posed in front of a Dunbar Elementary School portable. (Photo Courtesy of John A. Wright.)

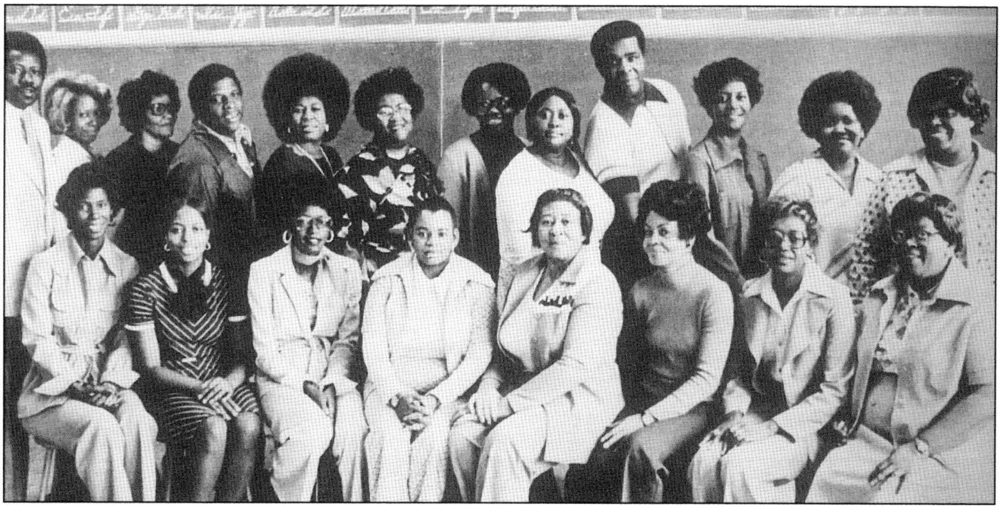

Dunbar School's last principal, Lawrence Wooten, and the school's teachers and some members of the support staff posed for this photograph in 1975. Almost all of the members transferred to schools in the Ferguson-Florissant School District after the court-ordered merger. They are, from left to right: (first row) Harriet Crouch, Verlean Nicks, Ruby Franks, Mary Pearson, Ollie Dowsing, LaGloria Hunter, Charlotte Christopher, Rose Palmer; (second row) Lawrence Wooten, Charlene Brown, Flora Page, Rufus Davis, Vera Mitchell, Evelyn Thompson, Martha Harvey, Rachel Hockett, Robert Wilson, Juanita Charles, Mamie White, and Addie Reed. (Photo Courtesy of John A. Wright.)

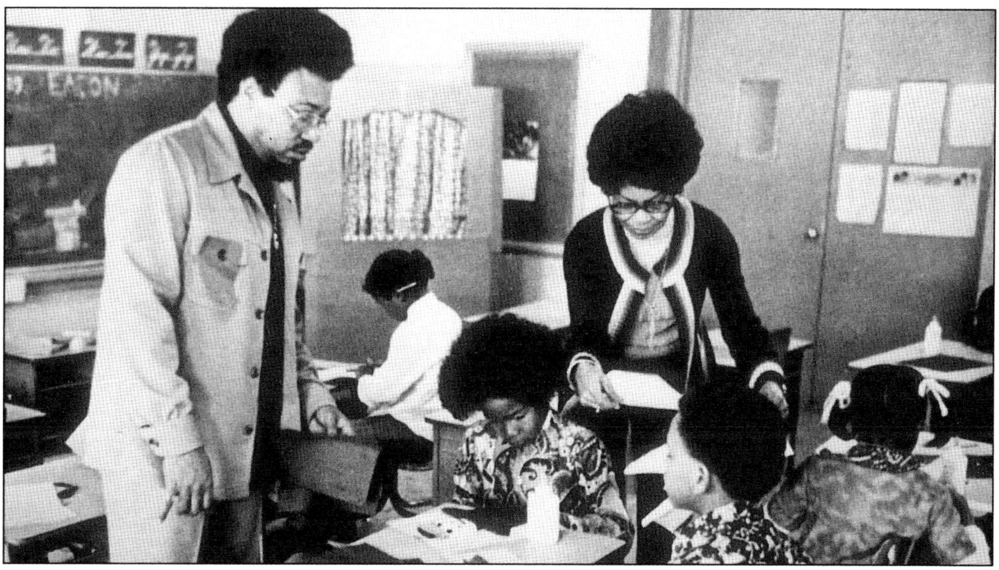

William Curtis, a Kinloch High School graduate and well-known local artist, is shown here with LaGloria Hunter, a teacher, supervising an art project. Curtis left the Webster Groves School District in St. Louis County to return to Kinloch to coordinate the District's Fine Arts program. When Kinloch School District merged with Ferguson-Florissant, he was appointed director of Adult Basic Education and later a high school assistant principal. (Photo Courtesy of John A. Wright.)

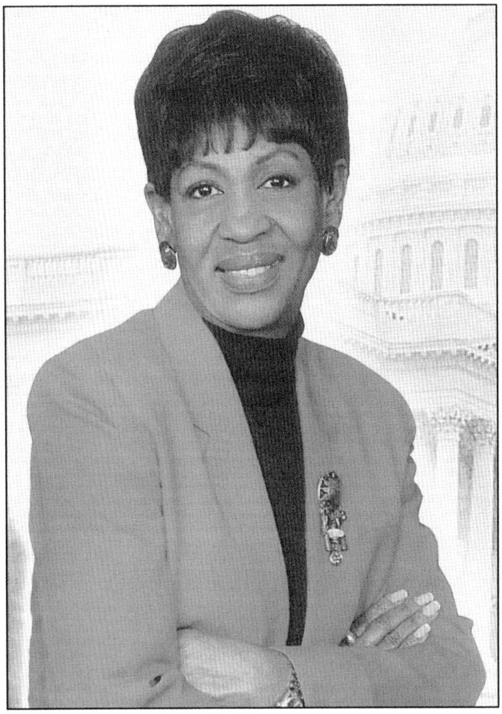

Maxine Waters, an early Dunbar alumni, is shown in this photograph. She went on to be elected in 1990 to represent the Twenty-Ninth District of California in the U.S. House of Representatives, after 14 years as an elected member of the California Assembly from South Central Los Angeles. (Photo Courtesy of Wiley Price.)

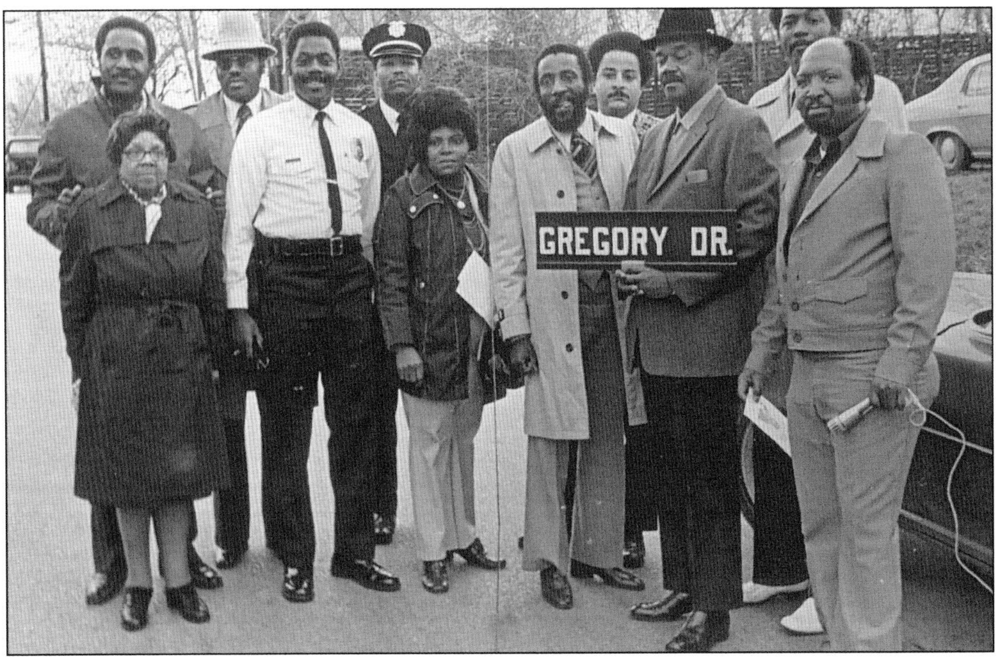

Dick Gregory (seventh from the right), a Dunbar alumni and comedian, is shown here on his return to Kinloch in the early 1980s to take part in the naming of a street in his honor. Gregory was one of the country's best known comedians in the 1960s. In 1966, he ran for mayor of Chicago and in 1968, for president of the United States. (Photo Courtesy of the 1983 Kinloch History Committee.)

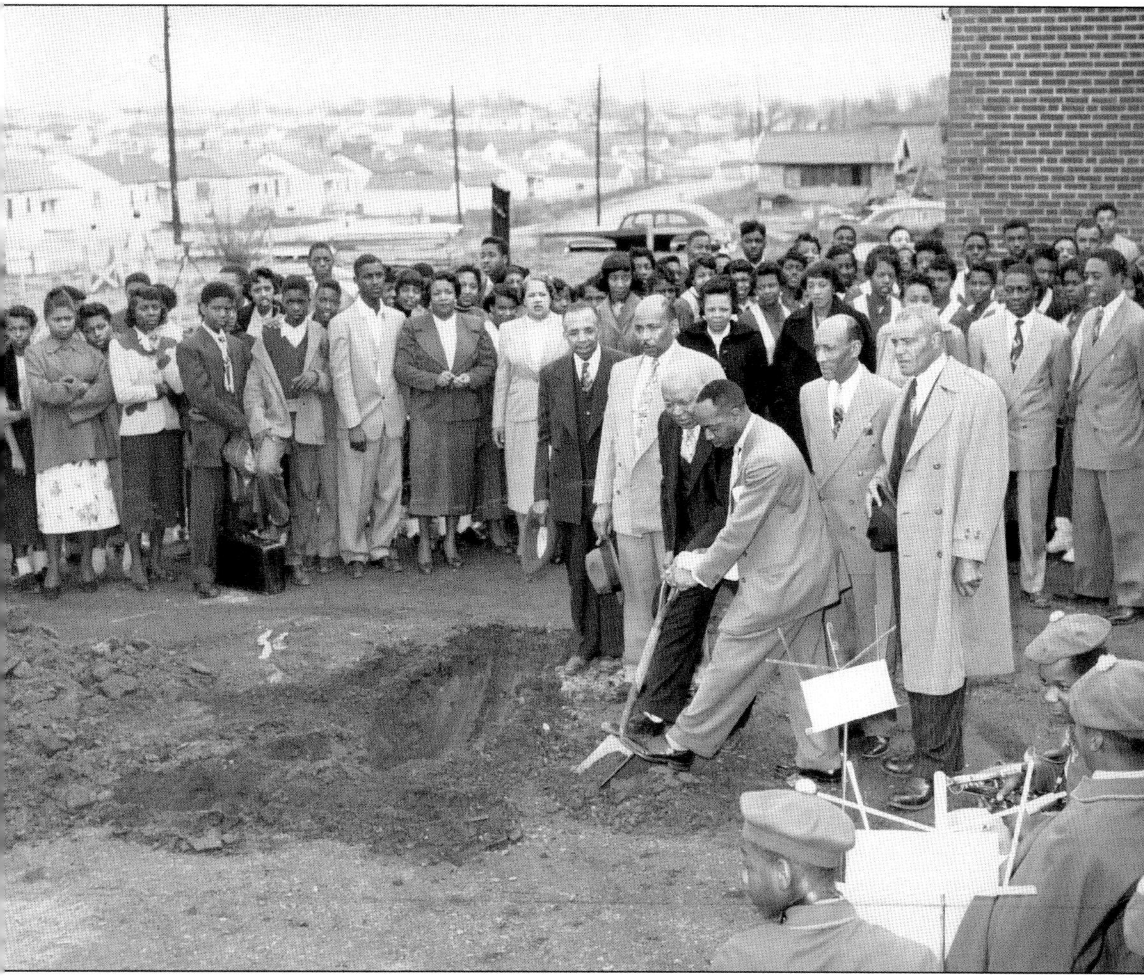

A groundbreaking ceremony for a $106,000 addition to Kinloch High School was photographed showing community members, students, faculty, and school board officials in attendance. Wielding shovels are Dr. J.S. Dorsey (dark suit), school board president, and S.L. Smith, superintendent of schools. In the group behind them, from left to right, are: Rev. J.J. Boyd, Willard Thornton, Victor Burton, and Atkis Boyd. (Photo Courtesy of *St. Louis Post-Dispatch.*)

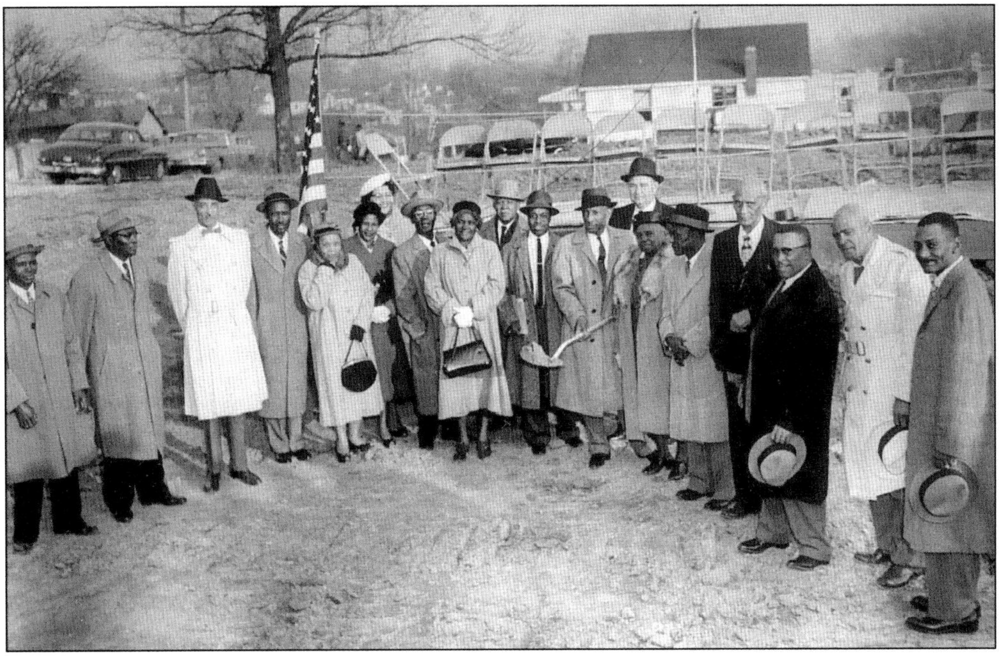

A groundbreaking ceremony for an addition to the south side of Kinloch High School is pictured here. School board President Victor Burton is pictured with the shovel. (Photo Courtesy of Ann Boyd.)

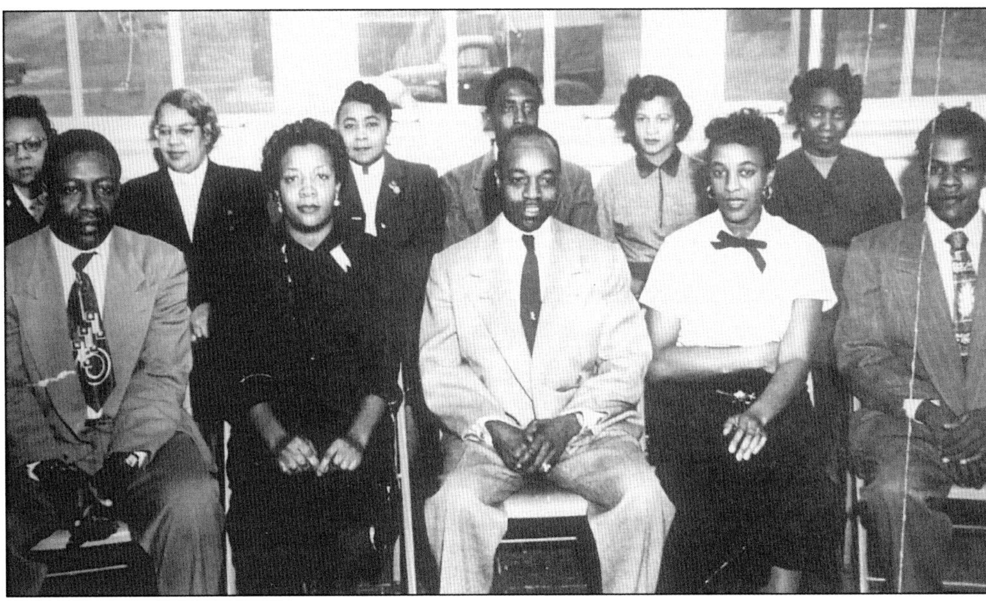

Kinloch High School's faculty with Superintendent of Schools Sylvester Smith in the late 1940s, from left, are: (first row) William Griffin, Essie Metcalf, Sylvester Smith, Bethel Buck, Joe Dorsey; (second row) Lucye Belue, Myrtle Hadnot, Josephine Davis, John Hartfield, Jacqueline Williams, and Barbara Stevens. (Photo Courtesy of Dorothy Lewis.)

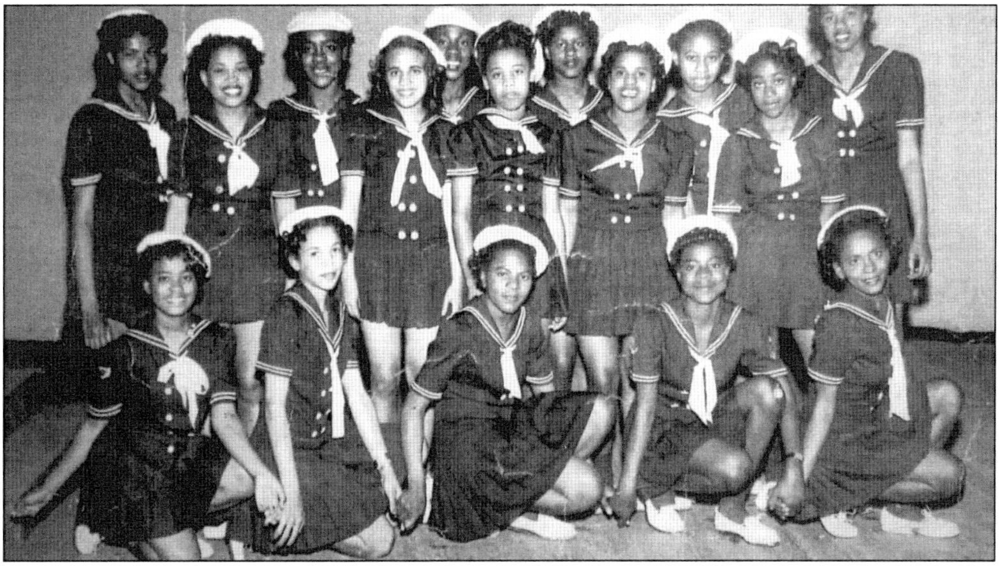

A 1940s Kinloch High dance group is shown here in costumes of navy and white. Dancers, from left, are: (first row) Ernestine Payne, Harriet Hayes, Samella Thompson, Lorraine Johnson; (second row) Juanita Johnson, Eleanor Drake, Kelly Bryant, V.T. Davis, Jackie Pollard , Peggy Anderson, Maybell Simms, Mary Ashby; (third row) Eunice Johnson, May Walker, Elizabeth Anderson, and Elizabeth Drake. (Photo Courtesy of Dorothy Lewis.)

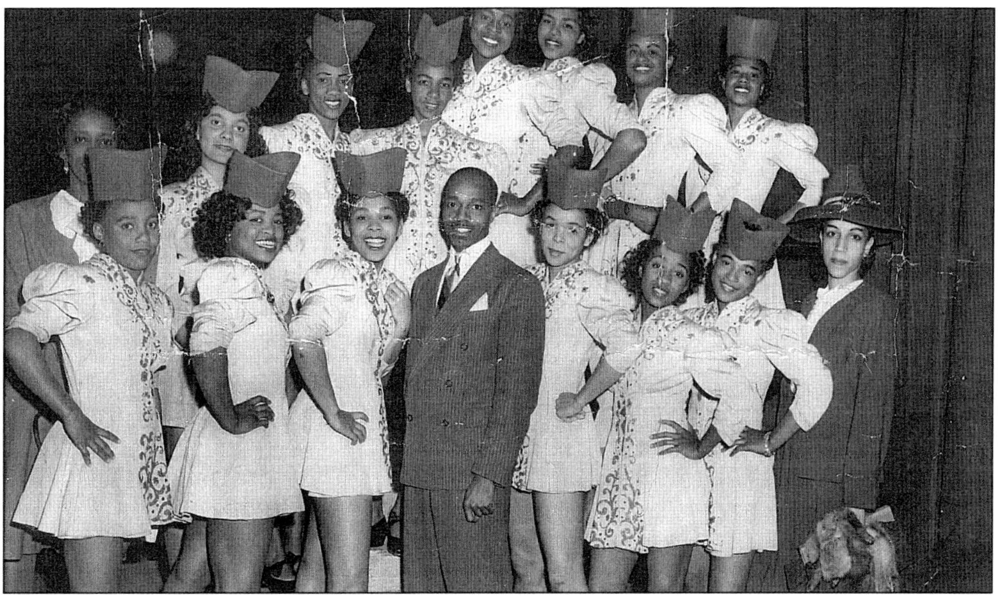

Instructor Sylvester L. Smith and his dance group pictured here performed in the Pine Street "Y" Circus at the Kiel Auditorium during the 1940s. From left to right, are: (first row) Edith Burns, Ernestine Payne, Geneva Purnell Dalton, Sylvester L. Smith, Harriet Hayes, Ernestine Payne, Dorothy Payne, Josephine Rowels; (second row) Nola Cothran, Annette Whitfield, Barbara Jean Smith, Lorraine Johnson, Eleanor Drake, Uretha Payne, and Jewell Anthony. (Photo Courtesy of Victoria Cothran.)

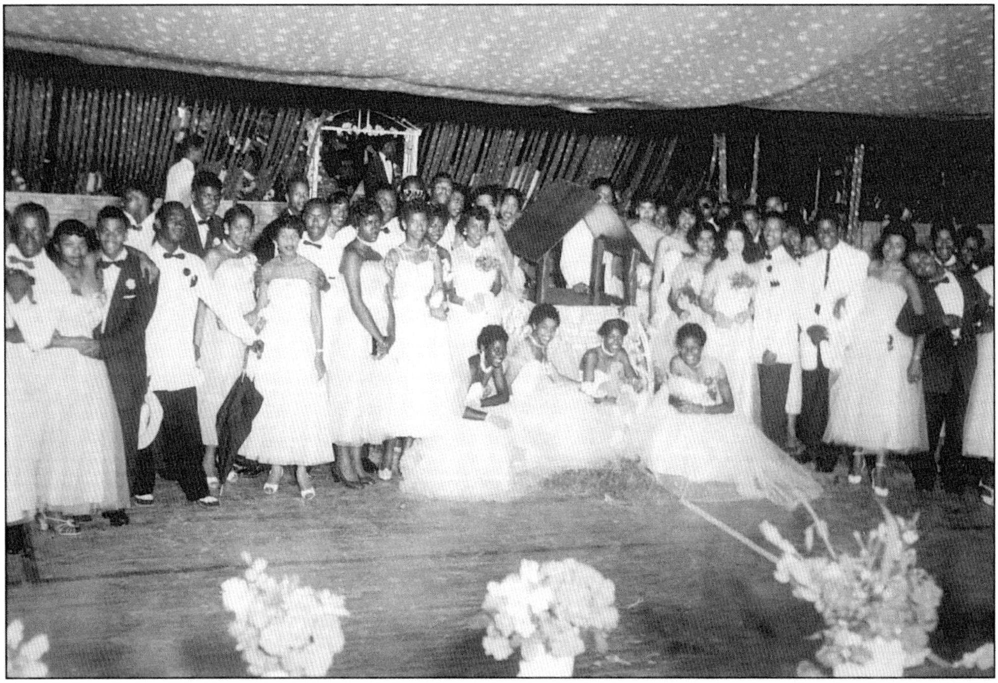

An early 1950s May Day queen's court and celebrants are shown here during an annual celebration. (Photo Courtesy of Dorothy Lewis.)

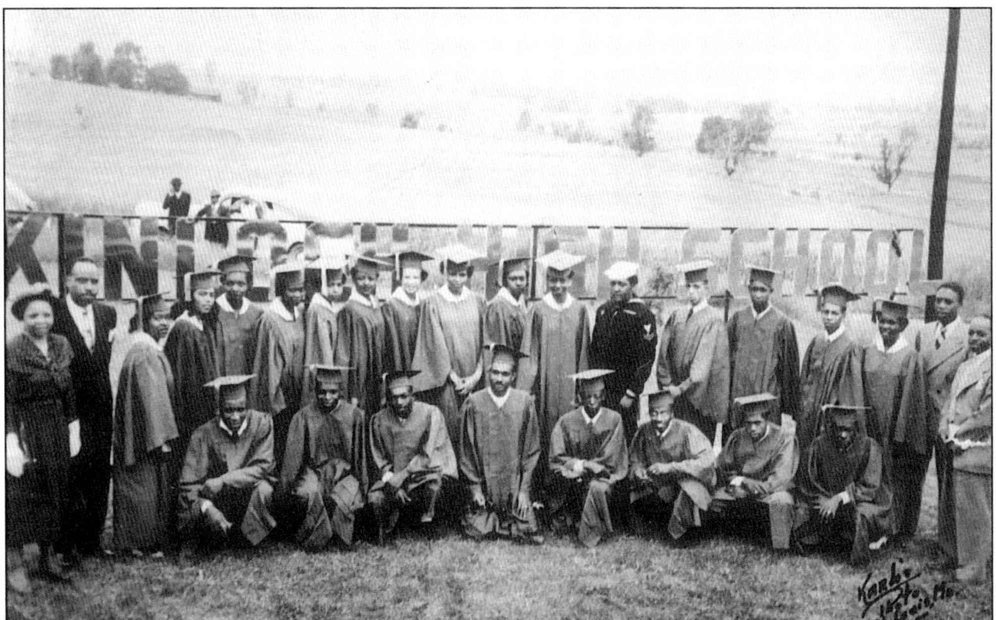

The 1948 graduating class of Kinloch High School is shown here with Principal Lucye Belue, with her husband Harold on the left, and Superintendent of Schools Sylvester L. Smith on the right. This is the first class to be photographed in front of the new Kinloch High School sign. (Photo Courtesy of Dorothy Lewis.)

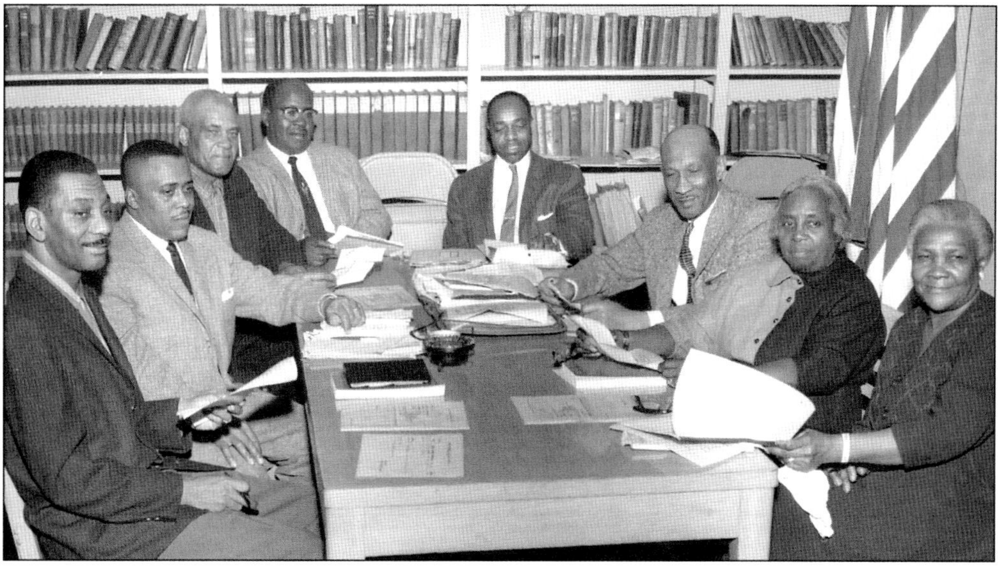

A very dignified and serious looking school board posed for this photograph as they addressed issues facing the district. From left to right, are: Woodrow T. Hughes, director; Larcell McQueen, treasurer; Atkis Boyd, director; Napoleon Williams, secretary; S.L. Smith, superintendent of schools; Victor Burton, president of the board; Alice Scales, vice president; and Mary Lee, chaplain. (Photo Courtesy of *St. Louis Post-Dispatch.*)

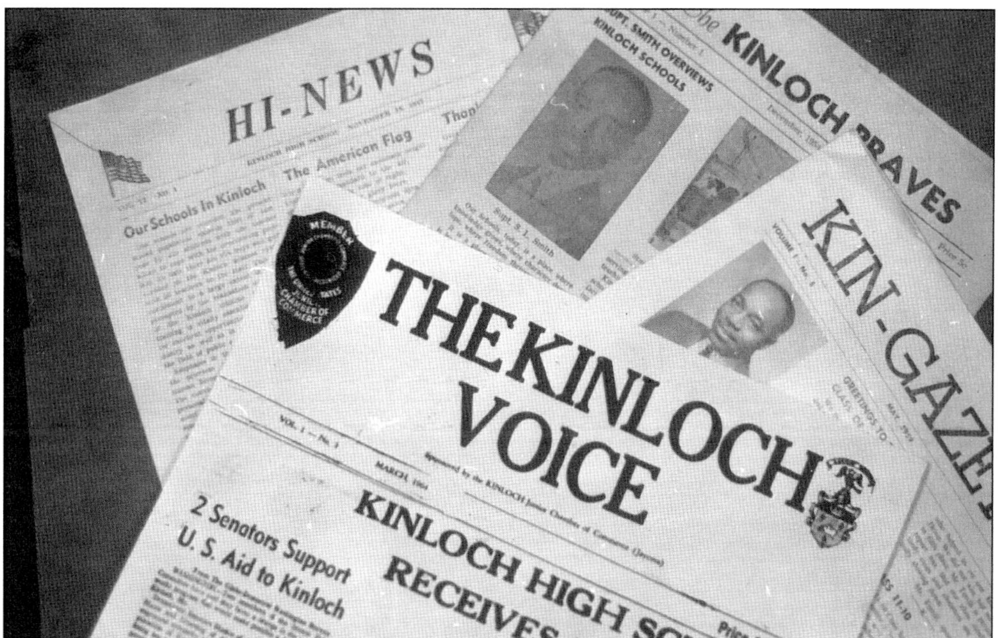

Shown here is an example of the types of publications produced by the Kinloch School District over the years to keep the community informed of school activities. (Photo Courtesy of John A. Wright.)

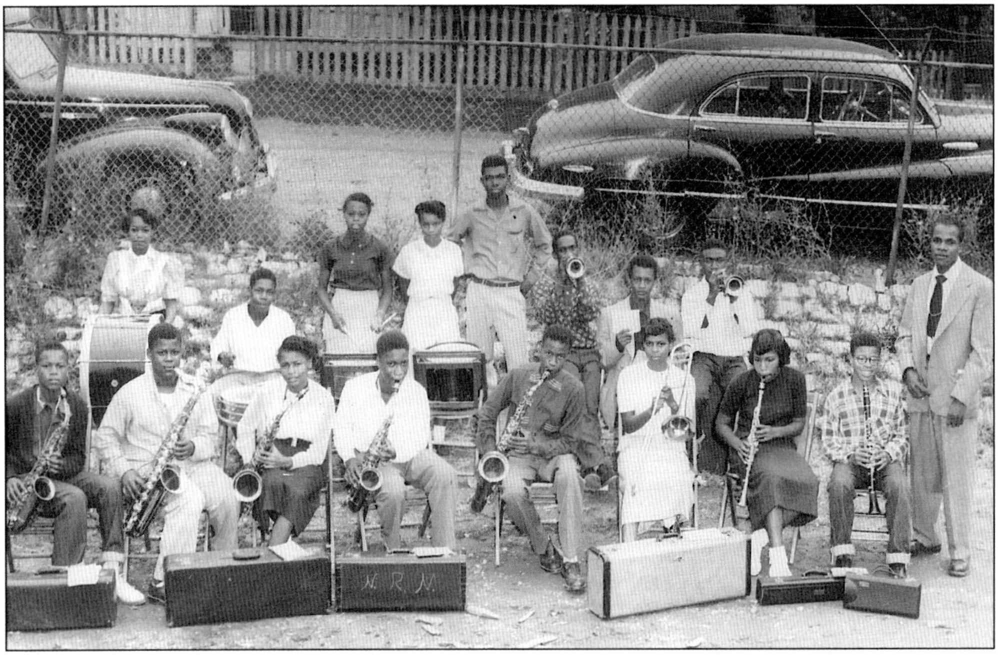

Joe Dorsey, Kinloch High School's band director, is shown in this early 1940s photograph with Kinloch's first band. (Photo Courtesy of John A. Wright.)

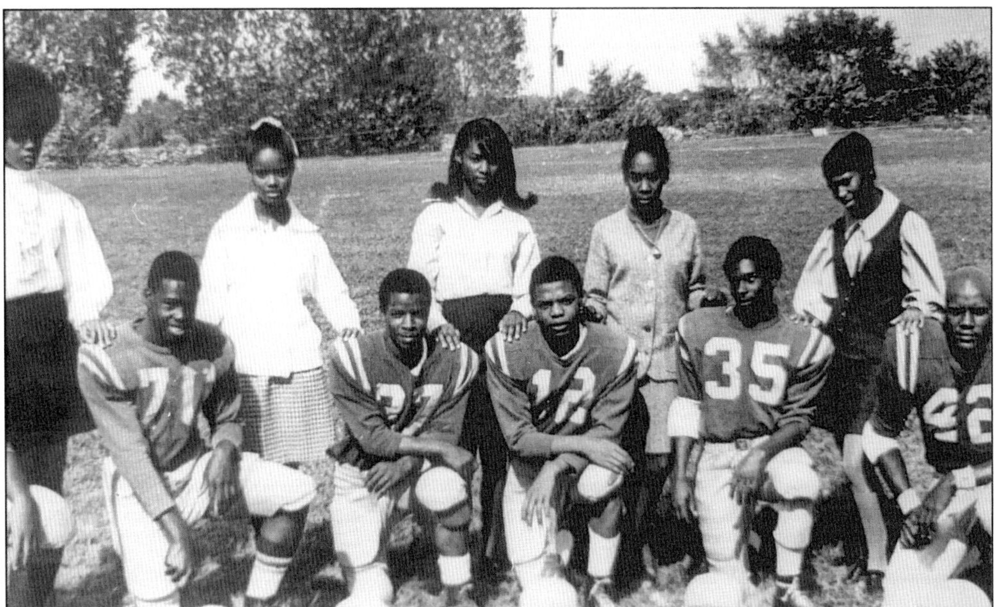

Members of the 1967–68 Kinloch High School football team were photographed during a break at football practice behind the high school. Kinloch High School maintained an active football team through the 1960s until its enrollment began to decline. From left to right, are: (front row) Montay Newton, Arnold Cornell, Lukie Henderson, Cecil Mitchell, Ernie Duke; (second row) "unidentified," Rosemary Wilkes, Elizabeth Olham, Marquita Herndon, and ? McKinnies. (Photo Courtesy of John A. Wright.)

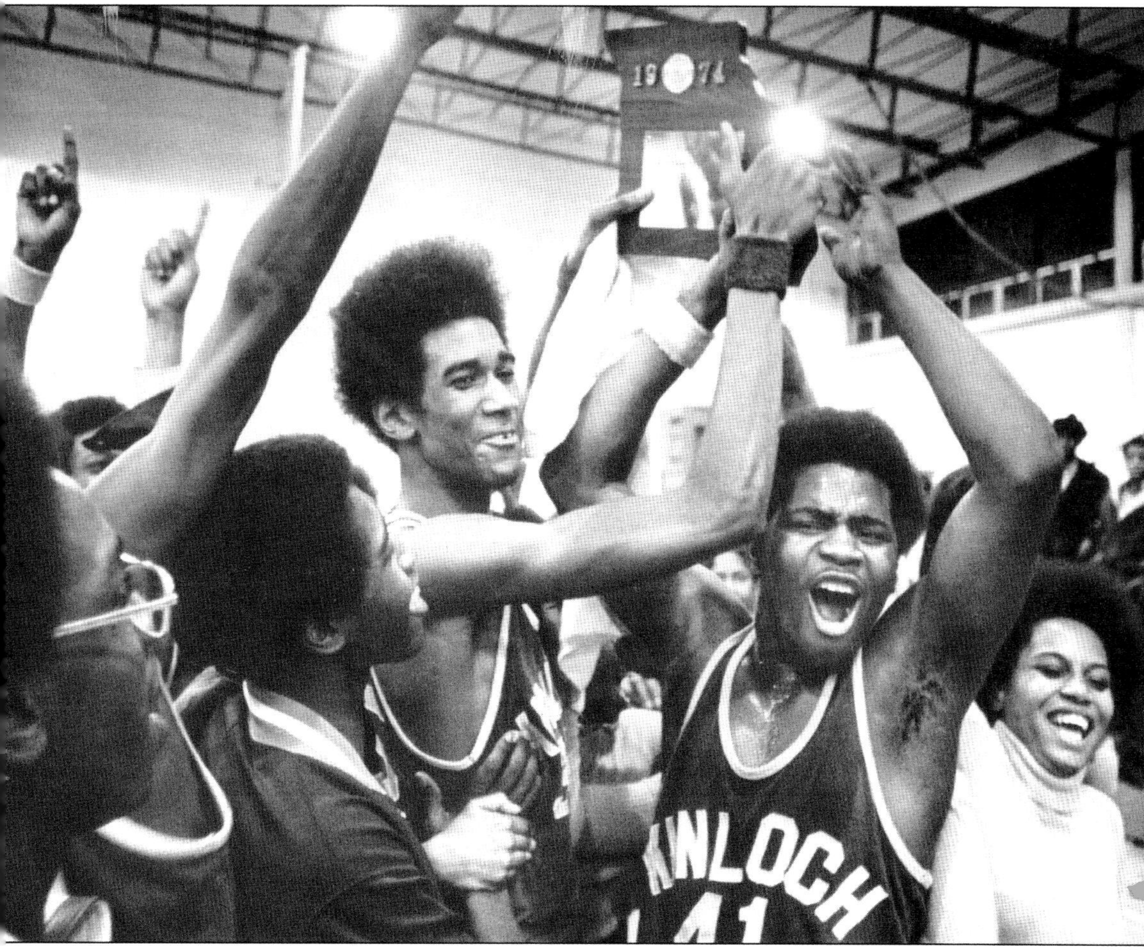

To the victors went the spoils after Kinloch's 2A regional high school basketball championship on February 22, 1974, at Priory. Kelvin Henderson (center) and Michael Cornell are shown here displaying the first-place trophy. (Photo Courtesy *St. Louis Post-Dispatch.*)

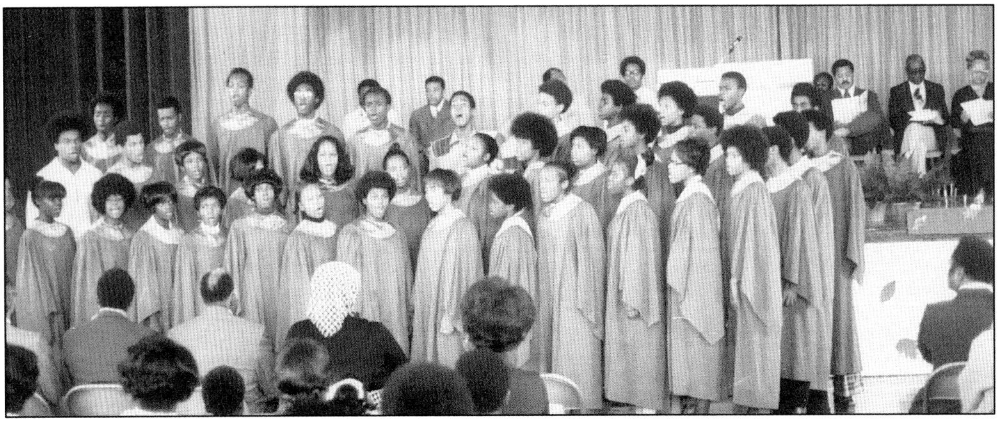

The choir, under the direction of Essie Metcalf for over 34 years, played a major role in the life of Kinloch High School. The choir's 1974 performance at the St. Louis Suburban Music Festival earned its members a standing ovation. This recognition was especially important because it was the only choir to receive such an honor. The adjudicator awarded the KSHS Choir four A-plus's and one A-minus. The 1973–74 choir members are shown here performing at a district function at the high school. (Photo Courtesy of John A.Wright.)

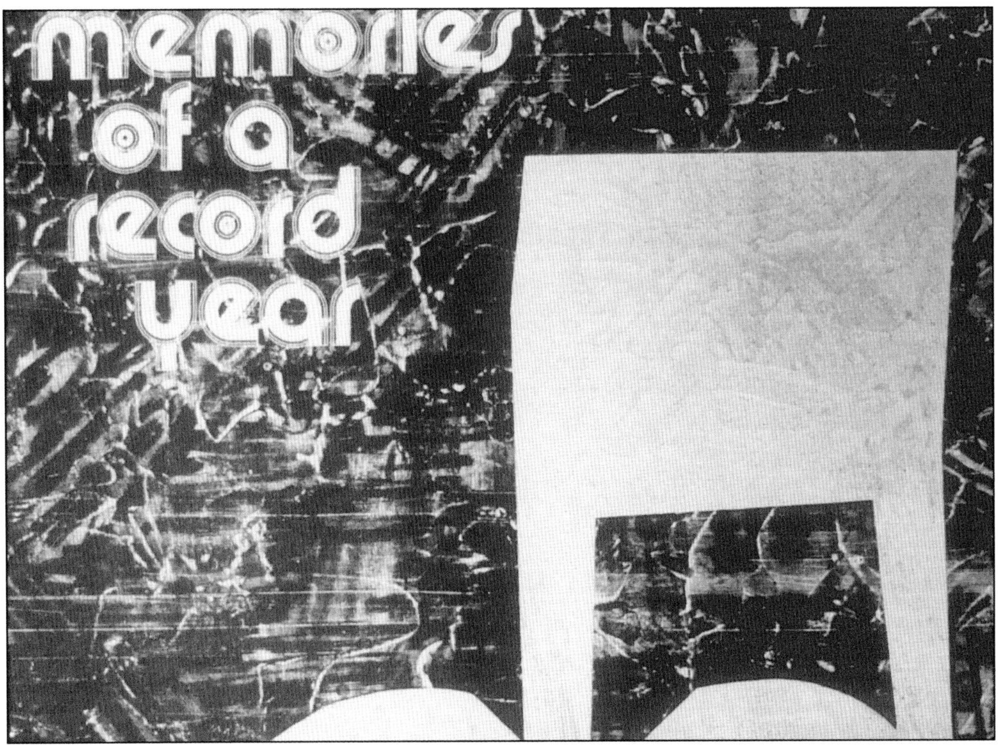

This record album pictured here was produced during the 1973–74 school year by the Kinloch Choir. Ron Metcalf, son of longtime director Essie Metcalf, was the guest director. Twelve selections were presented from the choir's varied repertoire. Besides a wide selection of negro spirituals, the album featured soloists Herbert Irons, Janet Dalton, Fannie Davis, and Phyllis Washington. (Photo Courtesy John A. Wright.)

Sylvester L. Smith, pictured here, moved to the community with his family as a child and completed his elementary and secondary education in the district before going to college. He returned to the community in 1937 to teach, and ultimately succeeded Clarence English as superintendent of schools. (Photo Courtesy of Sylvester Smith.)

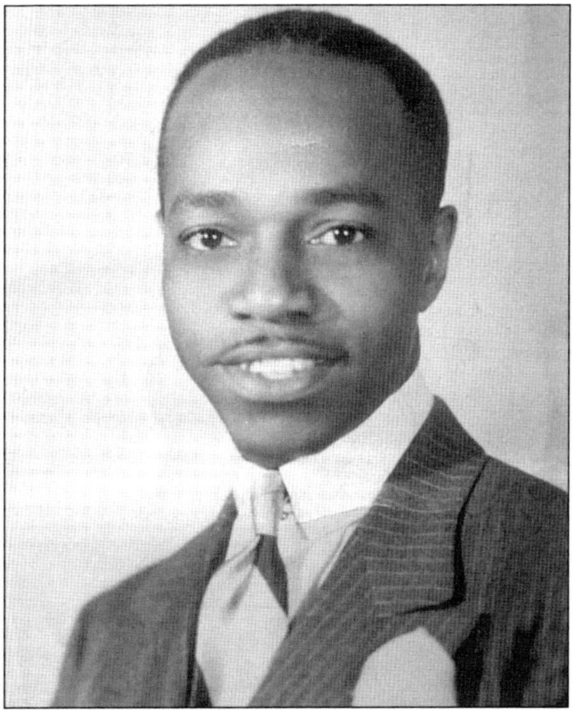

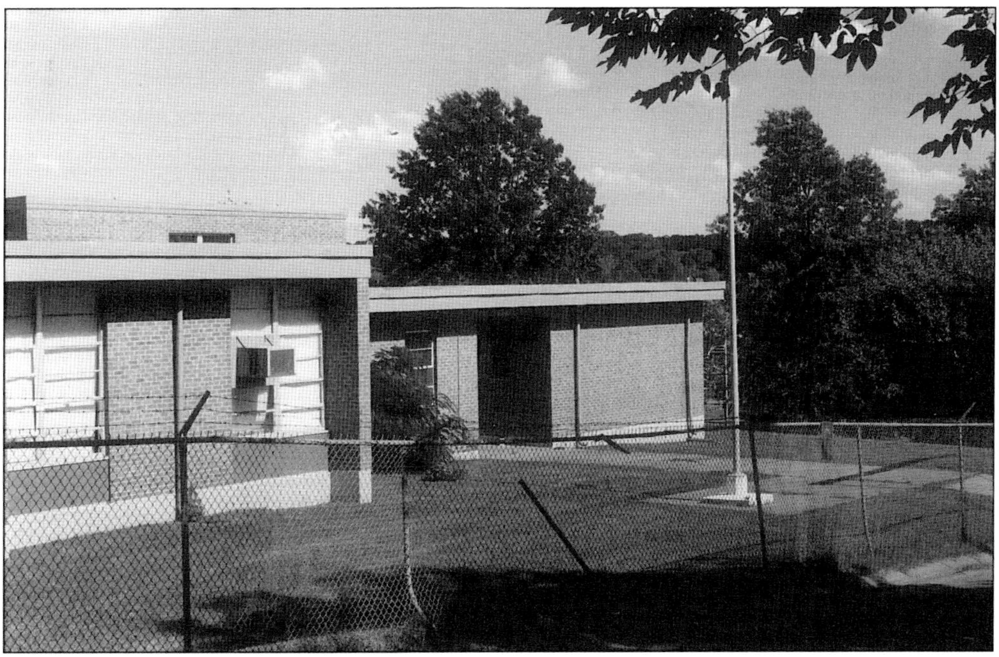

This is a photograph of Smith Elementary School. The school was named in honor of Sylvester L. Smith, superintendent of the Kinloch School District from 1944 to 1961. Smith Elementary was a key element in the redevelopment of the southeastern portion of the community since the government allowed the community to count the school as its share of redevelopment cost. (Photo by John A. Wright.)

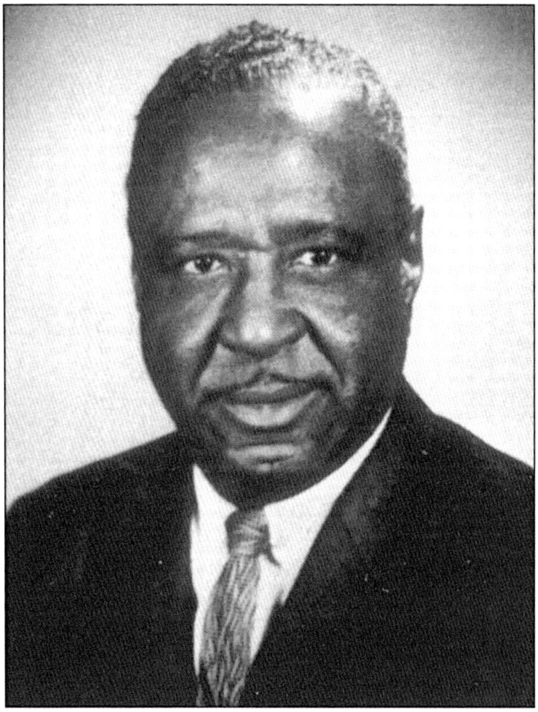

Shown here is Dr. Arthur Cortez Shropshire, who followed Sylvester Smith as superintendent of schools in 1961. Dr. Shropshire held the position until his retirement in 1973. As president of the Missouri State Association of Negro Teachers from 1942 to 1944, he successfully led the fight to equalize the salaries of black teachers to that of white teachers in the state. He was also instrumental in collecting and receiving out-of-state tuition owed to Missouri students who attended institutions of higher learning outside of the state. (Photo Courtesy of John A. Wright.)

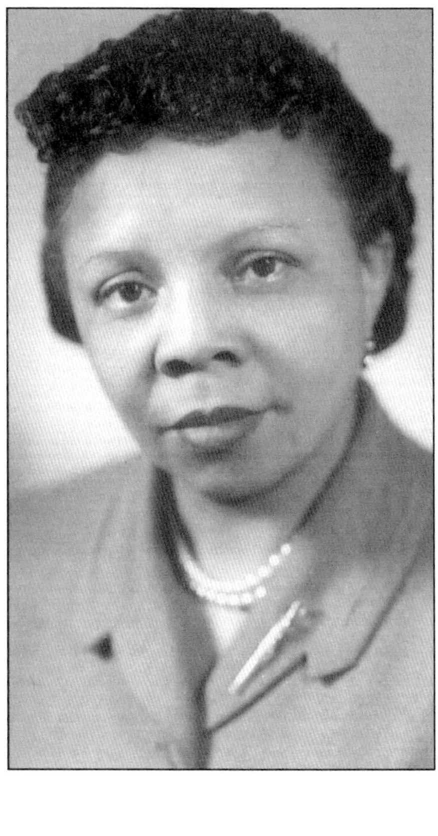

Lucye Belue, the principal of Kinloch High School from 1944–1974, is pictured here. Mrs. Belue came to Kinloch with her parents in 1912. She received her elementary education at Dunbar School in Kinloch and her secondary education at Sumner High School in St. Louis. Mrs. Belue will always be considered a "pillar of the community." (Photo Courtesy of John A. Wright.)

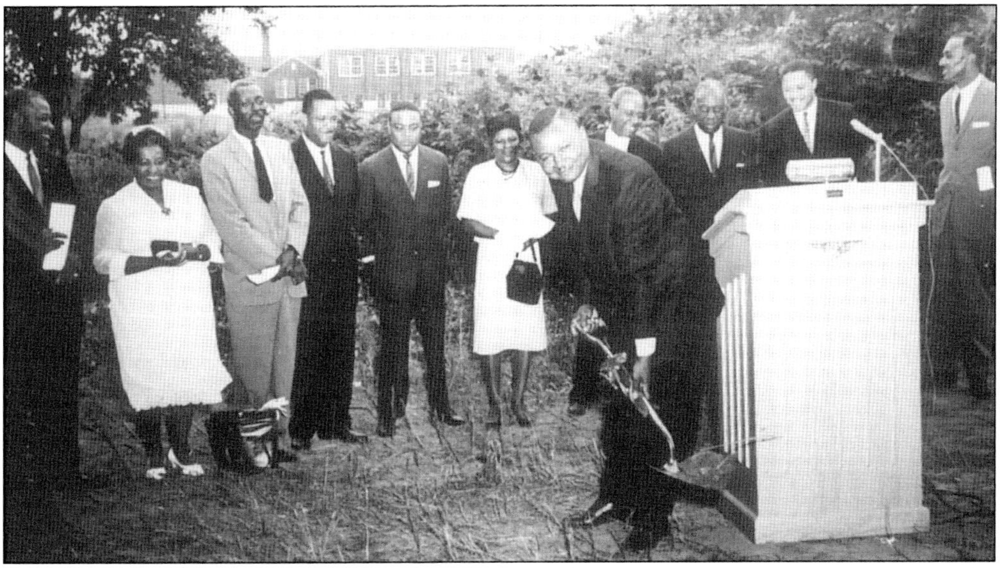

This groundbreaking ceremony, which is pictured here, was at the construction site for John F. Kennedy Junior High School. Wielding the shovel is Rev. John Mitchell, school board member, and behind him, from left to right, are: the architect, Rev. Gregory, board member John Page, unidentified, O.C. King, board member Minerva Scott, Superintendent Arthur Shropshire, board member Carlson Oliver, board member Samuel Boyd, and board member John O'Guinn. (Courtesy of Rev. John Mitchell Sr.)

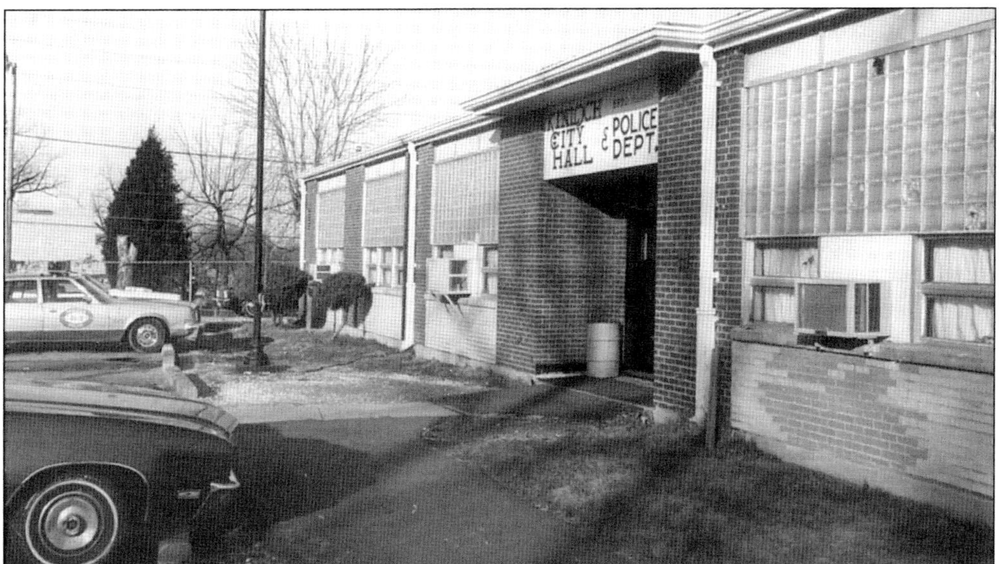

Kinloch City Hall, shown here, was once John F. Kennedy Junior High School. The building is the first known school in the United States named in honor of the late president. A school board meeting was in session when members learned of the president's death. To recognize and pay tribute to the late president's efforts on behalf of Americans in general and blacks in particular, a motion was made to name the new school in his honor. (Photo Courtesy of John A. Wright.)

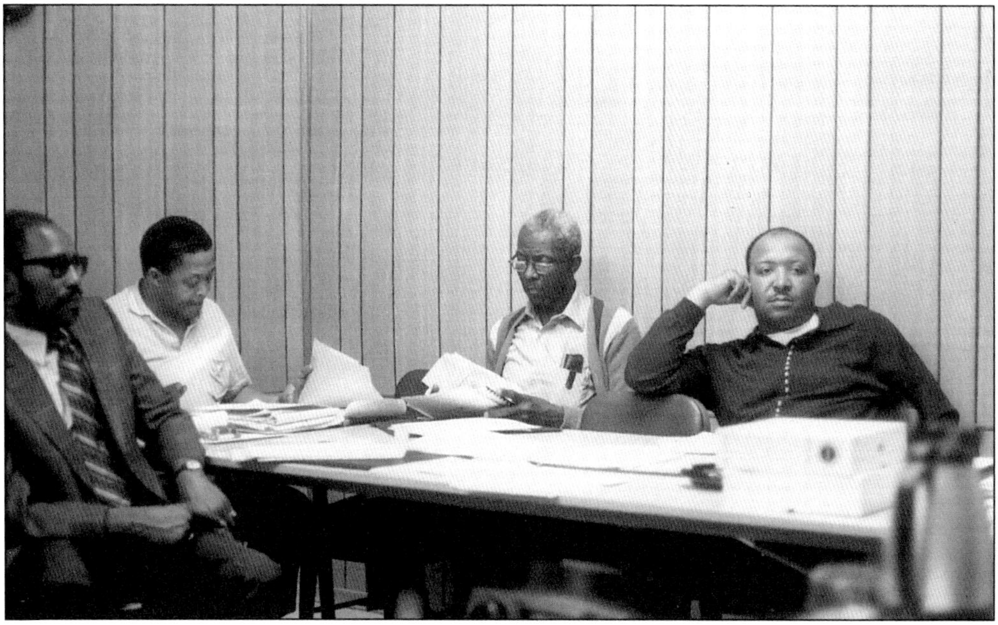

This picture was taken of school board members (left to right) Leroy Noah, Samuel Boyd, John Page, and Joseph Wells as they search for solutions for issues facing the district. The photo was taken just prior to the district receiving notification from the U.S. Department of Justice on August 31, 1971, that it would institute legal actions to bring about the desegregation of the Kinloch School District. A year earlier, a petition had been filed without success for the dissolution of the district. (Photo Courtesy of John A. Wright.)

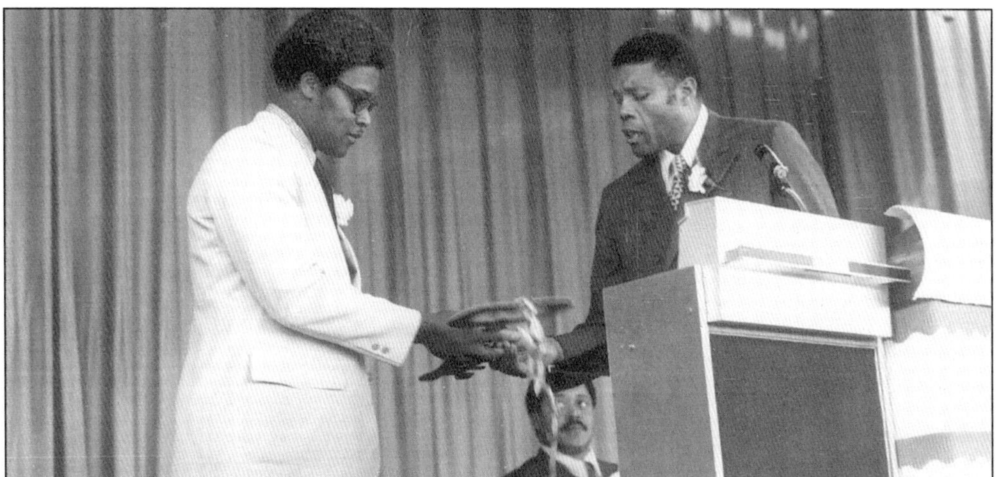

Mayor Robert Metcalf is presenting John A. Wright, the school district's sixth superintendent, with a key to the city during a welcoming ceremony at the high school in 1973. Wright came to the district from the Webster Groves School District in St. Louis County and continued with the Kinloch School District through the merger. He remained as an assistant superintendent in the newly formed district. (Photo Courtesy of John A. Wright.)

On August 27, 1973, Judge James H. Meredith issued an order requiring the State Board of Education, St. Louis County Board of Education, and their members and administrative officers to develop a plan to disestablish the racially isolated Kinloch School District within 60 days. Kinloch presented the petition shown here, as did the other two districts involved, to the U.S. Supreme Court. In June of 1976, the court ruled to uphold the merger of the Kinloch and Berkeley School Districts to the Ferguson-Florissant School District. (Photo Courtesy of John A. Wright.)

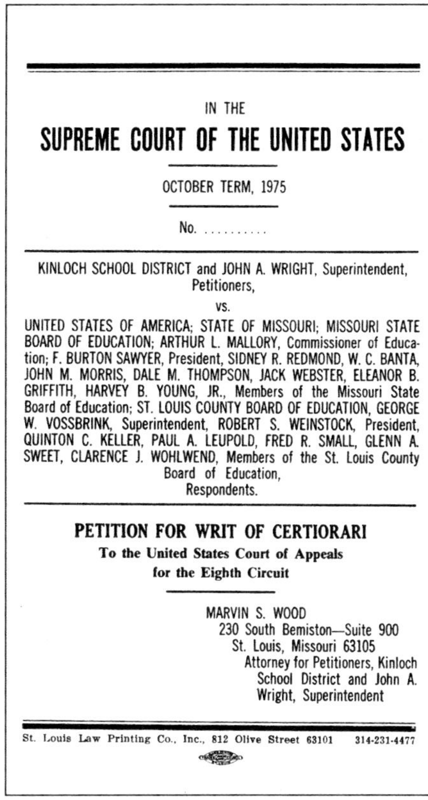

IN THE

SUPREME COURT OF THE UNITED STATES

OCTOBER TERM, 1975

No. . . . .

KINLOCH SCHOOL DISTRICT and JOHN A. WRIGHT, Superintendent,
Petitioners,

vs.

UNITED STATES OF AMERICA; STATE OF MISSOURI; MISSOURI STATE BOARD OF EDUCATION; ARTHUR L. MALLORY, Commissioner of Education; F. BURTON SAWYER, President, SIDNEY R. REDMOND, W. C. BANTA, JOHN M. MORRIS, DALE M. THOMPSON, JACK WEBSTER, ELEANOR B. GRIFFITH, HARVEY B. YOUNG, JR., Members of the Missouri State Board of Education; ST. LOUIS COUNTY BOARD OF EDUCATION, GEORGE W. VOSSBRINK, Superintendent, ROBERT S. WEINSTOCK, President, QUINTON C. KELLER, PAUL A. LEUPOLD, FRED R. SMALL, GLENN A. SWEET, CLARENCE J. WOHLWEND, Members of the St. Louis County Board of Education,
Respondents.

PETITION FOR WRIT OF CERTIORARI
To the United States Court of Appeals
for the Eighth Circuit

MARVIN S. WOOD
230 South Bemiston—Suite 900
St. Louis, Missouri 63105
Attorney for Petitioners, Kinloch School District and John A. Wright, Superintendent

St. Louis Law Printing Co., Inc., 812 Olive Street 63101 314-231-4477

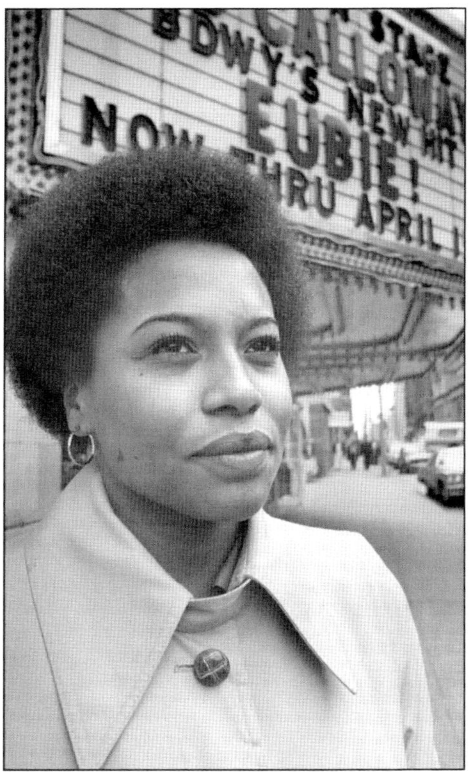

During its life, the Kinloch School District produced many outstanding graduates who have gone into all walks of life. Graduate, actress, singer, and dancer Jenifer Lewis, is pictured here in front of the Fox Theatre in St. Louis where she performed in *Eubie* in 1979. Jenifer has also performed on Broadway in *Dreamgirls, Comin' Uptown,* and *Ain't Misbehavin'*. In the past several years, she has made a number of television appearances on such shows as *In Living Color* and *Fresh Prince of Bel Air.* Her silver screen stints include a compelling turn as Zelma Bullock, Tina Turner's mother, in *What's Love Got to Do With It,* and Jackie in *Jackie's Back.* (Photo Courtesy of *St. Louis Post-Dispatch.*)

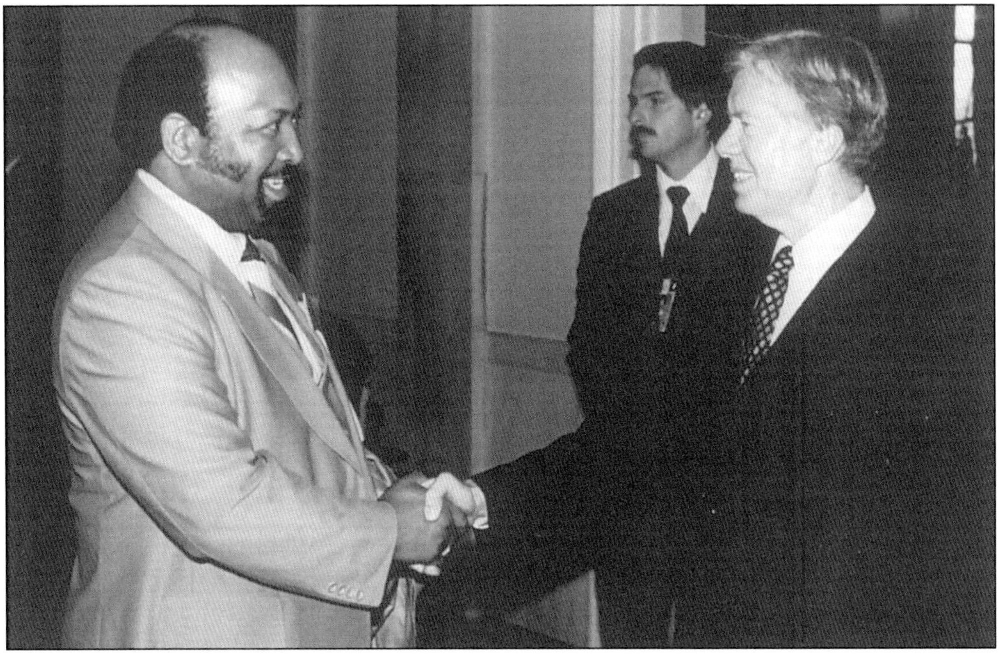

Kinloch graduate Joseph Wells, pictured here with President Jimmy Carter, was elected to the Kinloch School Board and later elected mayor of the city. Wells was also the first black elected member of the Ferguson-Florissant School Board. (Photo Courtesy of Joseph Wells.)

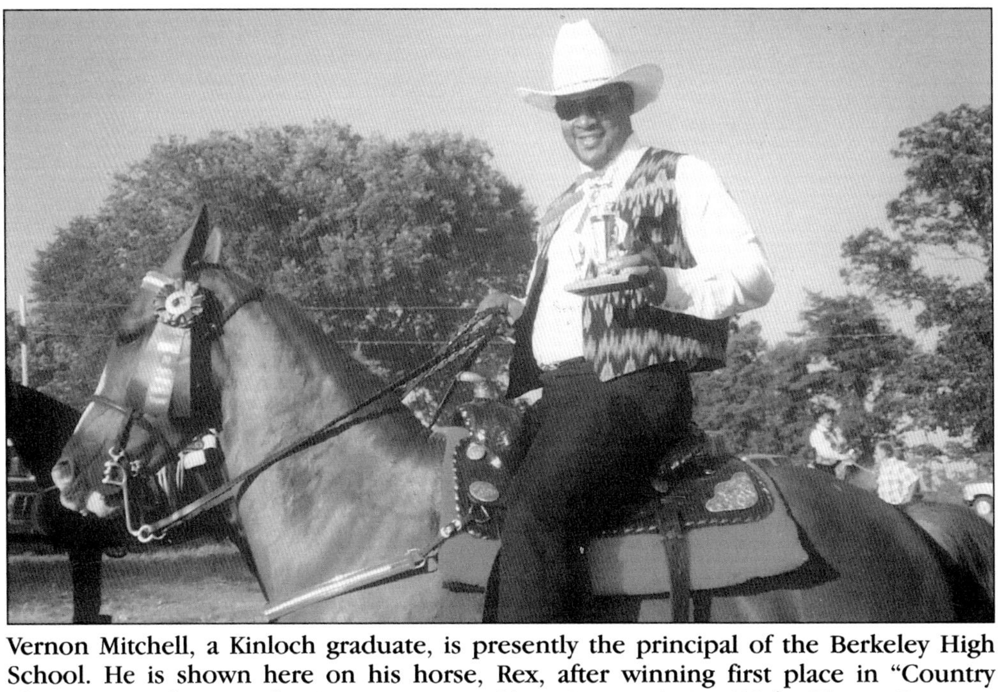

Vernon Mitchell, a Kinloch graduate, is presently the principal of the Berkeley High School. He is shown here on his horse, Rex, after winning first place in "Country Pleasure" at the Lincoln County Fair in Troy, Missouri, in 1996. (Photo Courtesy of Vernon Mitchell.)

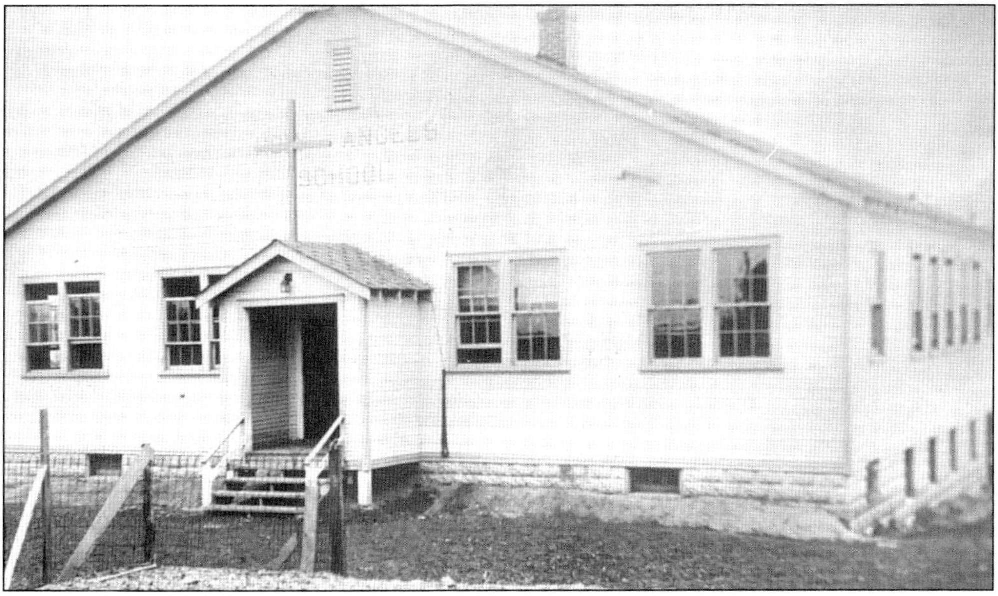

Holy Angels Elementary School, later renamed Our Lady of the Angels, opened in the fall of 1931, under the pastorship of Father Otto J. Moorman, S.J. It was staffed by the Sisters of Notre Dame and assisted by Miss Marie Gordon. The school's initial enrollment of 40 students in kindergarten through eighth grade soon grew to 147, as students came from as far away as Wellston, St. Louis, and Robertson. The school is shown here after receiving its first coat of paint. (Photo Courtesy of Holy Angels Church.)

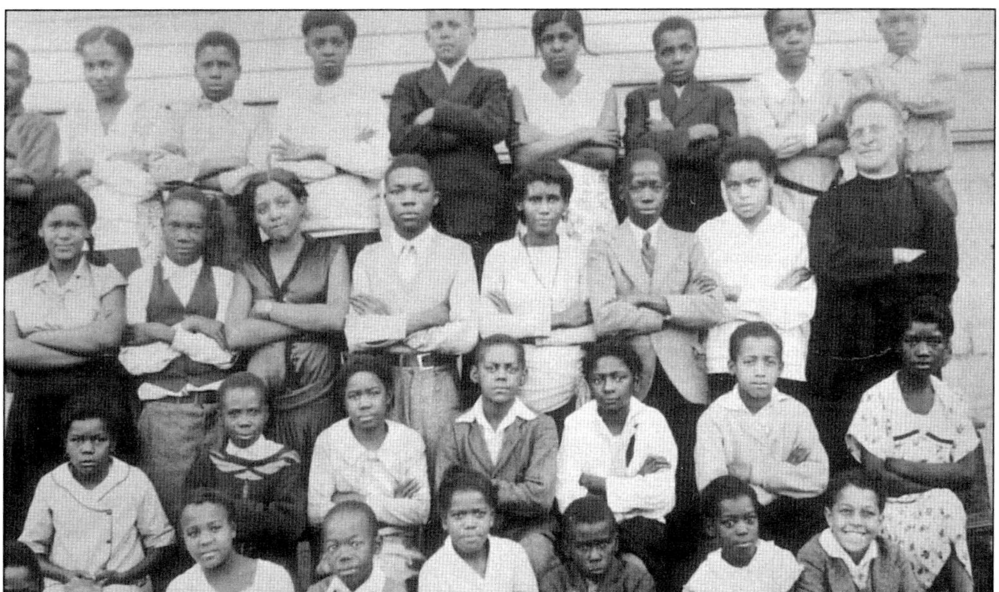

Pictured here are Holy Angel School's first enrollment of fourth, fifth, and sixth graders after it opened in 1931. With them is Father Otto J. Moorman. (Photo Courtesy of Midwest Jesuit Archives.)

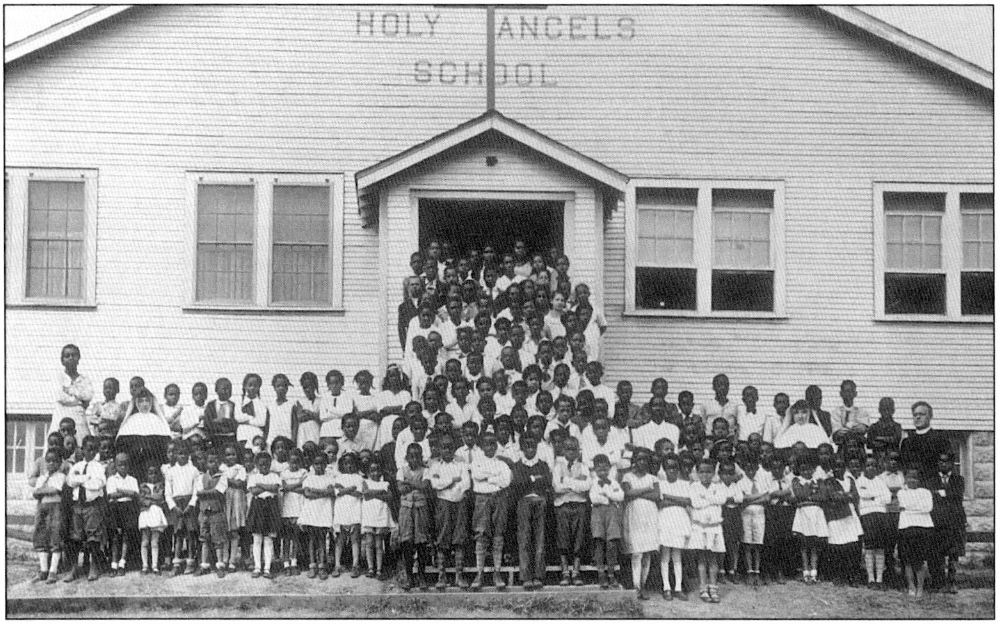

The enrollment of Holy Angels School continued to grow from its initial enrollment of 40 students, as can be seen in this picture taken a year after its opening. (Photo Courtesy of Holy Angels Church.)

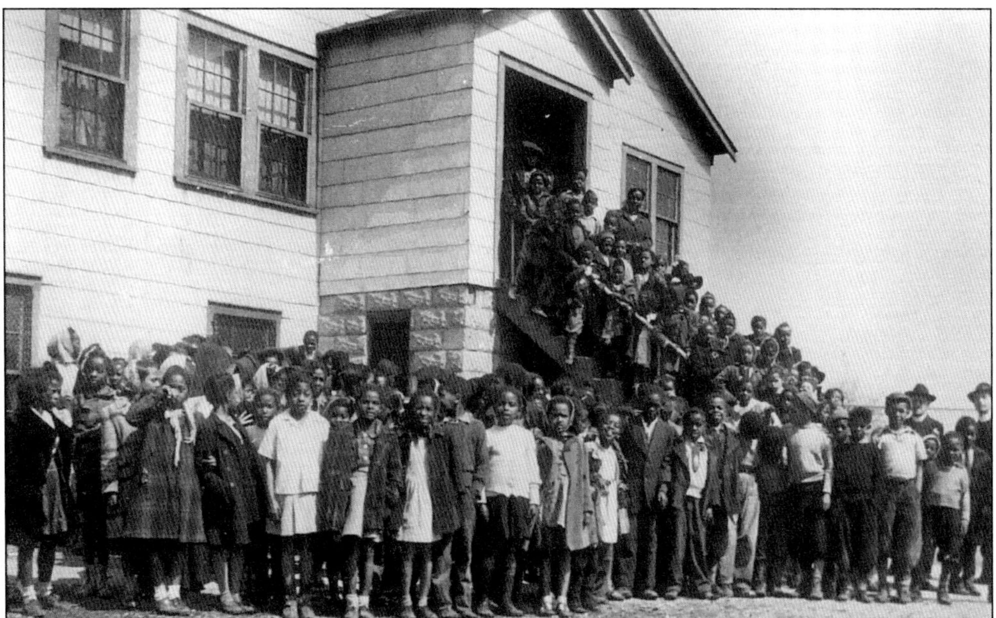

This picture of an ever-growing student body at Holy Angels School was taken in 1933. (Photo Courtesy of Holy Angels Church.)

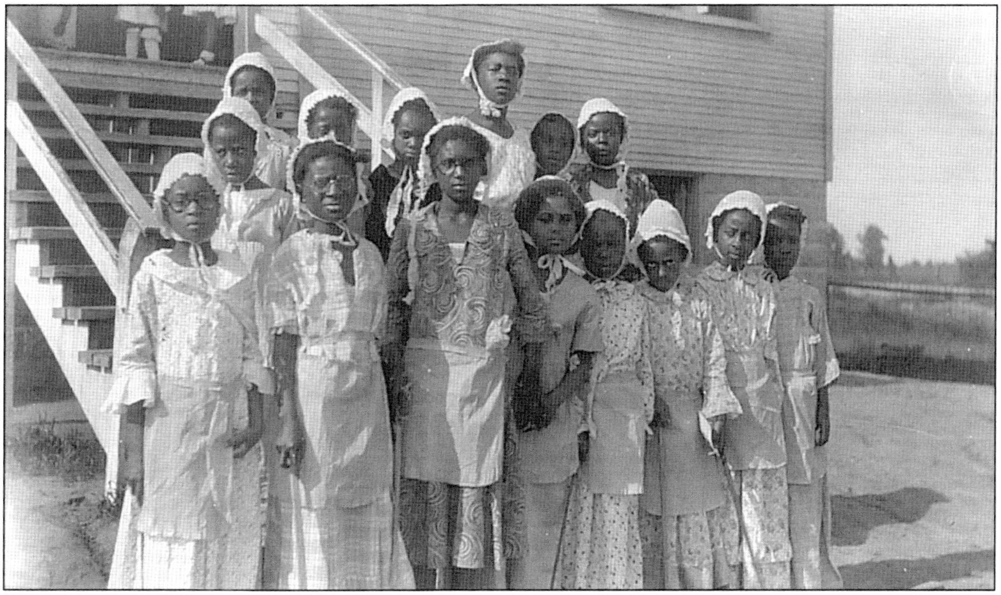

School plays and other fine arts activities were an ongoing part of school curriculum at Holy Angels. These students had roles in a 1932 play entitled *Premature Grandmothers*. (Photo Courtesy of Holy Angels Church.)

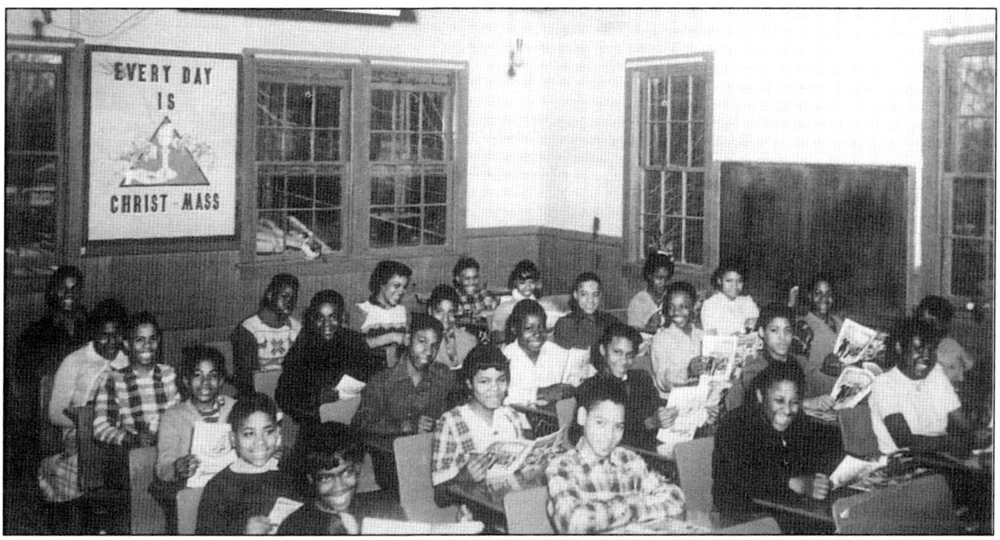

This 1951–52 school year photograph is of the seventh and eighth graders of Holy Angles School. Even though the two grades shared a room, they received separate instructions from one teacher, Sr. Clarita. Students, from left to right, are: (front row) Patricia Whitener, Ernest Simmons, Rosemary Hankins, Charles Thompson, Lucille Dunn, and John Simmons; (second row) Henry Parker, Edna Cornell, Fred Reed, Roy Cornell, and Harvey Alexander; (third row) Claudette Farrell, Carlene Farrell, Otha Johnson, Billy Simmons, and Lesabee Harrington; (fourth row) Annie Lee Ross, Billy Vaughn, Henry Bradford, Bobby Miller, Hazel Bradford, and Leonard Wright; (fifth row) unidentified, Lester Bryant, Magnolia Williams, and Lavern Taylor. (Photo Courtesy of Pat Whitener.)

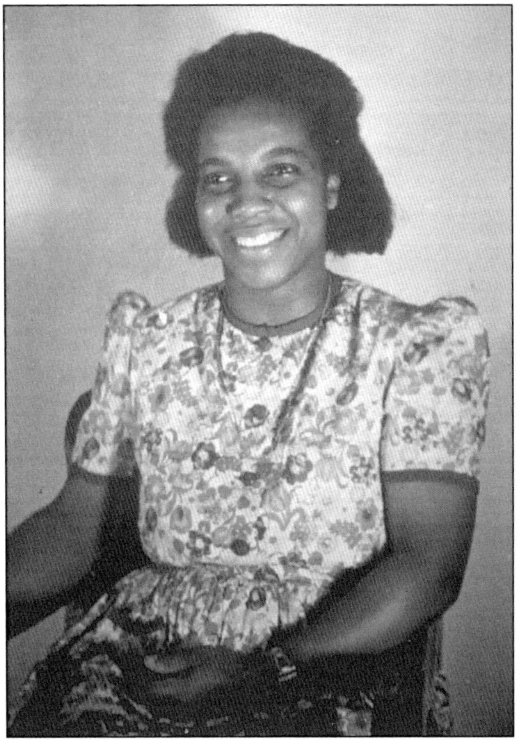

Miss Marie Gordon, the only black teacher at Holy Angels School for many years, is shown here. It is reported that she and her sister Rebecca wanted to become nuns and, after meeting no success, took a vow of chastity and remained unmarried. Along with her teaching duties, she served as the choir director, altar and church decorator, and assistant to the priest in preparation for mass and special occasions. (Photo Courtesy of the Midwest Jesuit Archives.)

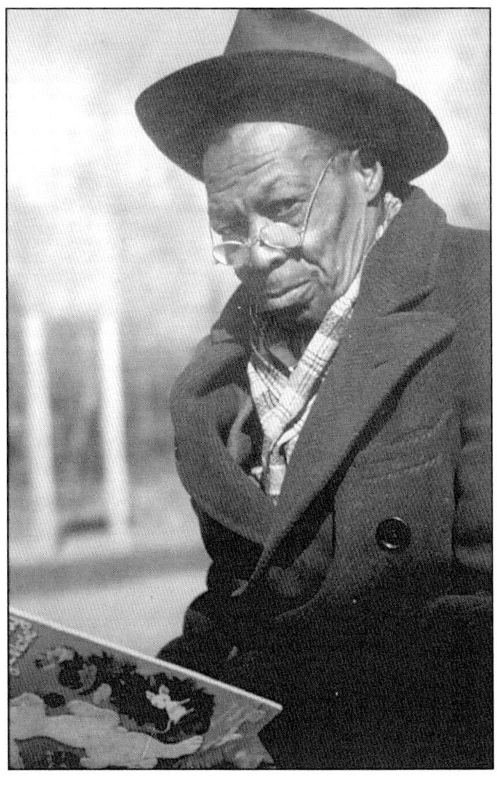

George "Paw" Gordon, pictured here, was the faithful custodian, handyman, and driver for Holy Angels Church for many years. He and his daughters lived in a small brick home built for them a few hundred feet from the church by one of the parish's benefactors. In the evenings in the early years of the parish, Gordon taught woodcraft to students and taught adults how to play a horn. (Photo Courtesy of Holy Angels Church.)

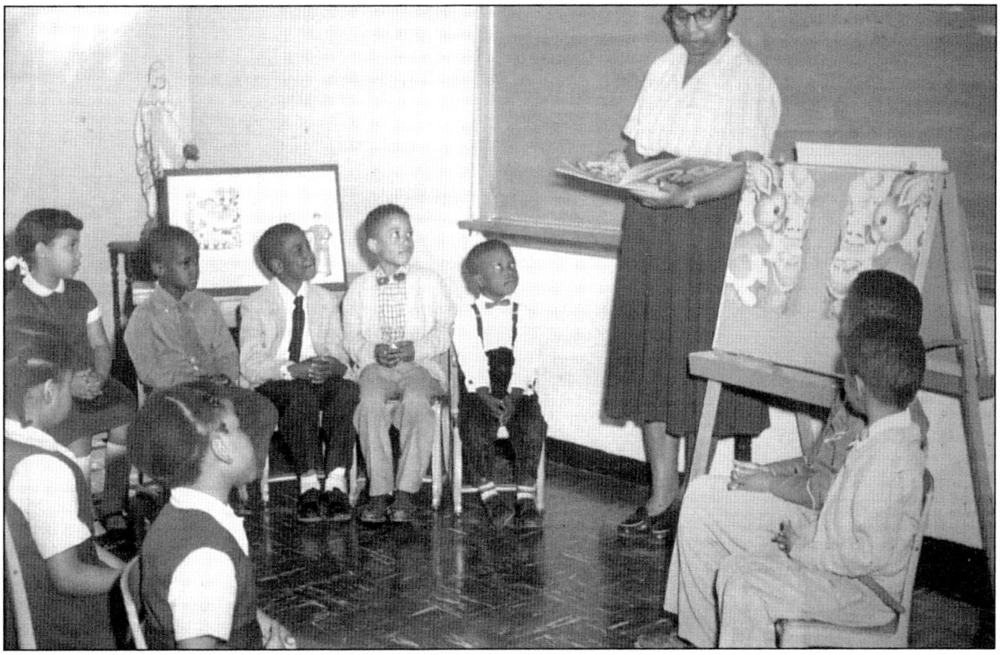

In this 1950s photograph, Miss Marie Gordon is shown with a class of attentive kindergartners. Miss Gordon also taught first and second grades and music. She remained the only black teacher at Holy Angels School until 1956, when the Oblates, an order of black nuns, took over the teaching duties from the Sisters of Notre Dame. (Photo Courtesy of Holy Angels Church.)

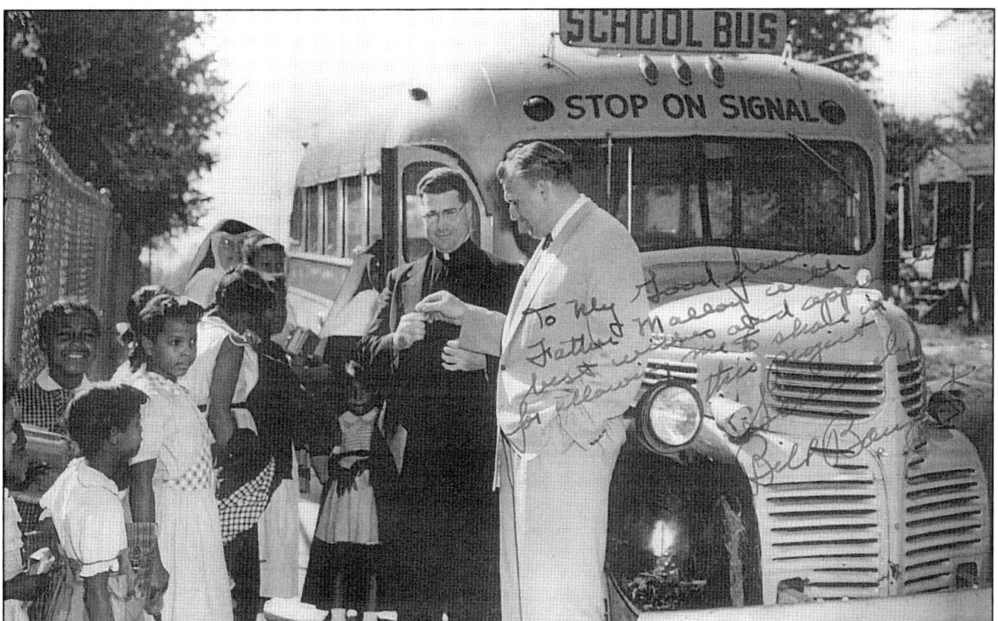

Father Patrick J. Malloy is shown here accepting the keys to the school's new bus while students patiently wait to take a look inside. (Photo Courtesy of Holy Angels Church.)

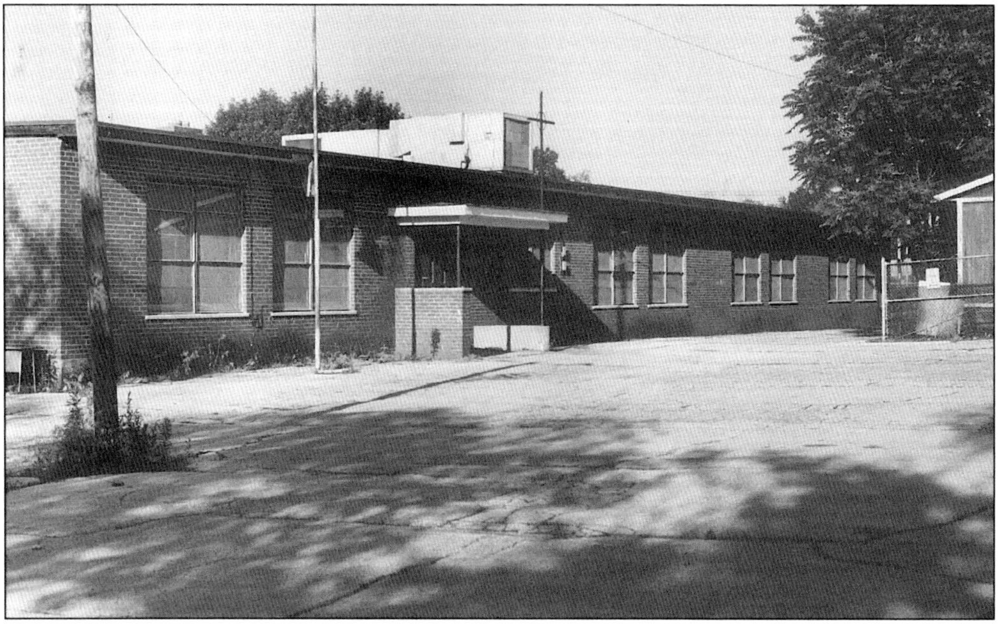

This second Holy Angels School was opened in 1955. The new school was constructed on the site of the old school's playground. Children were provided education from kindergarten through eighth grade. (Photo by John A. Wright.)

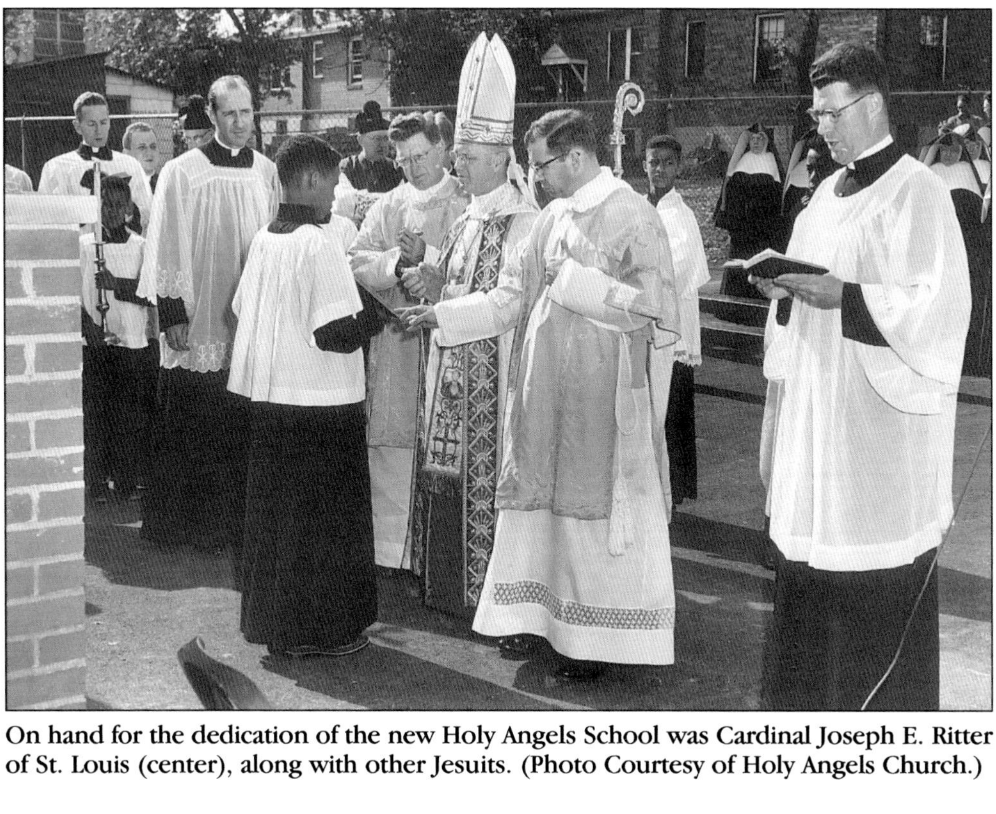

On hand for the dedication of the new Holy Angels School was Cardinal Joseph E. Ritter of St. Louis (center), along with other Jesuits. (Photo Courtesy of Holy Angels Church.)

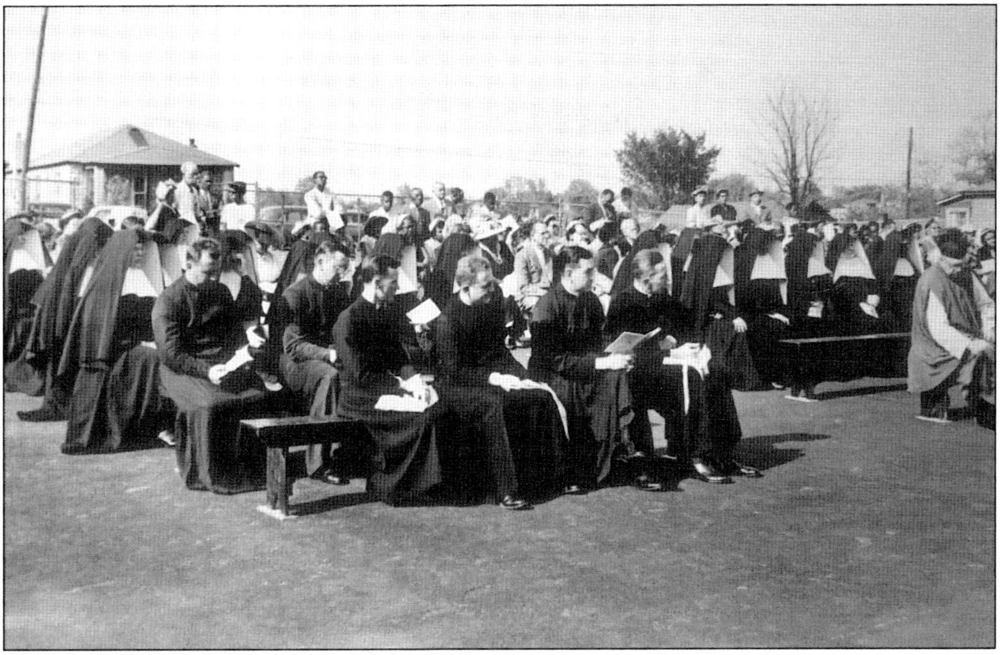

Seated on the school's cafeteria benches are bishops, Jesuit priests, Sisters of Notre Dame, and parishioners, who were photographed at the opening ceremony of the new Holy Angels School in 1955. Of the nuns present, only three taught at the school. They were accompanied by other nuns from the Order's Mother House. (Photo Courtesy of Holy Angels Church.)

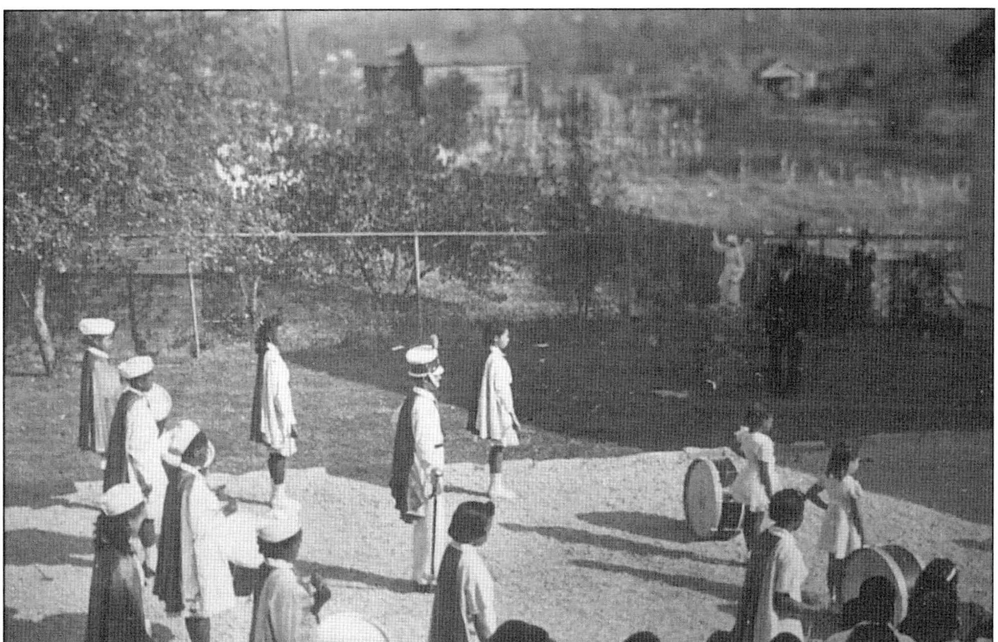

The Kinloch drum and bugle corps is shown here performing during the opening ceremony of Holy Angels School. (Photo Courtesy of Midwest Jesuit Archives.)

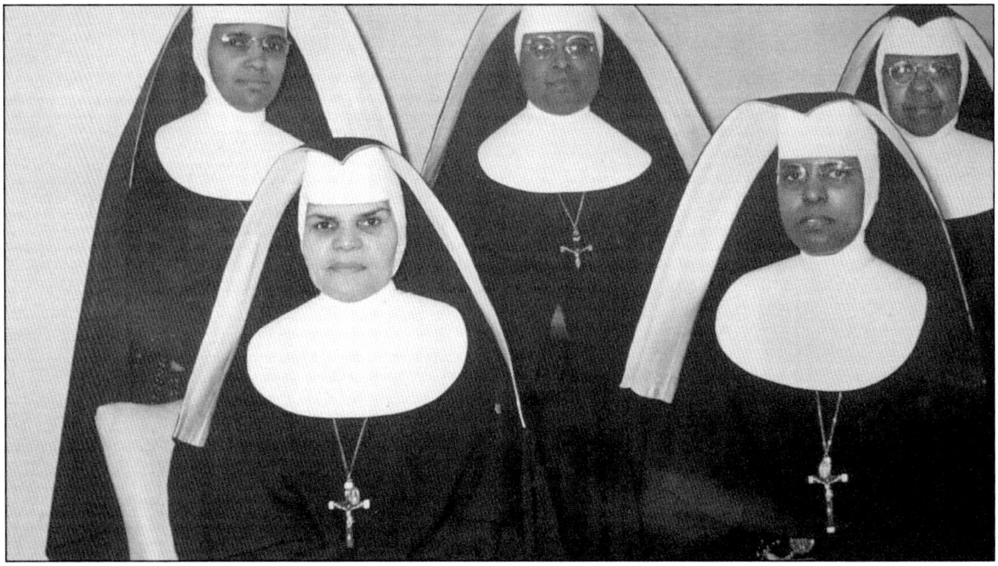

The nuns shown in this photograph are members of the Oblate Order. They took over teaching duties at the school from the Sisters of Notre Dame at the beginning of the 1955–56 school year and remained until the 1970s. The nuns seated, from left to right, are: Mother Providencia, Sr. Duchesne, Sr. Trinita, Sr. Christella, and Sr. Clotel. (Photo Courtesy of Holy Angels Church.)

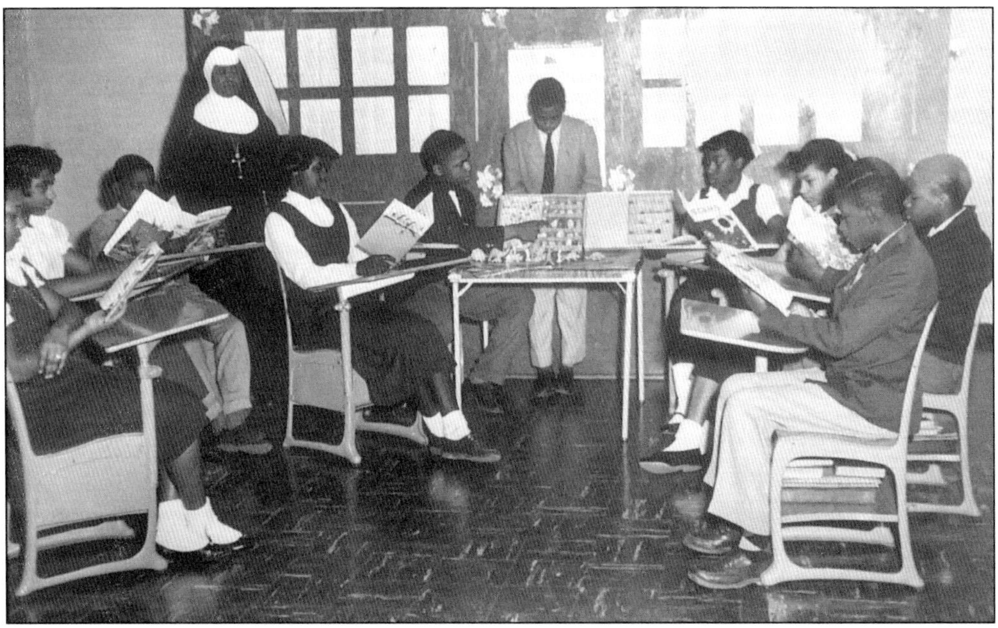

This mid-1960s photograph of a neatly dressed class is shown with their teacher Sister Christella, an Oblate nun. As shown in this picture, the girls were dressed in their uniforms of blue jumpers, white blouses, and white socks. Boys were required to wear shirts and ties and, for special occasions, sport jackets. A uniform of blue pants, white shirts, and blue ties was adopted for boys in the 1970s. (Photo Courtesy of Holy Angels Church.)

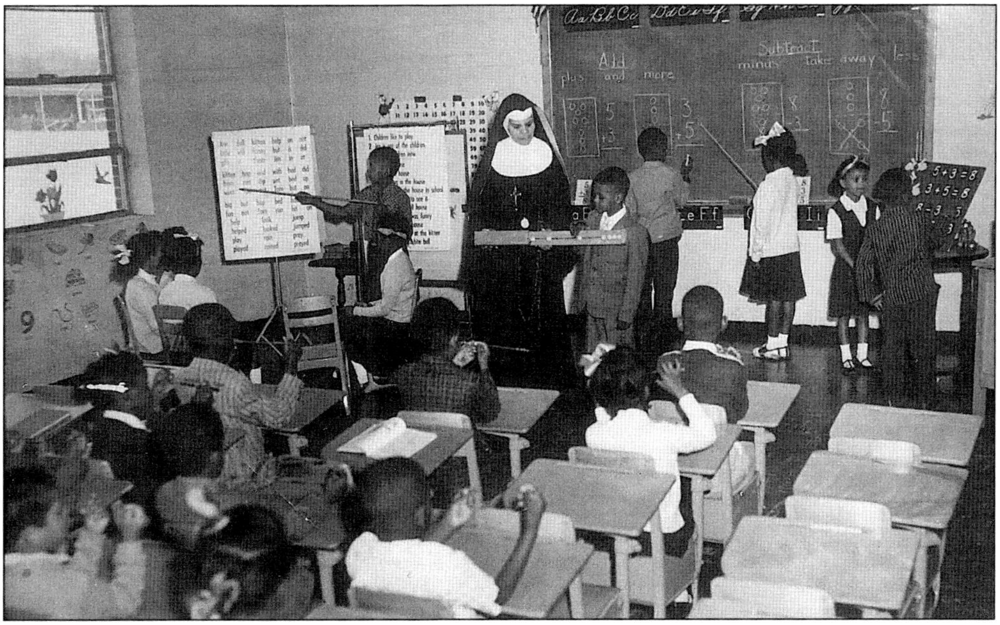

Sister Providencia is shown here teaching a math lesson while some students are working independently on a reading lesson. (Photo Courtesy of Holy Angels Church.)

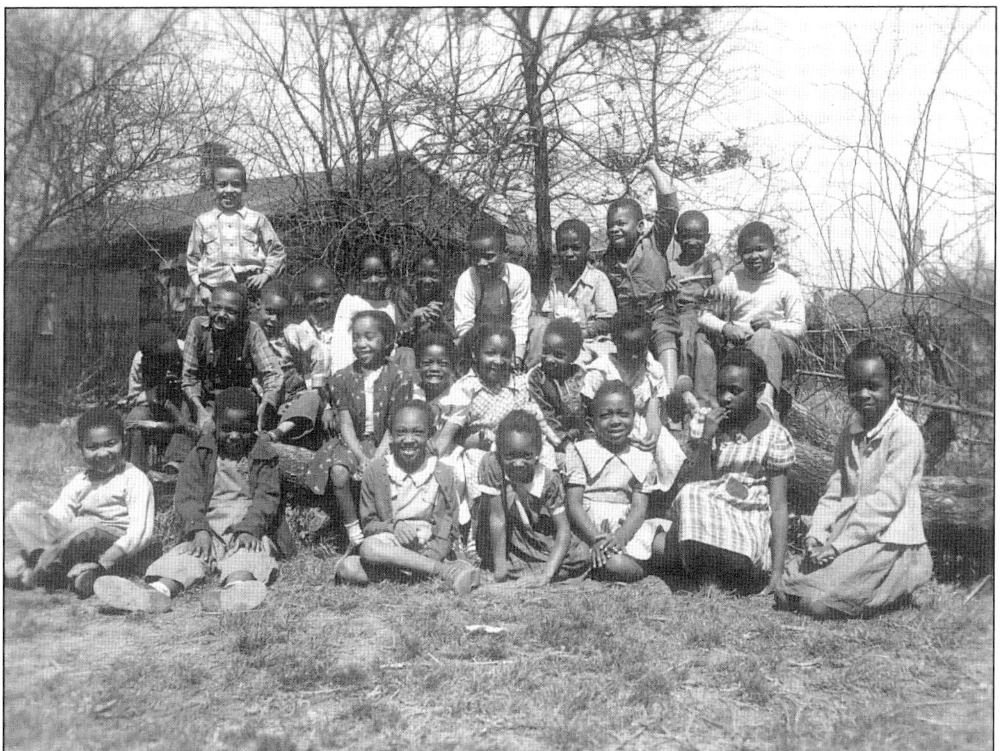

These Holy Angles School students are enjoying themselves during a break on their grassy playground behind the school. (Photo Courtesy Holy Angels Church.)

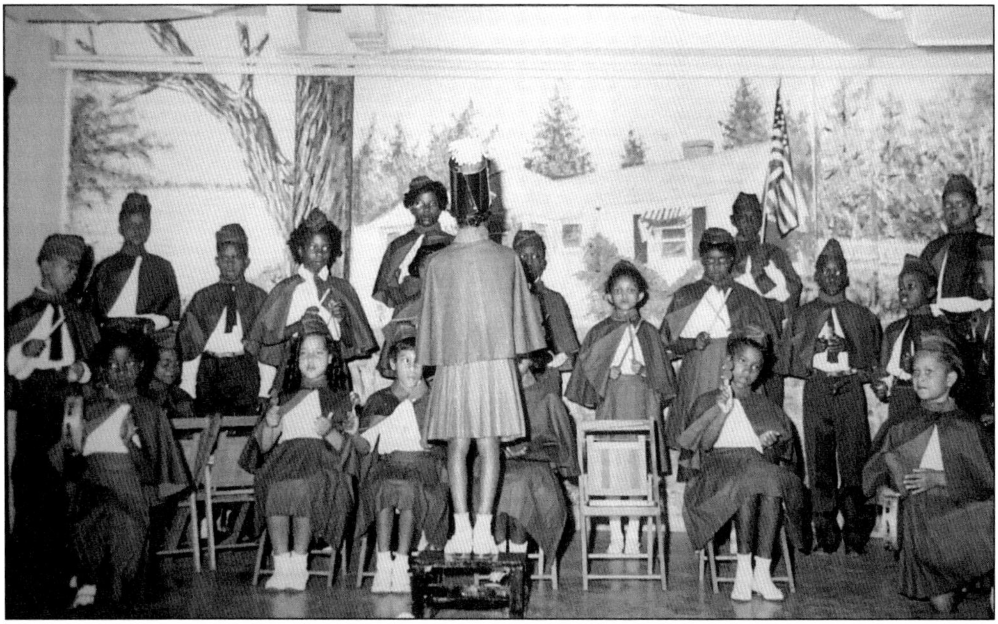

Each spring for several years, the classes of Holy Angels participated in well-staged musical skits. The events were attended and supported by family and friends, and gave young performers an opportunity to demonstrate their talent. This rhythm band is performing in a 1967 musical program at Holy Angels School. (Photo Courtesy of Holy Angels Church.)

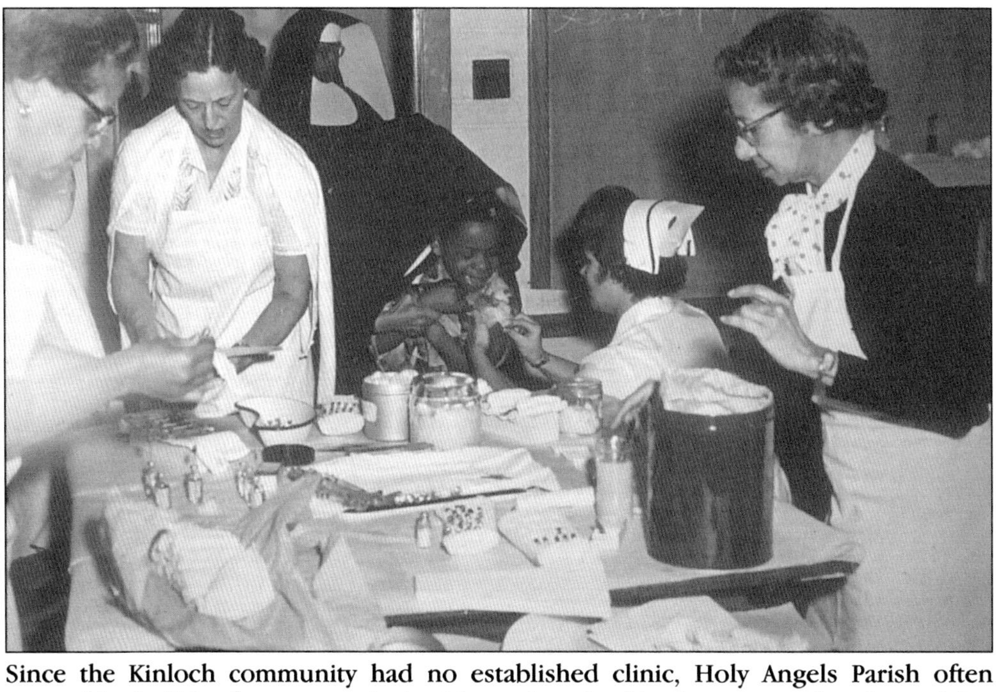

Since the Kinloch community had no established clinic, Holy Angels Parish often opened its facilities for community health services. In this picture a student is receiving an immunization shot. (Photo Courtesy of Holy Angels Church.)

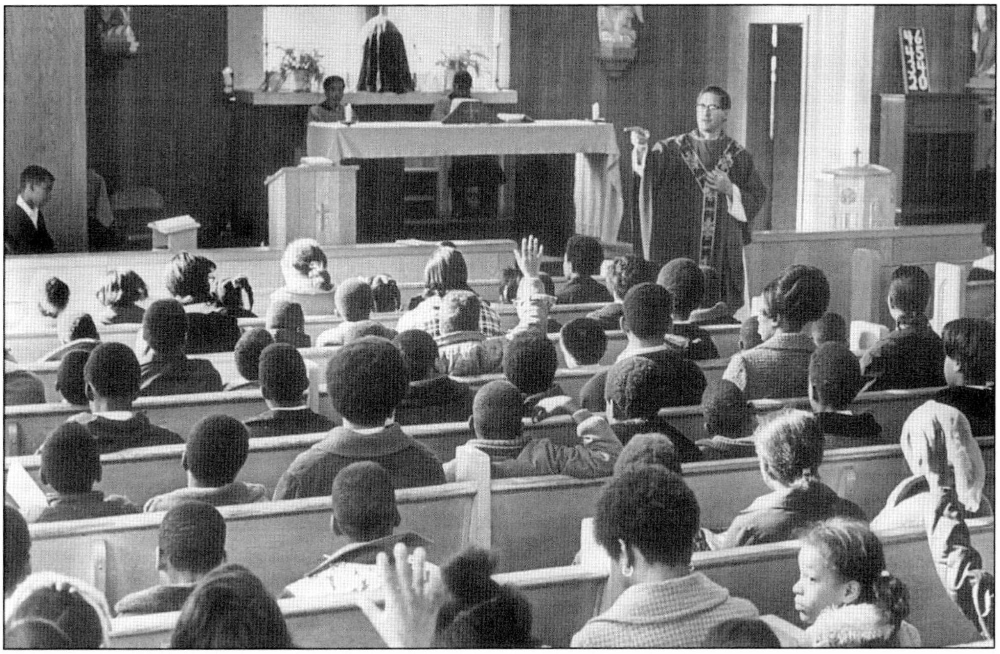

Holy Angels School students are shown here with Father Anthony Seibert during their religious instruction in the 1970s. (Photo Courtesy Holy Angels Church.)

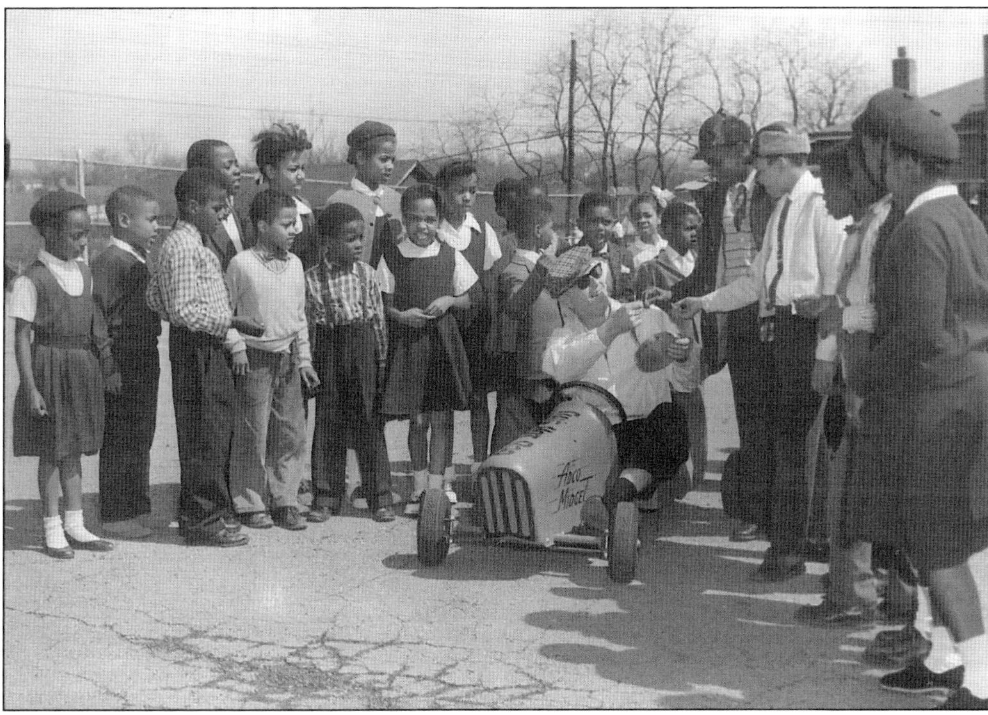

Father Joseph Scheer is pictured here in his hot rod equipped with a lawnmower-type motor. The machine was named for his dog, Fui. Children paid 10¢ to ride around the yard three times. (Photo Courtesy Holy Angels Church.)

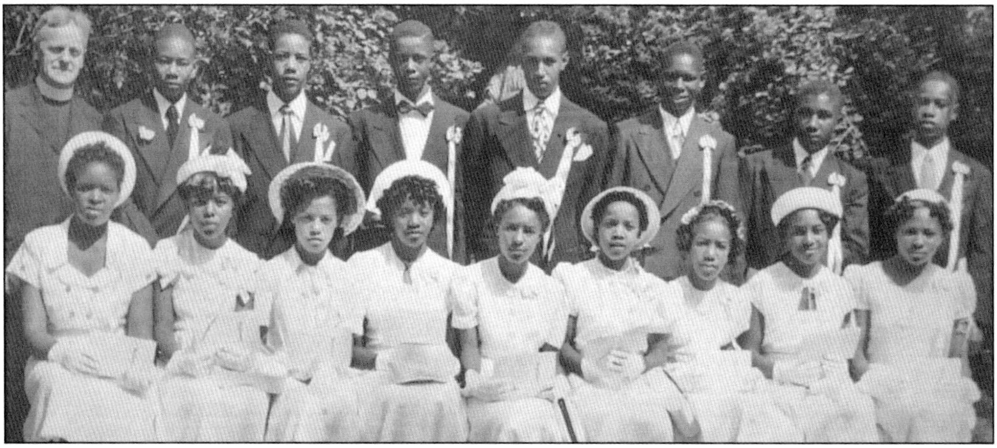

This 1947 class posed with Fr. Otto Moorman after their graduation ceremony at Holy Angels Church. At that time, for graduation the girls were required to wear white clothing and accessories. The boys were required to wear blue suits and white shirts. These students furthered their education at either Kinloch High School or St. Josephs Catholic High School in the City of St. Louis. Graduates, from left, are: (seated) Bessie Mae Turner, Delores Jackson, Virginia Johnson, Elva Jean Alexander, Bernice Houston, Audrey Owens, Lavina Lewis, Jean Stewart, Grace Fulghum; (standing) Fr. Otto Moorman, Raymond Vaughn, Robert Brady, Fred Ward, Ernest Wells, Fred Williams, and Nathaniel Battle. (Photo Courtesy of Midwest Jesuit Archives.)

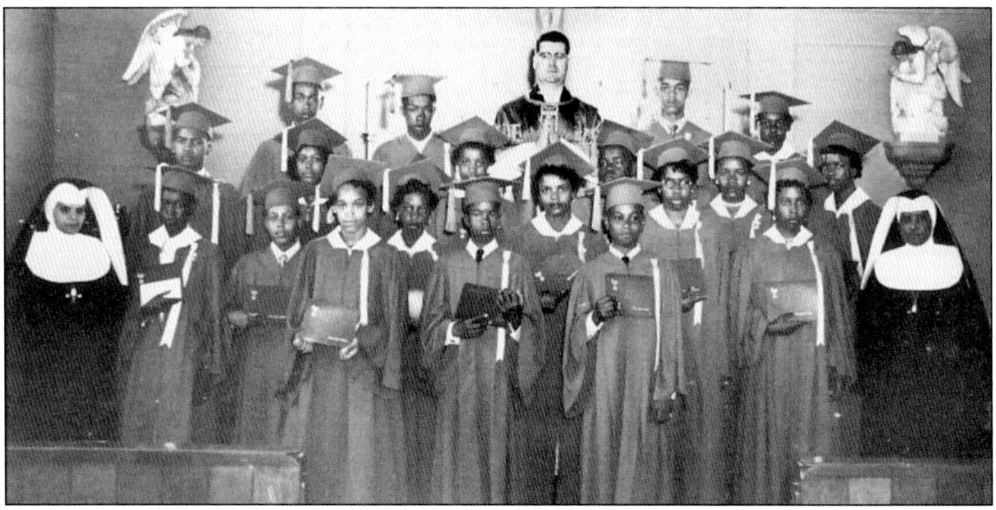

These serious looking eighth grade graduates were photographed in Holy Angels Church following their graduation ceremony on Sunday, June 10, 1956. This was the second class of graduates since the new school opened in 1955. One graduate, Edmond Squires, is currently an elementary principal in St. Louis. The graduates, their teachers, and the parish priest, from left to right, are: (first row) Mother Providencia, Katherine Hodge, Thomas Vaugh, Darlene Owens, Ronald Thompson, Willie Bathey, Peggy Whitener, Sister Christella; (second row) Barbara Daugherty, Robert Bradford, Loretta Johnson, Wanda Stewart, Rose Marie Ross, Edmond Squires, Regina Owens, Marcella Murray, Raymond Brucannon, Gordon Miller, William King, Fr. Patrick J. Malloy, William Hamler, and Essie Mae Bailey. (Photo Courtesy of Edmond Squires.)

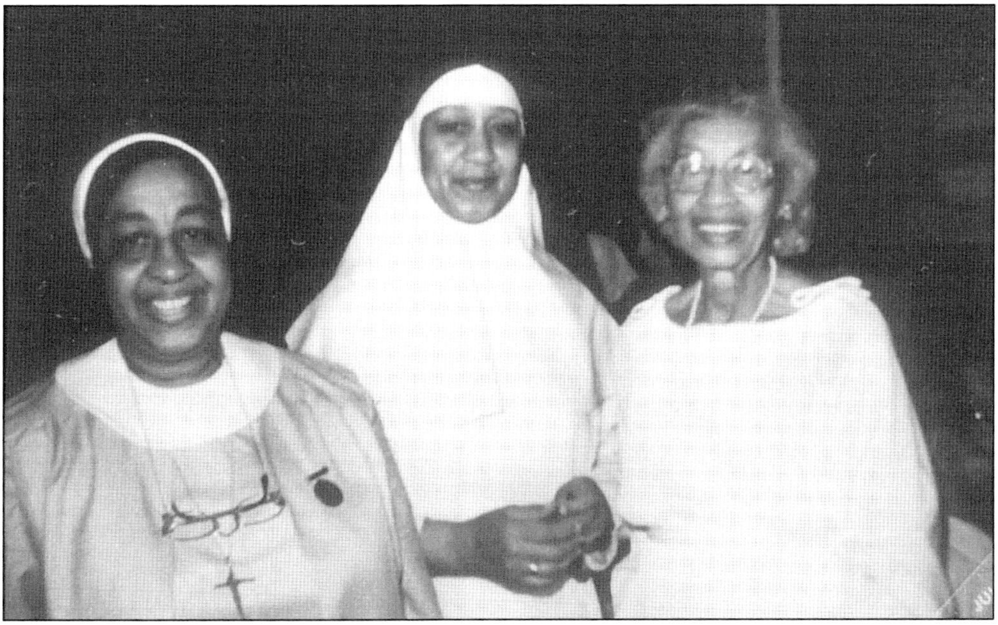

Mrs. Annabell Allen (right), a longtime resident of Kinloch and faithful member of Holy Angels Catholic Church, is shown in this 1980s photograph with two of her four daughters. Sister Mary Immaculata, (Olivia—left) joined the Franciscan Handmaids in 1948, and Sister May Aquinas, (Yvonne—center) later joined a cloistered order of Dominicans. The Allen children were educated at Holy Angels Elementary School. (Photo Courtesy of Victoria Cothran.)

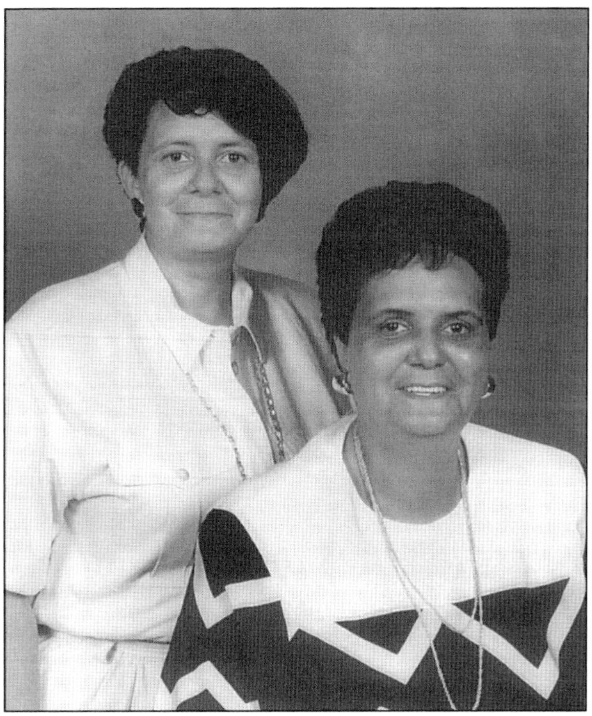

Delores and Victoria Cothran, alumni of Our Lady of the Angels School, returned to the school and the community after receiving their college education. Delores, on the left, taught at the school for over 39 years. Victoria became the school's first lay principal.

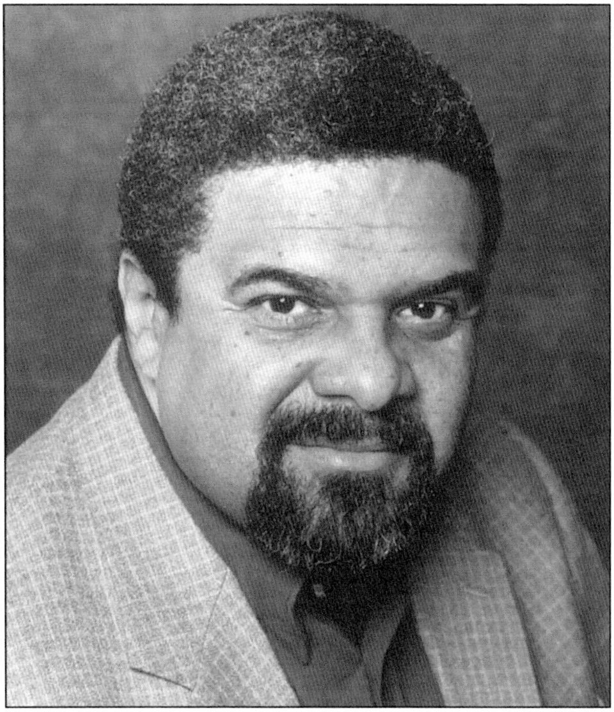

John Cothran Jr., an alumni of Holy Angels School, began his stage career in Holy Angels School's spring musicals and went on to star in television, film, and theatre. He has appeared in over one hundred theatre productions and numerous films, including *Boyz in the Hood*, *Kiss the Girls*, and *Poetic Justice*. Among his television performances are parts in *Star Trek*, *Touched By an Angel*, *Brewster Place*, and *Seinfeld*. (Photo Courtesy of John Cothran Jr.)

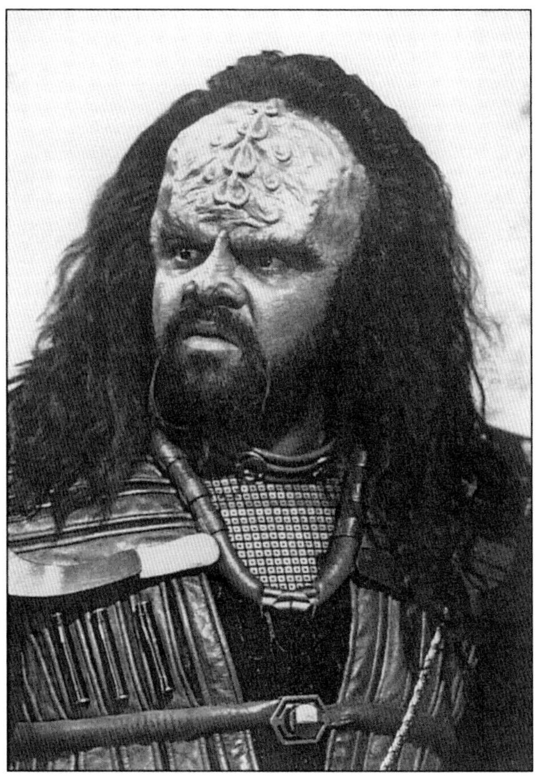

John Cothran Jr. is shown here in costume for his appearance in the television series *Star Trek*. (Photo Courtesy of John Cothran Jr.)

Three

A DIVERSITY OF FAITHS

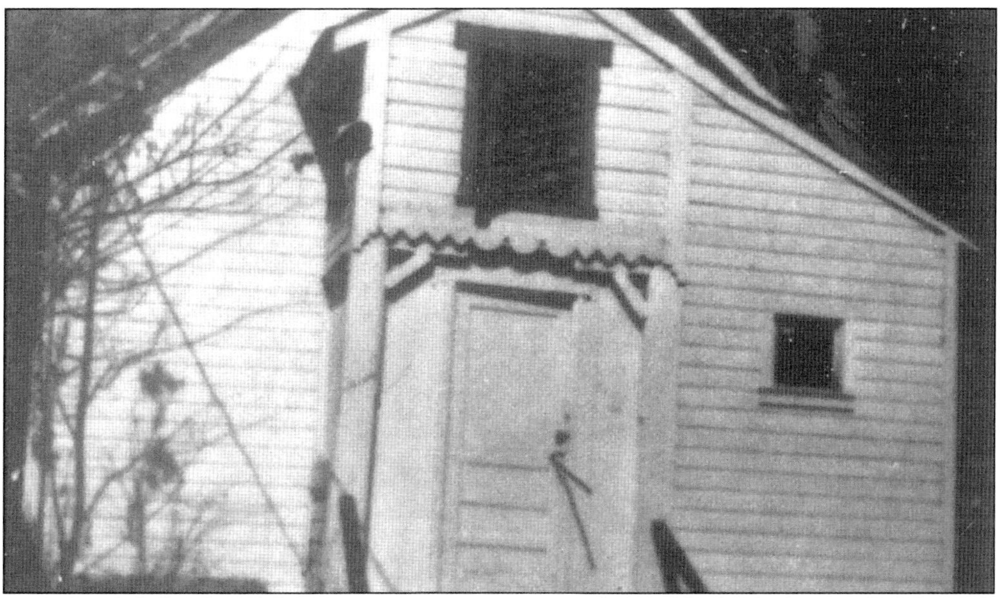

The church has traditionally been a formative and controlling influence in the lives of Kinlochians in spiritual matters, as well as in other areas of life. There were more churches than any other institutions in the community. Over the years, churches have served as an instrument of expression and action in civic, cultural, and educational concerns. They have also provided inspired leadership in the community's struggle for a fuller life. Mount Olive Missionary Baptist Church in Ferguson, shown here, was the sole place of worship for black Kinlochians until 1901. (Photo Courtesy of Ferguson Historical Society.)

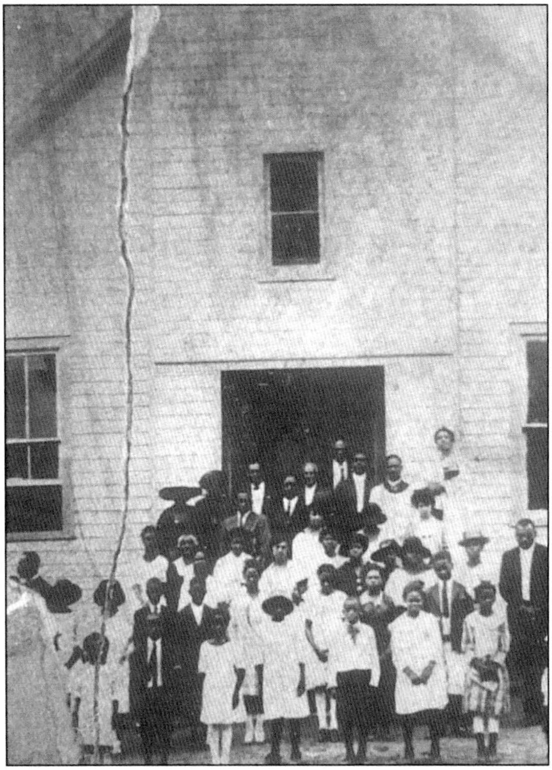

Shortly after the Kinloch Park Subdivision was established, some of the black families felt a deep need for a place to hold religious services in their own community. In April 1901, after meeting in private homes, the group organized upon receiving approval from the Mount Olive Missionary Baptist Church in Ferguson and established a church. The new church was named First Missionary Baptist Church that same month. Members are shown here outside of the church's first building at 5836 Washington Avenue. (Photo Courtesy of First Missionary Baptist Church.)

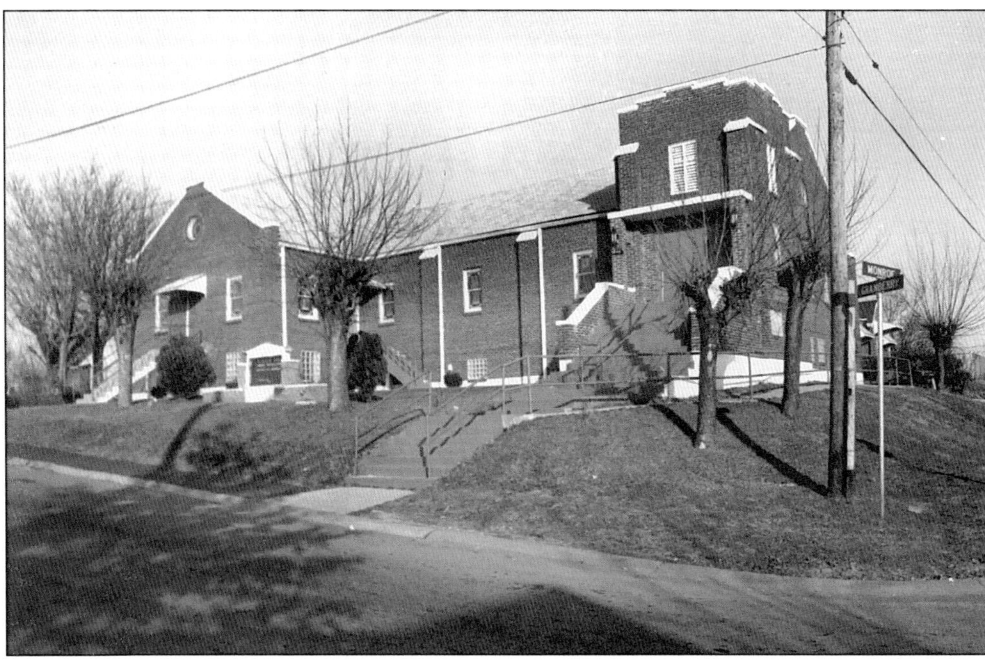

In 1955, members of First Missionary Baptist Church marched into their present building shown here at 5944 Monroe Street. Their previous building was destroyed by fire on September 20, 1950. (Photo by John A. Wright.)

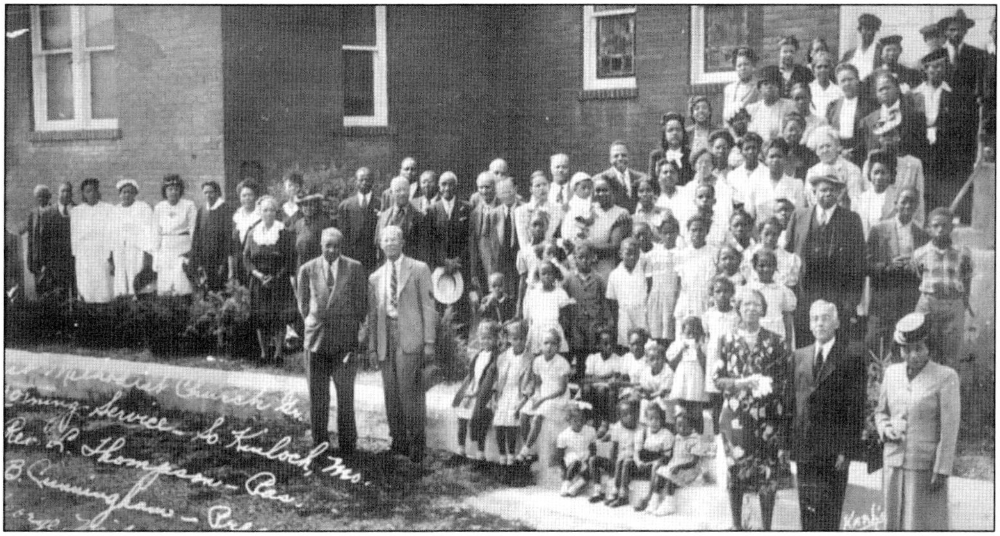

This is a picture of a 1946 Sunday school class at First United Methodist Church. The church is the second oldest in the community. It was organized in 1904 as the First Methodist Episcopal Church by Rev. B.J. Abbott, pastor of Union Memorial Methodist Church in St. Louis, where many of the local congregation were members. The first members of the new church were Mr. and Mrs. John Wheeler, Mr. and Mrs. William Phoenix, Mr. and Mrs. William Winfrey, Lulla Braggs, George Williams, Louise Abernathy, James Minor, and Una Catherine Williams. (Photo Courtesy of Samuel and Bernice Boyd.)

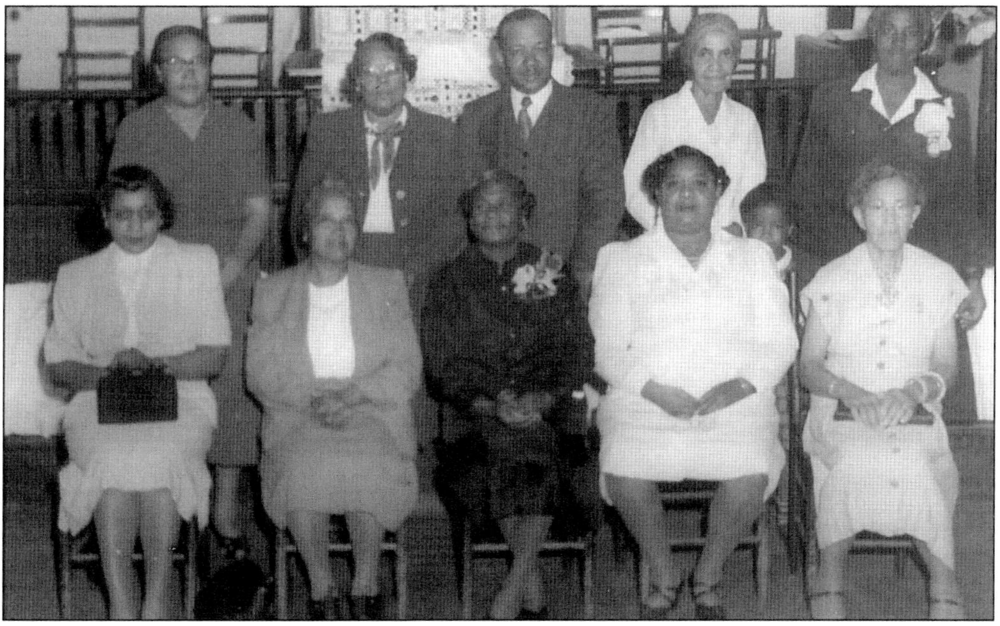

This early photograph is the First United Methodist Church Steward Board. They are, from left: (first row) ? Banks, Virgie Edwards, Vinne Simmons, Rosena English, Dale Cross; (second row) Victoria Boyd, Lucille Cameron, Rev. W.T. Mitchell, Alpha Robinson, and Naomi Drake. (Photo Courtesy of Ann Boyd.)

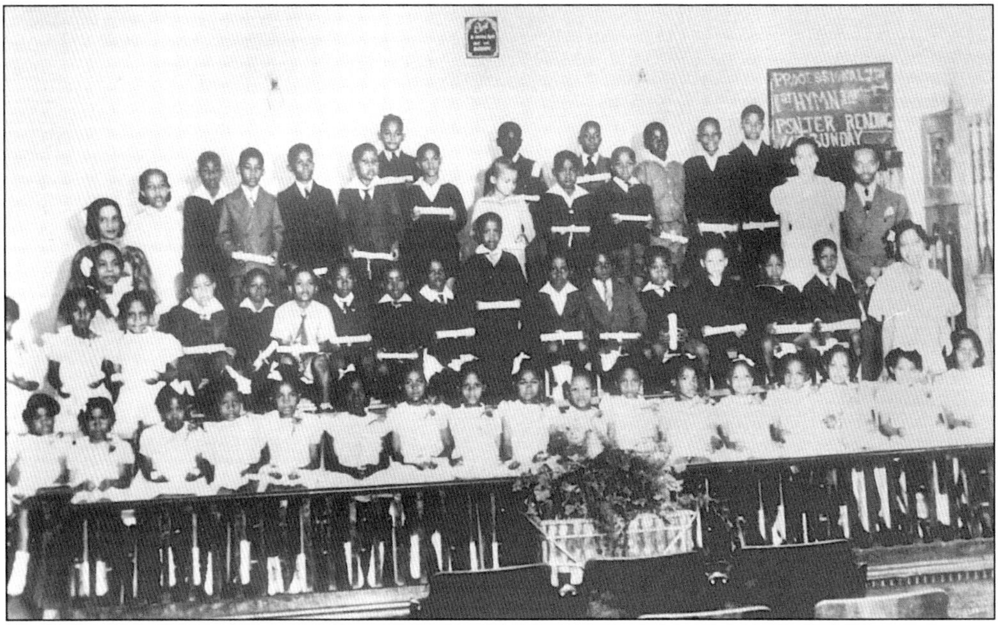

This 1939 Dunbar School first grade class celebrated promotion to second grade at First United Methodist Church. The church often served as a site for school events prior to the construction of the Kinloch High School auditorium. (Photo Courtesy of Samuel and Bernice Boyd.)

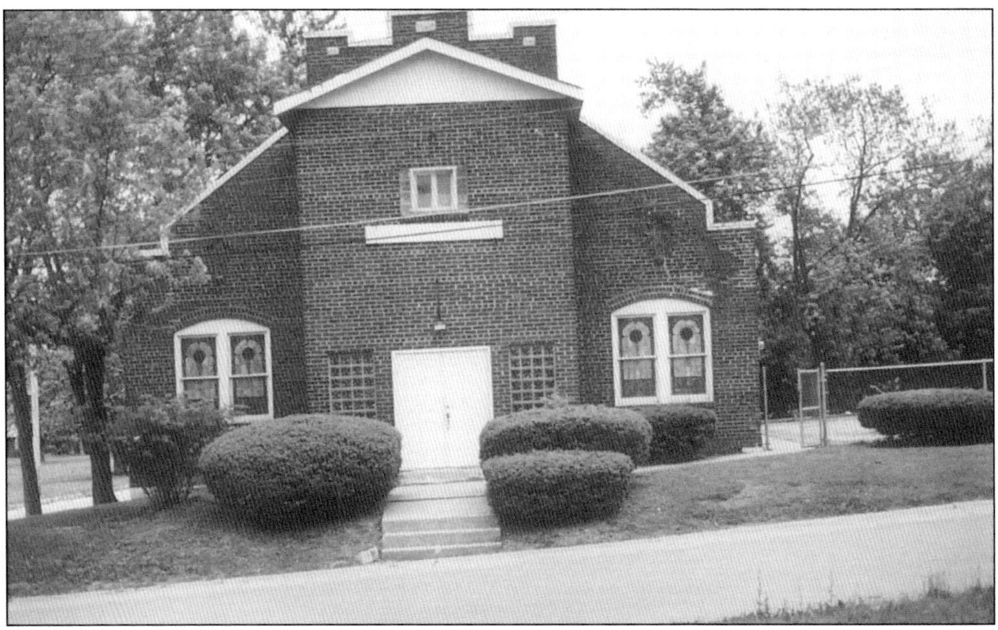

Under an apple tree in her front yard on King Street, Mother Brown started the Kinloch Church of God in Christ around 1914. Work continued on the sanctuary the next year under the pastorship of Elder Cleveland Bell and his assistant Elder M.H. Norman. In 1949, fire damaged the church and another building. In 1952, members marched into the church shown in this photograph. (Photo by John A. Wright.)

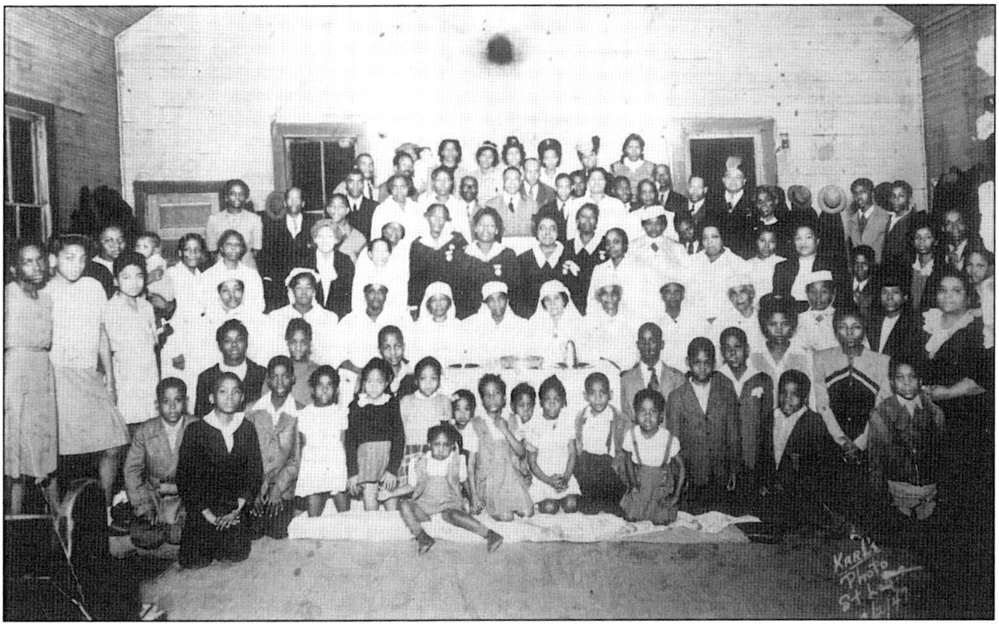

Members of the Mothers Board of Kinloch Church of God in Christ are shown here during a revival in 1947. (Photo Courtesy of Marion Holbrook.)

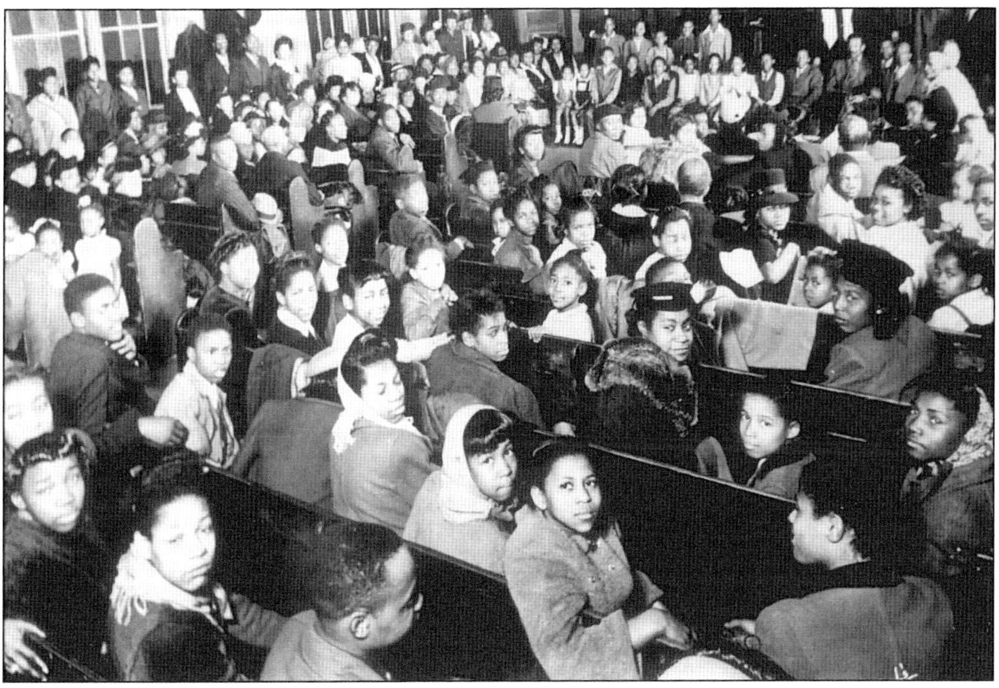

This photograph captured the closing of Rev. Eddie Sangster's last revival in Kinloch at the old Church of God in Christ on February 9, 1947. (Photo Courtesy of Clifford and Doris Eldridge.)

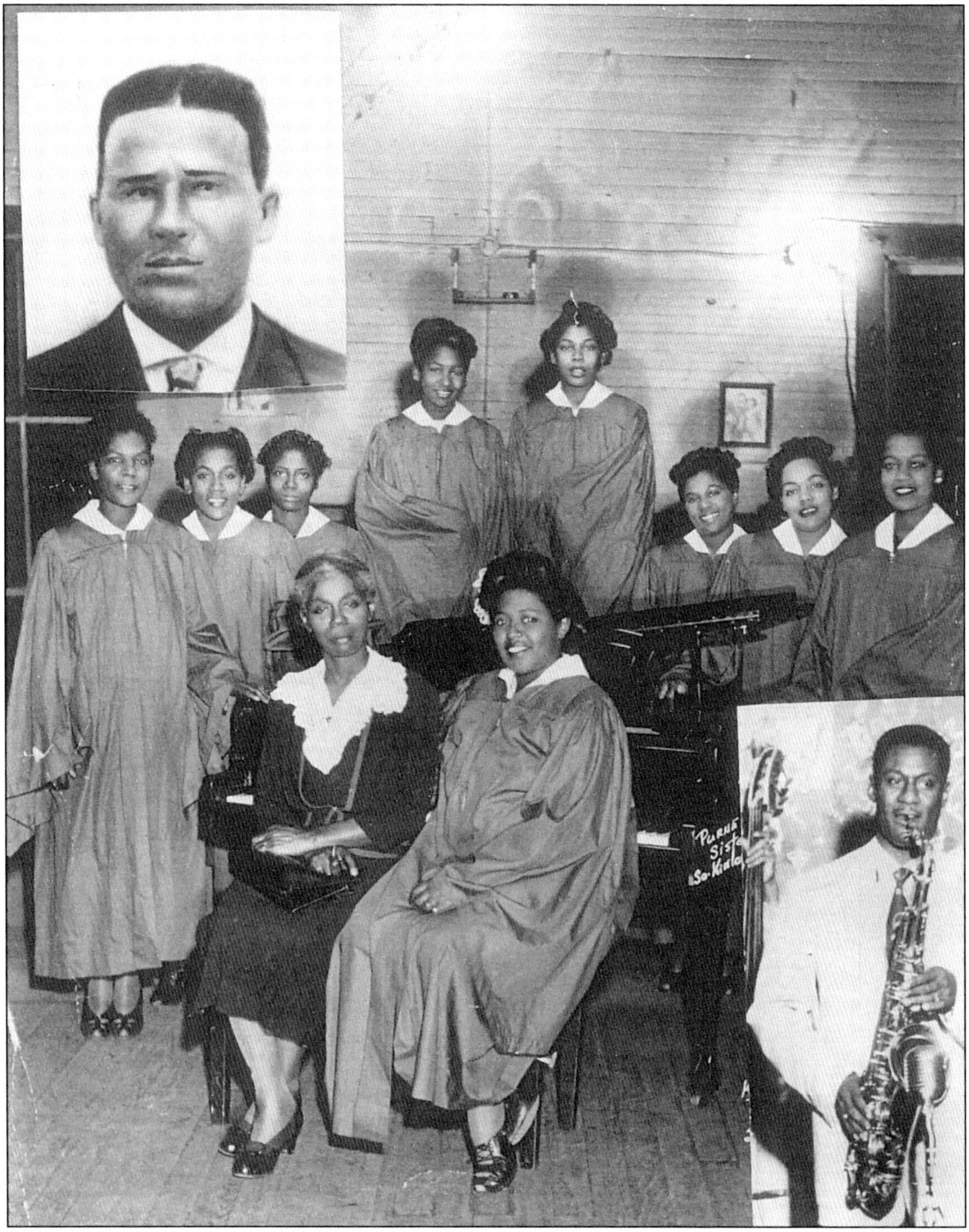

The Purnell sisters, a well-known singing group at the Church of God in Christ in Kinloch, are pictured here with their parents and brother. These nine sisters performed throughout Kinloch and the St. Louis area during the 1940s and '50s. They are, from left to right: (seated) Ethel Purnell and Clee Ethel Lyons; (bottom right corner) Curtis Purnell (their only brother); (second row) Leila Williams, Mary Bristol, Morzie Polk, Venecee Brooks, Geneva Dalton, Lillie Boyd, Lesie Oliver, Esther Webb; and (top left hand corner) Marshall Purnell (their father). (Photo and portrait Courtesy of Geneva Dalton.)

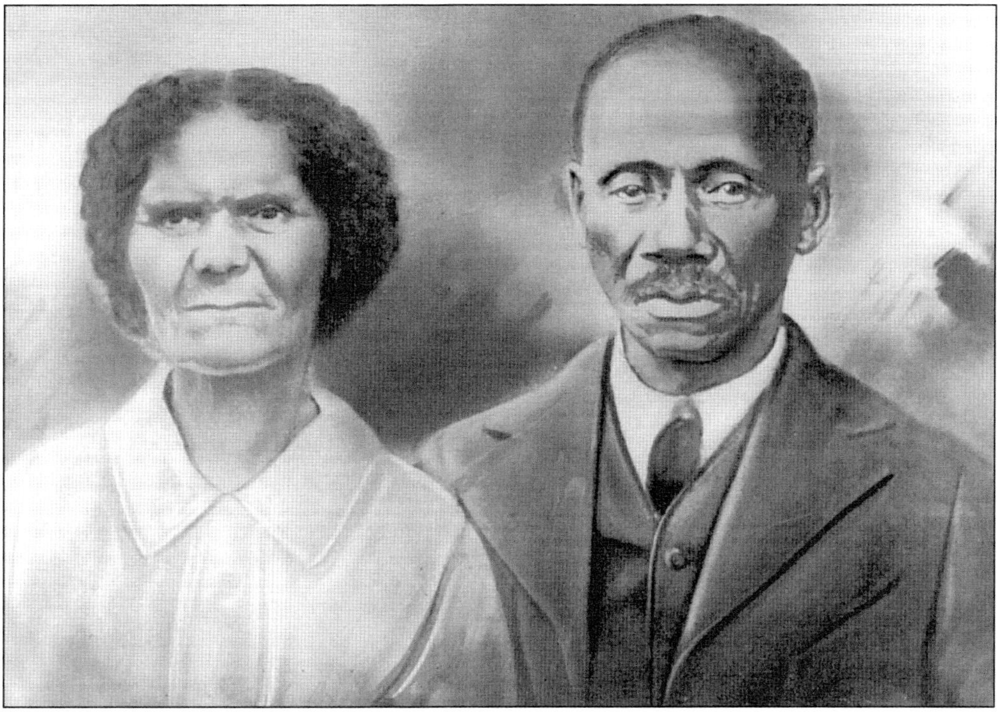

Pictured here are Fred and Sally Davis, longtime members of the Church of God in Christ who came to Kinloch in the 1920s. They were former slaves and later sharecroppers in Arkansas. Sallie and Fred are remembered as having constantly preached family unity to their 11 children, a message that has been preserved through succeeding generations. (Photo Courtesy of Lesie Oliver.)

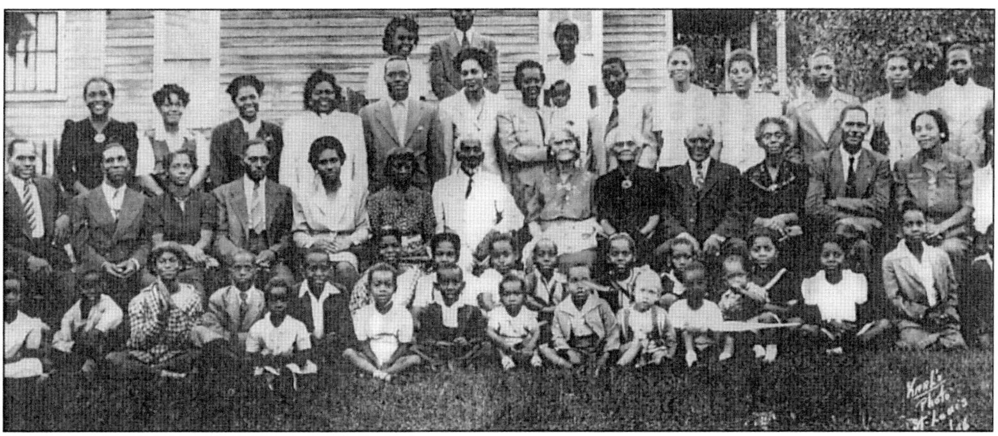

Five generations of family members gathered in Kinloch on September 27, 1946, to honor Fred Davis on his 109th birthday. Fred is the seated gentleman in the second row in the white suit and white beard. His wife Sallie (age 90) is seated to his left. Family members include Billy Davis, a former Fifth Dimension singer and his wife Marilyn McCoo. (Photo Courtesy of Lesie Oliver.)

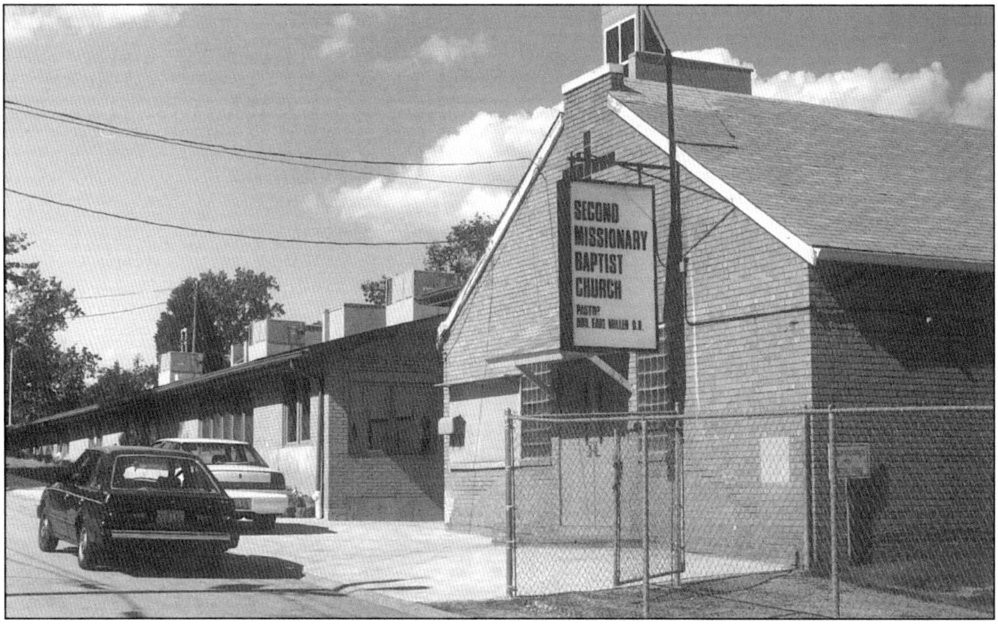

The Second Missionary Baptist Church shown here was constructed in 1979, but was organized May 16, 1914, under the leadership of Reverend Costello. Prior to 1918, when the church bought its present site and constructed, services were held in a small frame structure "down on the ditch or creek" as it was called. (Photo by John A. Wright.)

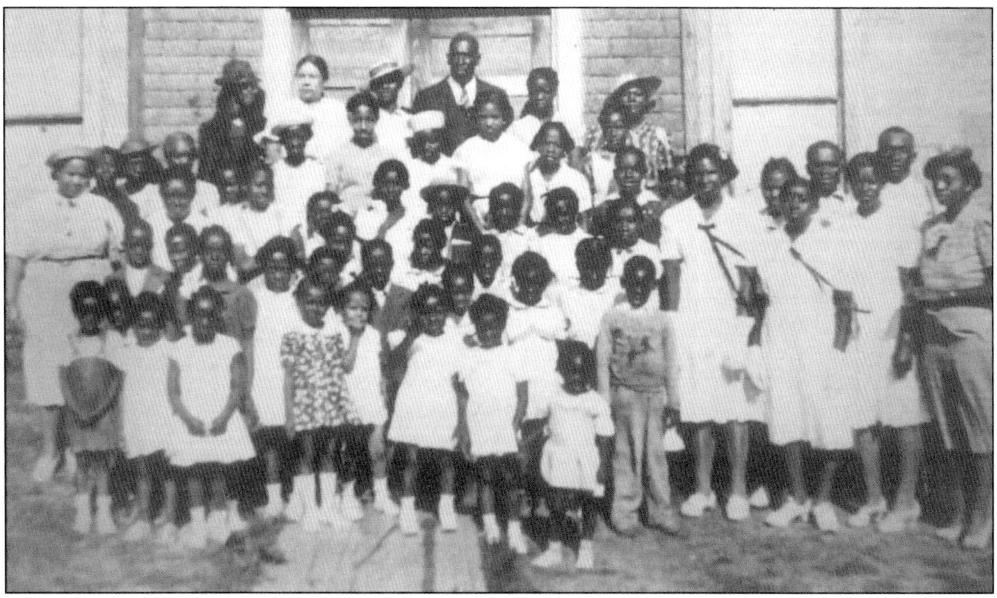

This picture of the Second Baptist Church's Sunday School class was taken in 1938. Hattie Stevenson, pictured on the far right, served as Sunday school superintendent, and Reverend H.S. Lee (middle of the back row) served as pastor. Rev. Lee walked from Robertson to Kinloch each Sunday to conduct services. (Photo Courtesy of William Arnett.)

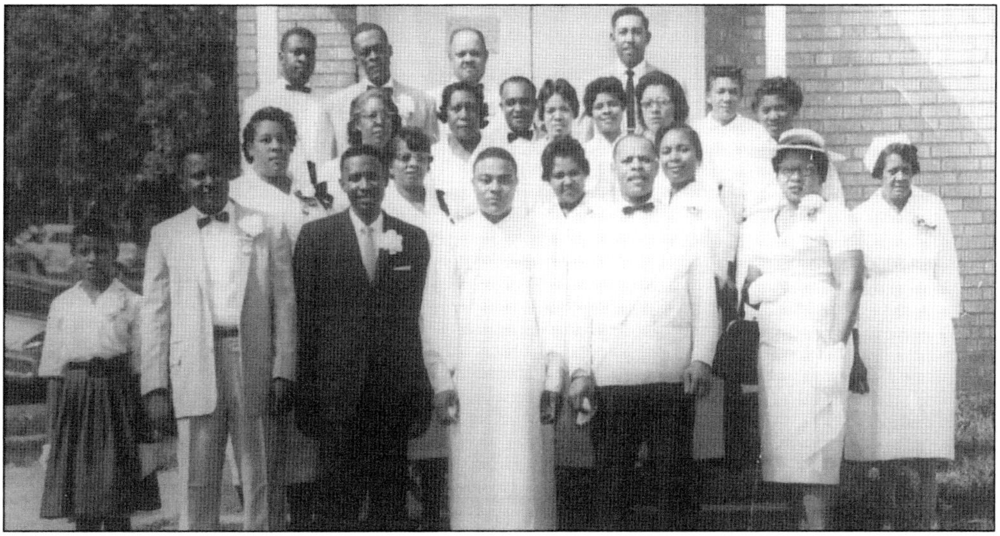

Second Baptist Church's Usher Board members and pastor posed for this photograph between 1946 and 1948 at an annual meeting. Board members, from left, are: (front row) unidentified, John Mitchell Sr., William Arnett, Pastor O.C. King, Mrs. Robinson, Johnny Griffin, Mamie Arnett, Mrs. Walters; (second row) Rosie Mitchell, Mrs. Goggins, Mrs. Howard, Rose Mills, Mrs. Jennings, J.C. Payne, Jackie Coleman, Mary Howard, Aloise McKent, Mrs. Whitely; (last row) Miller McClendon, Dave Bozeman, unidentified man, and Samuel McKent. (Photo Courtesy of William Arnett.)

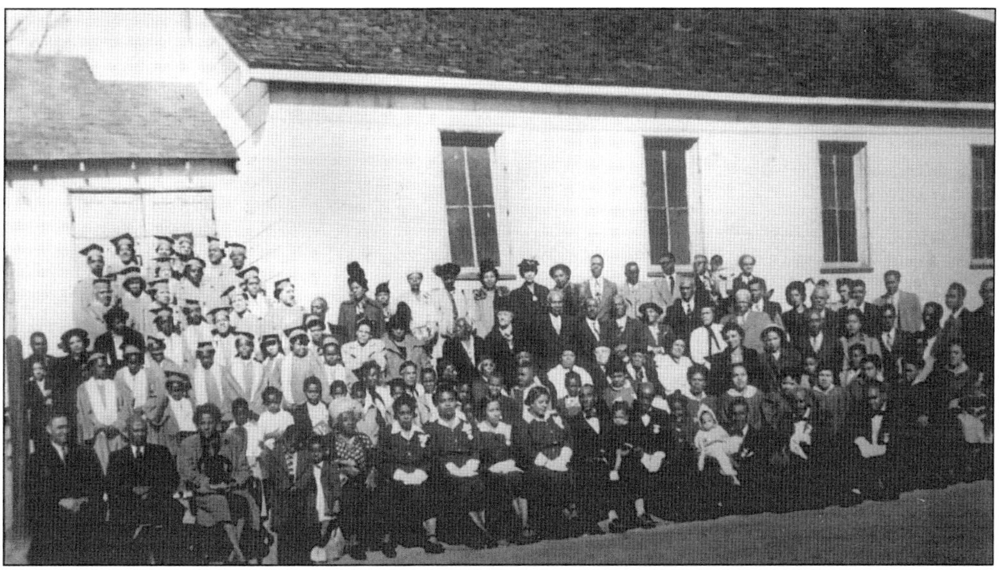

Ward Chapel African Methodist Episcopal Church on Scott and Monroe Streets, organized in 1914, is shown here with early members. The church was established by Rev. J.W. Garner, Henry and May Bass, Charles and Lucy Dixon, Charley and Dora Jones, Lillie Wright, Brother Mayo, Georgia Roberts, Ella Tomlinson, Mamie Perkins, Sam Bruner, and Rev. and Mrs. Alexander Brandon. Before the church was erected, members worshiped in a tent on the old car line. (Photo Courtesy of Rev. Ann MacDonald.)

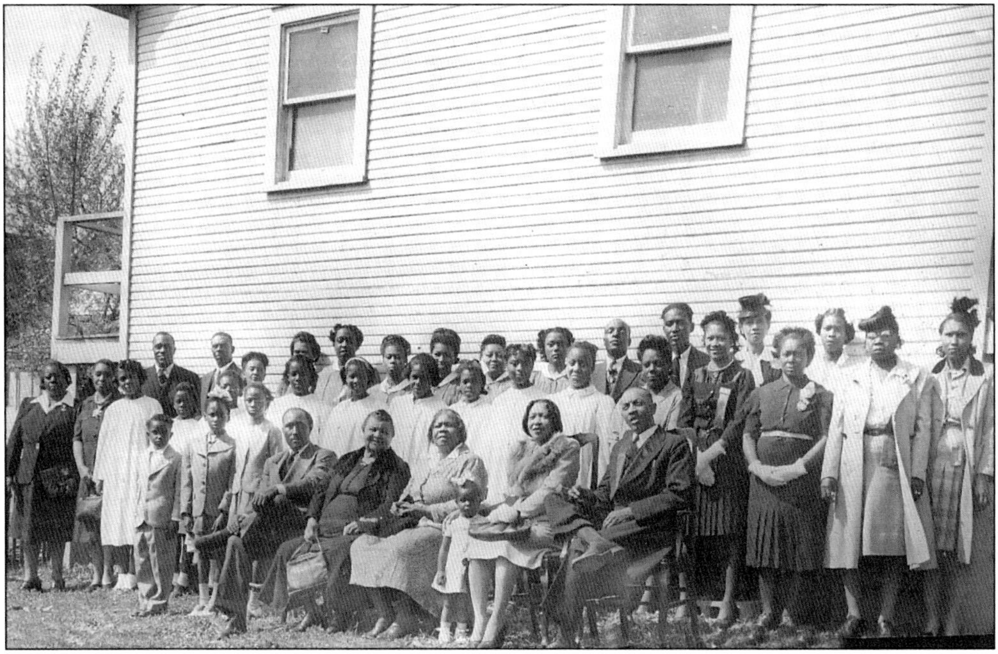

Church members of Coleman Chapel pose outside of their church at 908 Fifth Avenue in the late 1930s. The church and Sunday school were organized on December 28, 1924, by Rev. M.S. Coleman in his home. The first teachers were Rev. Coleman and Eloise Williams. Corina Johnson served as secretary and Johnnie Brand as treasurer. (Photo Courtesy of William Arnett.)

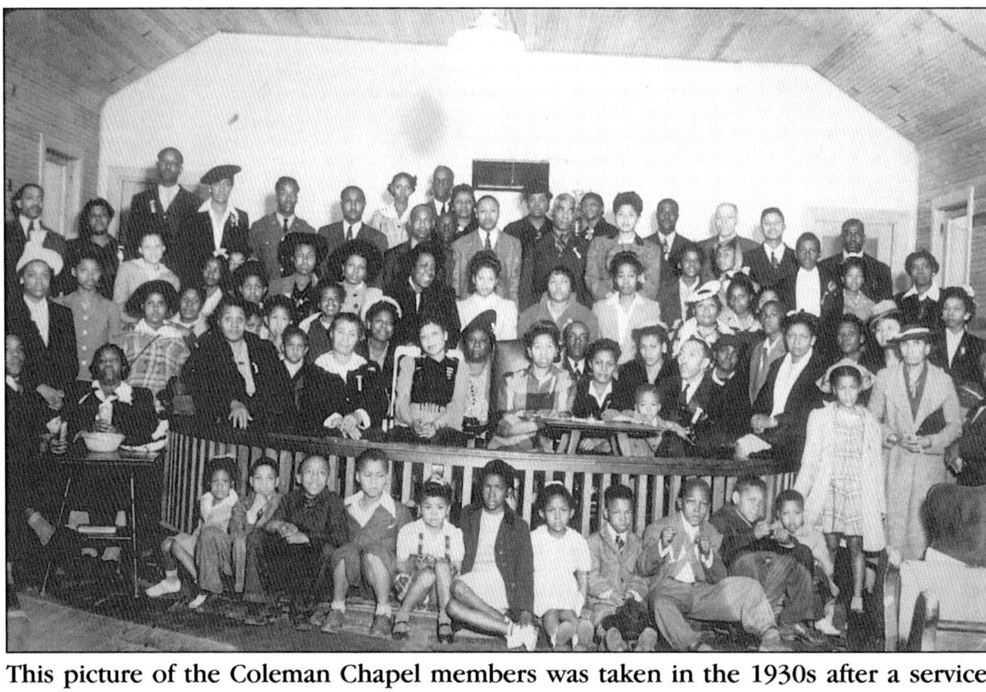

This picture of the Coleman Chapel members was taken in the 1930s after a service. (Photo Courtesy of William Arnett.)

The Coleman Temple Messengers Four provided gospel music throughout Kinloch and St. Louis. They are, from left: Curtis Brown, Leo Brown, George Hopper, and William Arnett. (Photo Courtesy of William Arnett.)

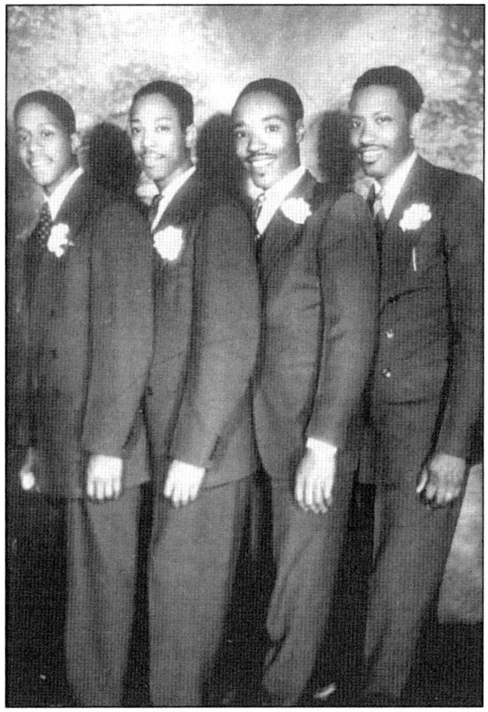

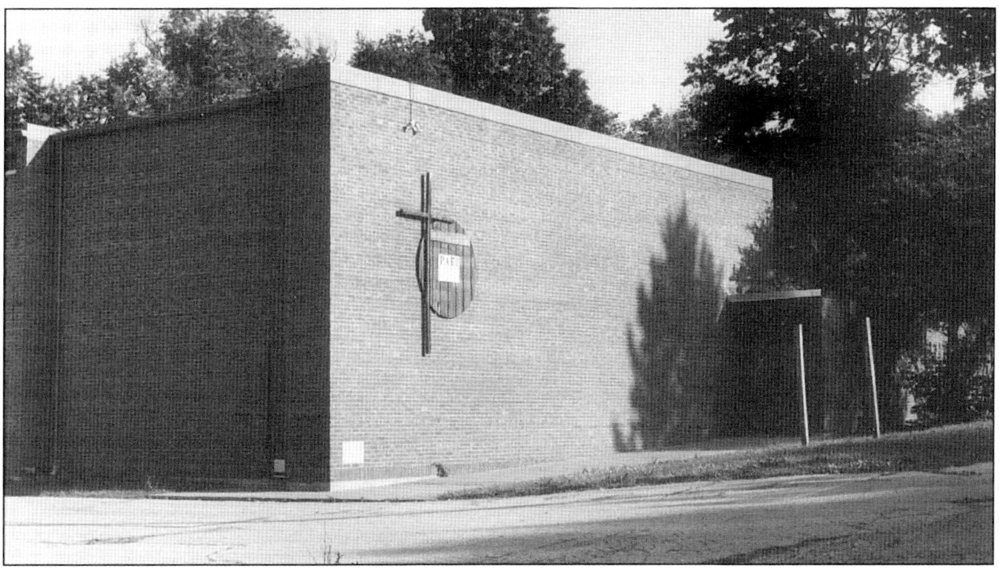

St. Michael's Lutheran Church shown here was constructed in 1970. It began as a home bible class initiated by the Otherine Wilson and Ida Squires families, Kinloch residents, who were members of St. Phillip's Church in St. Louis. Under the leadership of Rev. Andrew Schulze, their pastor, the class grew in number and moved from homes to larger quarters in the YWCA building owned by Irene Cohen. Later the group rented a building on Carson Road for bible classes and worship services. On September 29, 1946, the first church was dedicated and named for the Festival of the Day—St. Michael and All Angels. (Photo by John A. Wright.)

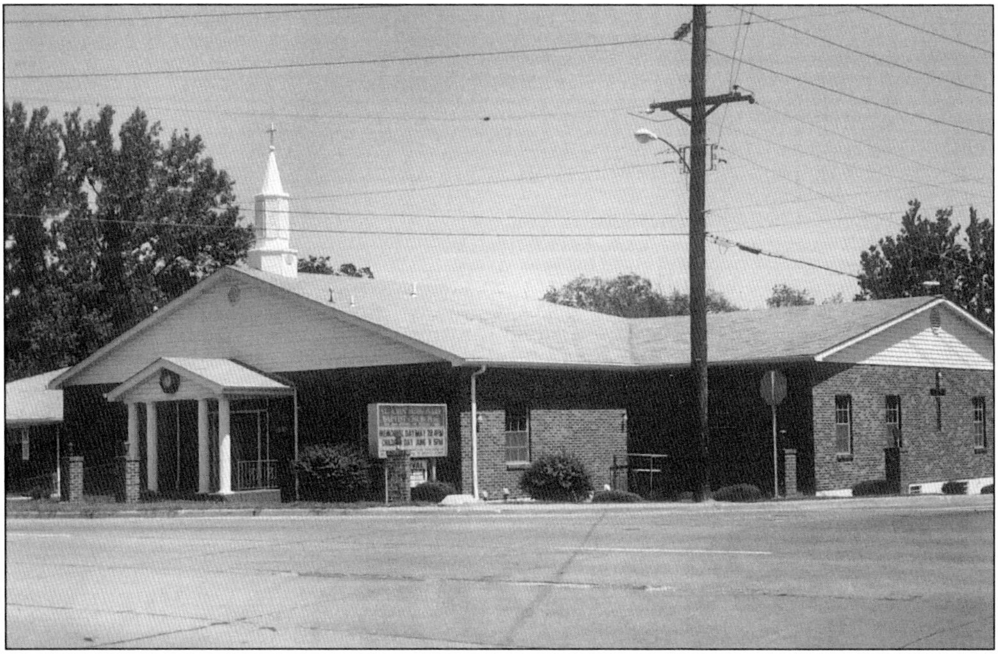

St. John Missionary Baptist Church was founded on September 11, 1966, under the leadership of Rev. John Mitchell Sr. Services were first held in Rev. and Mrs. Mitchell's home at 8246 Ardmore until January 14, 1968, when the members marched into the new church. (Photo by John A. Wright.)

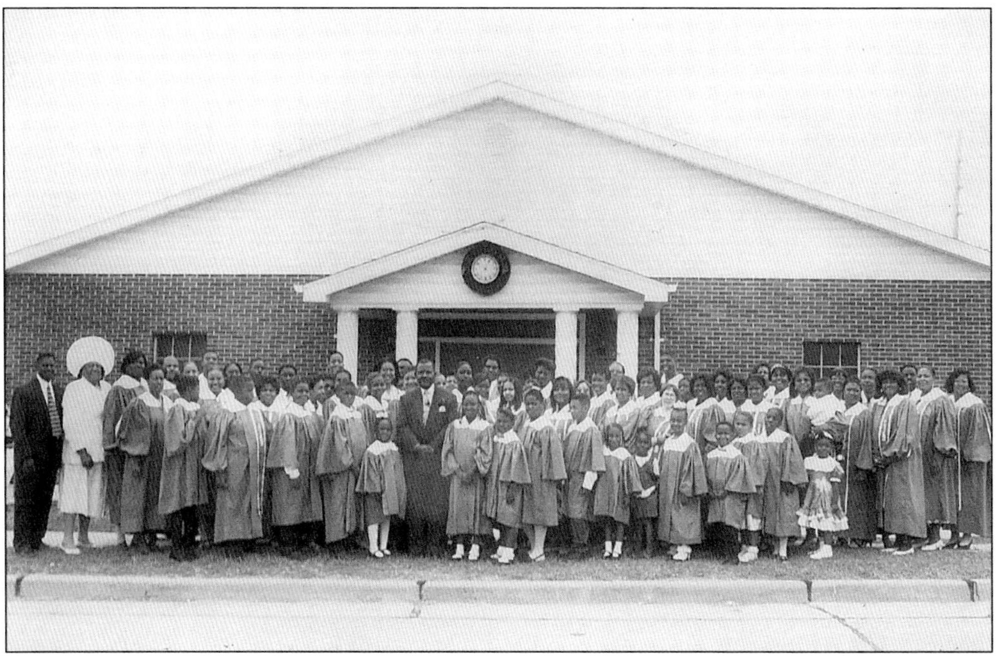

The members of St. John Missionary Baptist Church's choir posed in their robes in front of their new church at 5409 Hanley Road (formerly Case Avenue). (Photo Courtesy of Rev. and Mrs. John Mitchell Sr.)

Rev. John Mitchell is pictured here with his wife of 54 years, Rose. Rev. Mitchell served on Kinloch School District's Board of Education and was active in the construction of Kennedy Jr. High School. The couple have ten children, who have all been active members of the community. Three of their children work for the Ferguson-Florissant School District—Glenda Miles and Madeline Mitchell-Perry are teachers, and Vernon Mitchell is a principal. Glenda was an elected trustee for the St. Louis Community College District. John Jr. is pastor of Southern Missionary Baptist Church in Kinloch. (Photo Courtesy of Rev. and Mrs. John Mitchell Sr.)

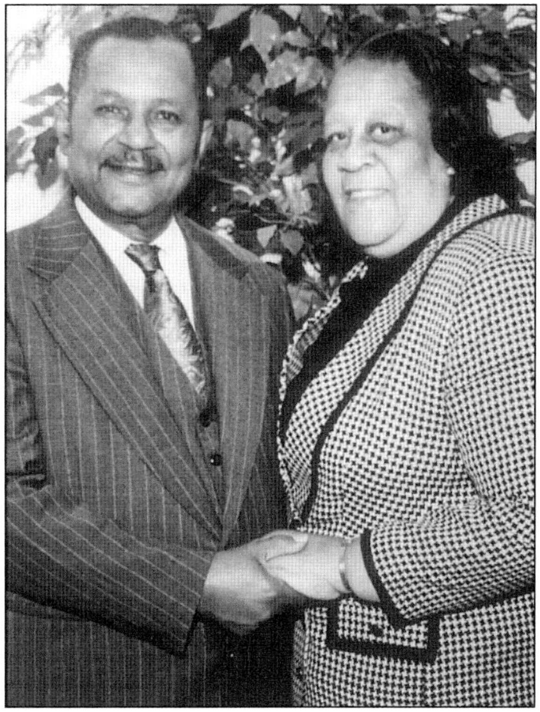

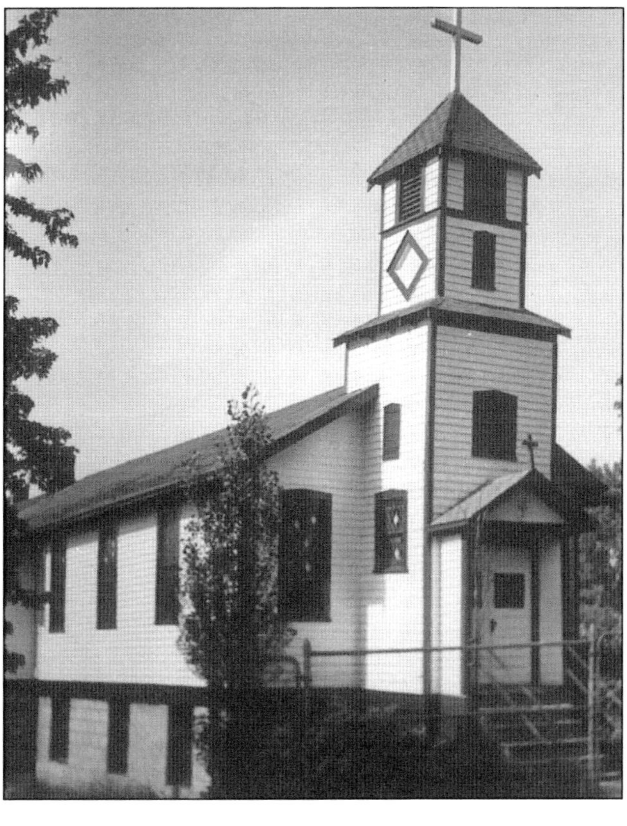

Holy Angel Parish in Kinloch is the oldest continuing black parish in the St. Louis Archdiocese. Prior to acquiring the building pictured here, parishioners met in Boyd's Funeral Home. This building was originally a Methodist church in the City of Jennings. It was hauled to Kinloch in 1925, and erected on Lix Avenue across from the present fire house on Martin Luther King Avenue. (Photo Courtesy of Midwest Jesuit Archives.)

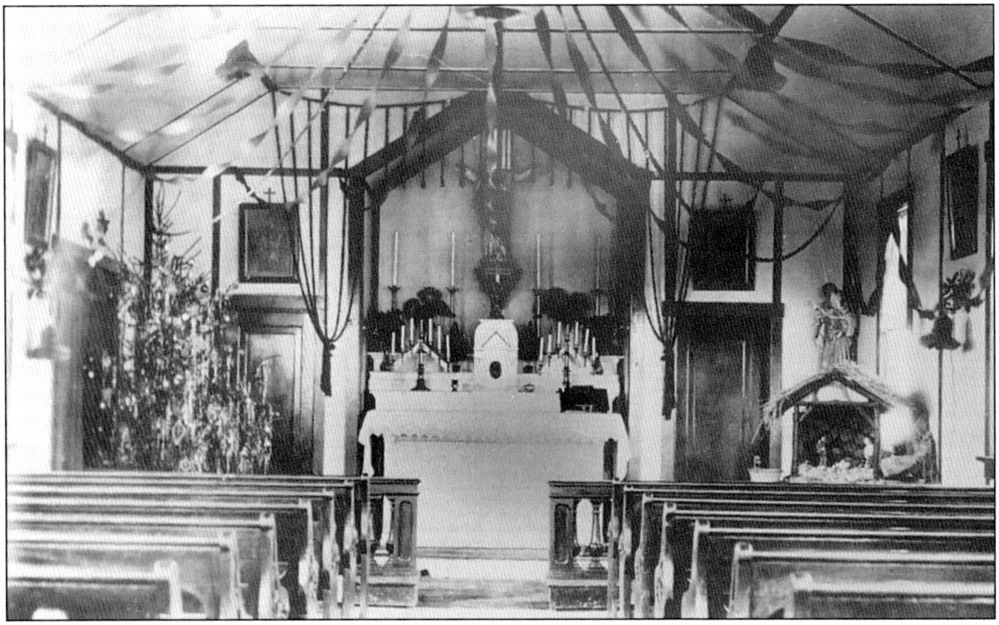

This picture of the sanctuary at Holy Angels Church was taken during the Christmas season in 1925. The church was moved to its present location on Scott Street in the fall of 1927, when the land owner refused to renew the church's lease. (Photo Courtesy of Holy Angels Church.)

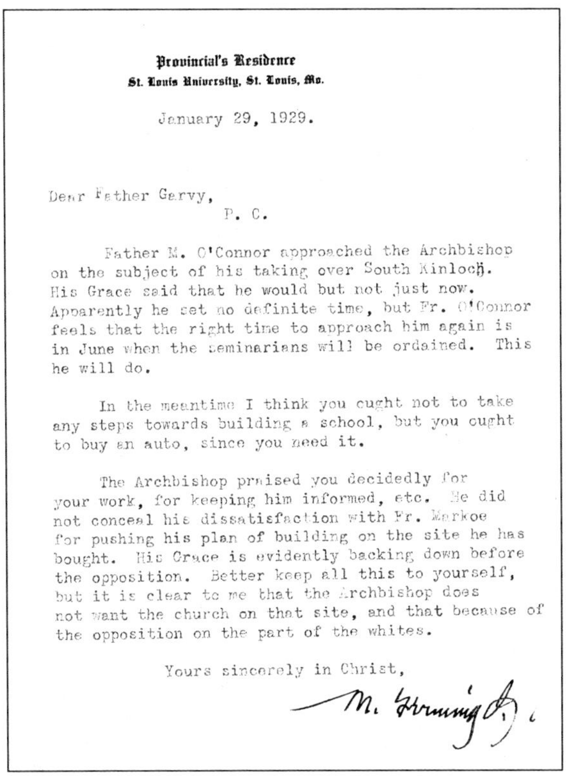

Provincial's Residence
St. Louis University, St. Louis, Mo.

January 29, 1929.

Dear Father Garvy,
P. C.

Father M. O'Connor approached the Archbishop on the subject of his taking over South Kinloch. His Grace said that he would but not just now. Apparently he set no definite time, but Fr. O'Connor feels that the right time to approach him again is in June when the seminarians will be ordained. This he will do.

In the meantime I think you ought not to take any steps towards building a school, but you ought to buy an auto, since you need it.

The Archbishop praised you decidedly for your work, for keeping him informed, etc. He did not conceal his dissatisfaction with Fr. Markoe for pushing his plan of building on the site he has bought. His Grace is evidently backing down before the opposition. Better keep all this to yourself, but it is clear to me that the Archbishop does not want the church on that site, and that because of the opposition on the part of the whites.

Yours sincerely in Christ,

M. Germing S.J.

This letter was sent to Father Garvey, pastor of Holy Angels, informing him of the Archbishop's concern about the church being constructed on its present site because of opposition from the white community. (Letter Courtesy of Holy Angels Church.)

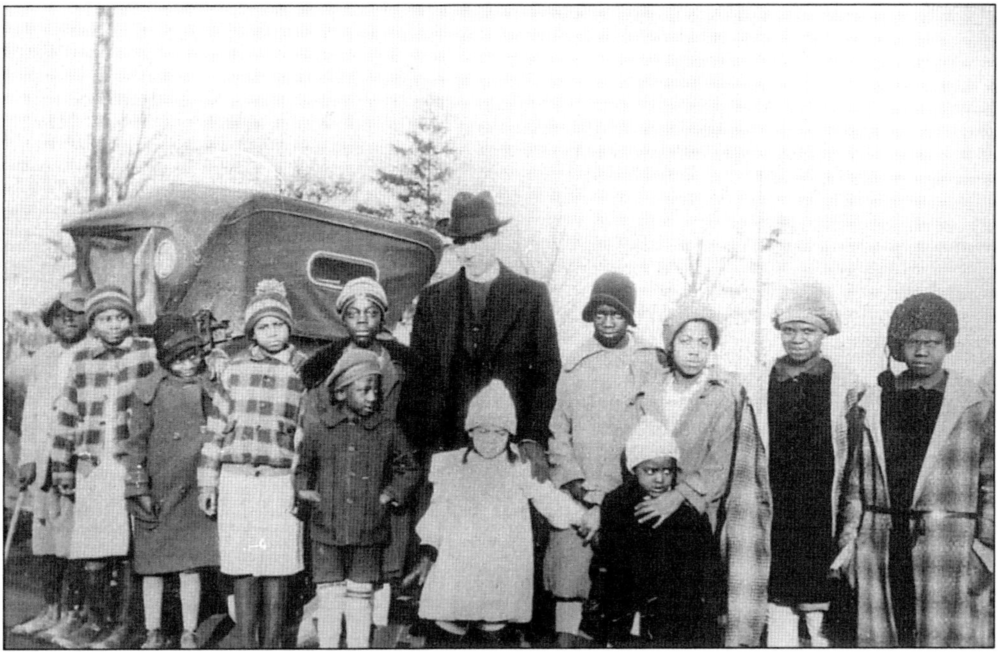

This 1930s picture was taken with Father Garvey and some young members of Holy Angels Church after a Sunday morning service. (Photo Courtesy of Holy Angels Church.)

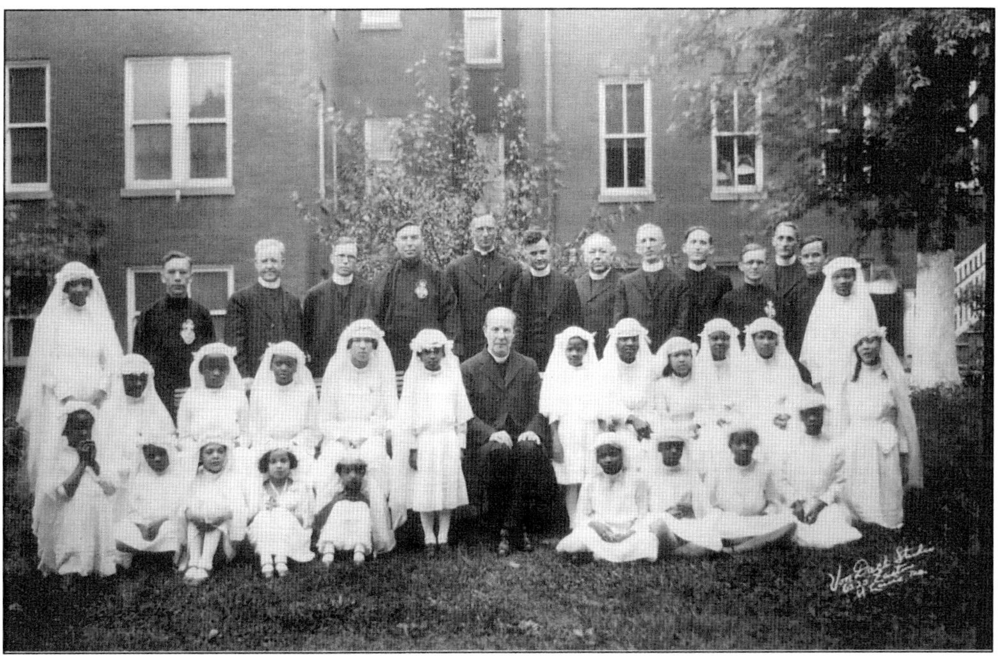

These attractive young ladies dressed in white posed with several priests in the early 1930s after their confirmation ceremony. In the early days of Holy Angels, priests at St. Stanislaus Seminary were very involved with the church. (Photo Courtesy of Holy Angels Church.)

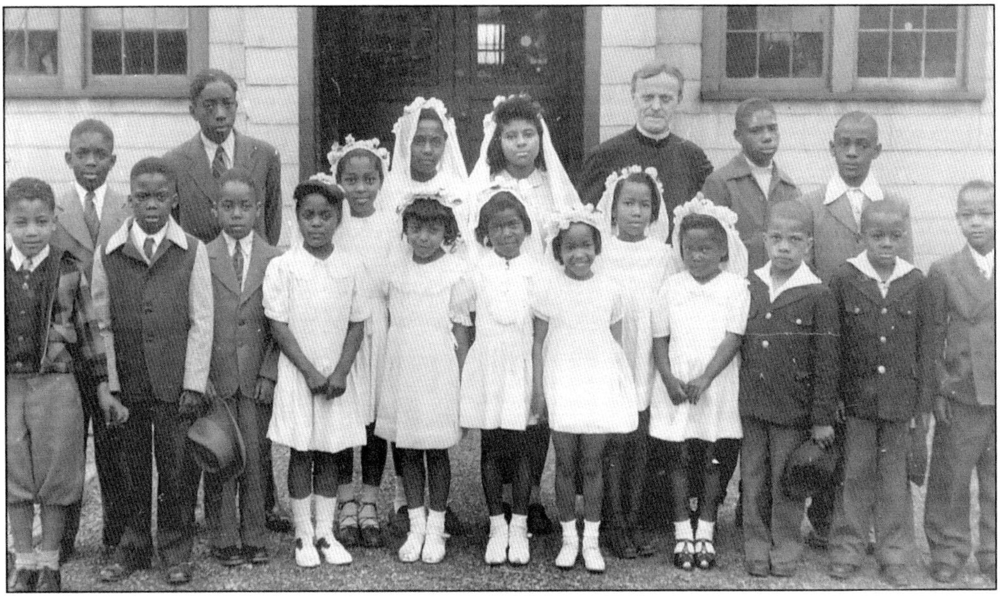

On a Sunday morning in 1944, this group of children posed with Fr. Otto Moorman for their First Communion photograph. Children were prepared for this special event in their lives by Fr. Moorman. They are, from left to right: (front row) Jimmy Vaughn, James Johnson, Med Daugherty, Maynetta Stewart, Geraldine Sample, Marie Smart, Ruth Owens, Lavilna Lewis, Verna Whitener, John Simmons, Lester Bryant, Juan Parades; (second row) Lewis Barnes, Harold Barnes, Ruthie Mae Barnes, Uethless Stegal, Fr. Moorman, Melvania Royal, and Byron Alexander. (Photo Courtesy of Holy Angels Church.)

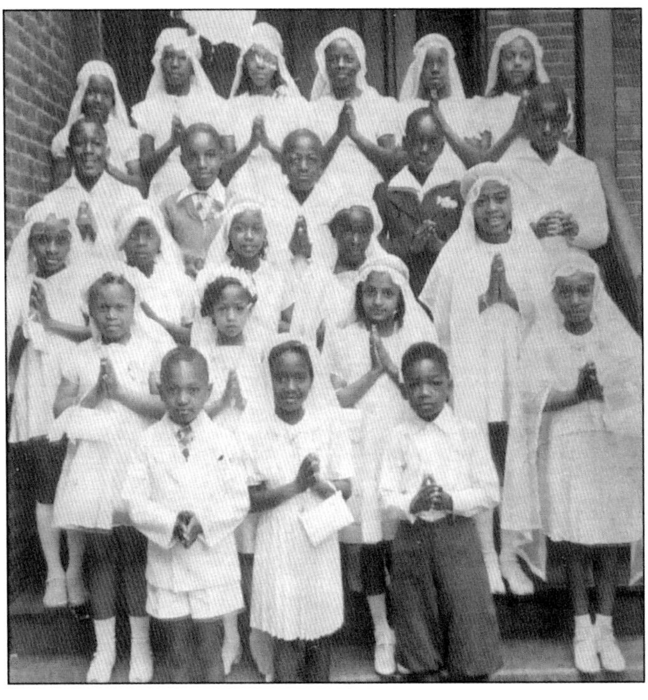

Pictured here are boys and girls who posed for this 1940s photograph after their First Communion ceremony. (Photo Courtesy of Holy Angels Church.)

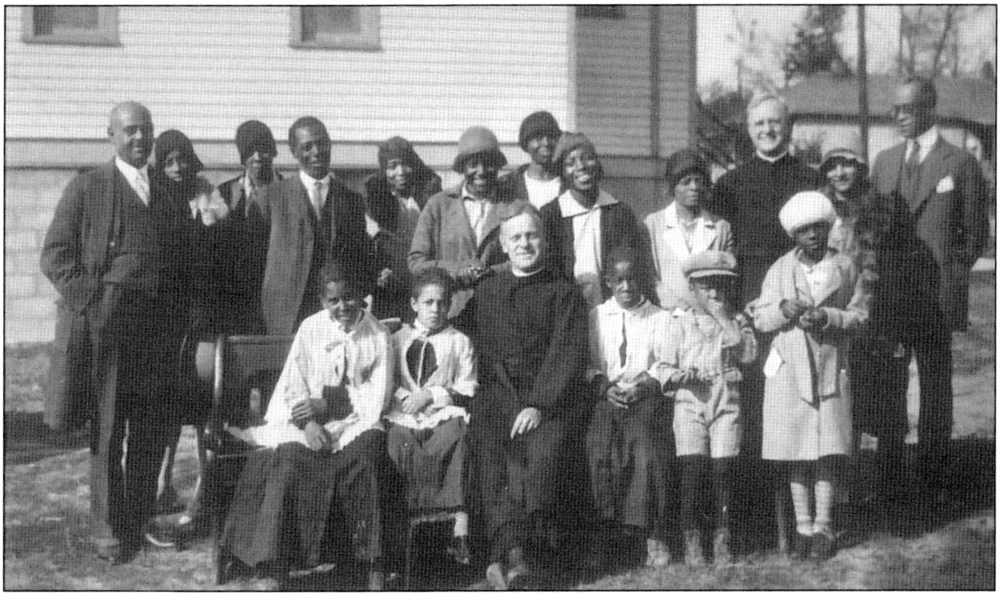

These dignified-looking and well dressed Holy Angels parishioners and the parish priest, Fr. Otto Moorman, were photographed in the 1930s outside of the church. During the Depression, Father Moorman established a community soup kitchen, which served several hundred meals weekly. (Photo Courtesy of Midwest Jesuit Archives.)

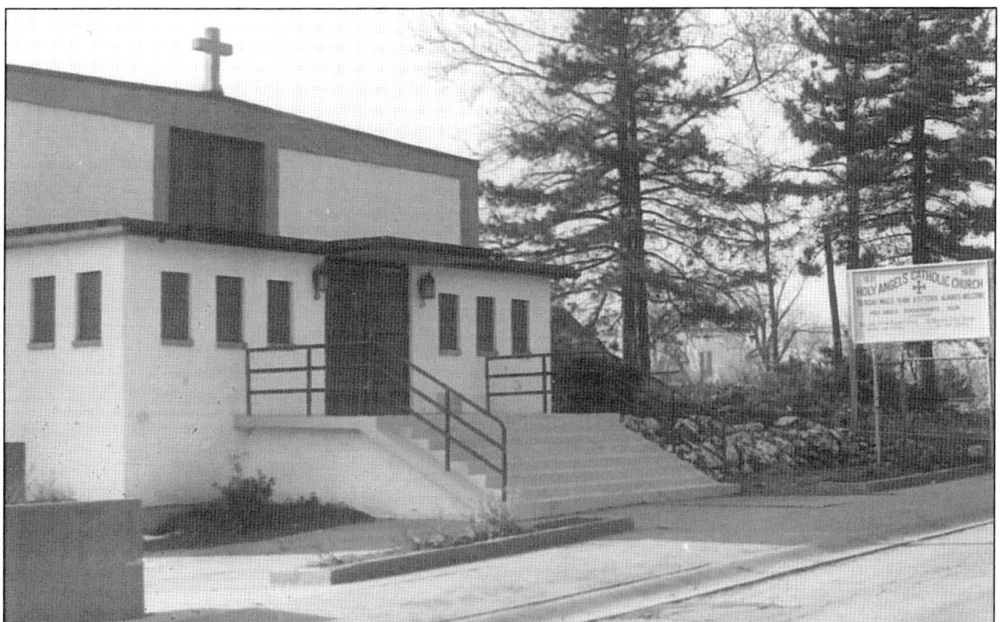

Before his retirement, due to poor health, Father Moorman was able to get funding for this new Holy Angels Church. (Photo by John A. Wright.)

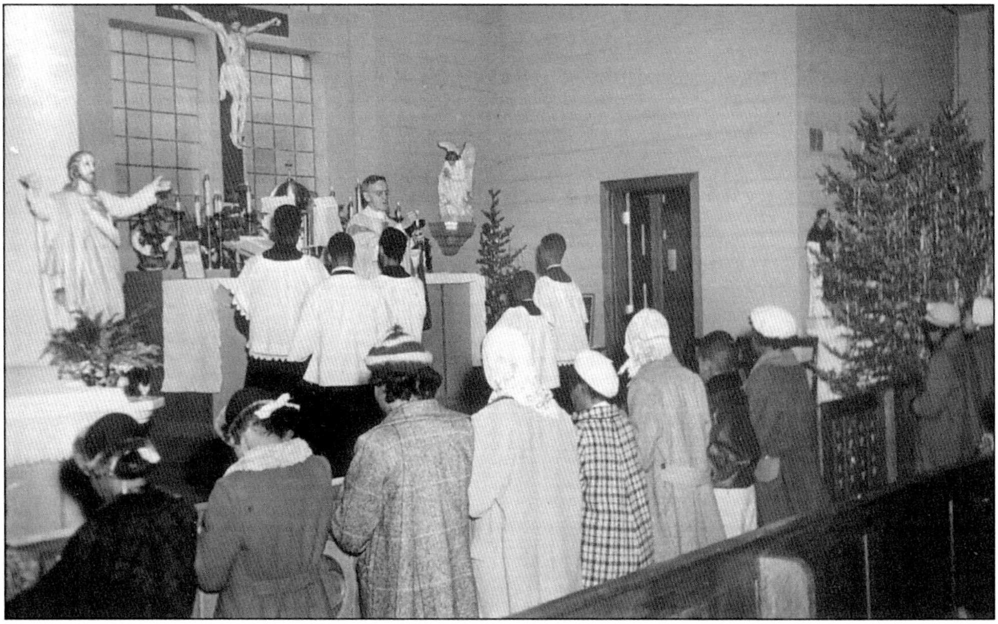

Father Moorman is shown celebrating his last mass at Holy Angels on Christmas Day in 1952. (Photo Courtesy of Midwest Jesuit Archives.)

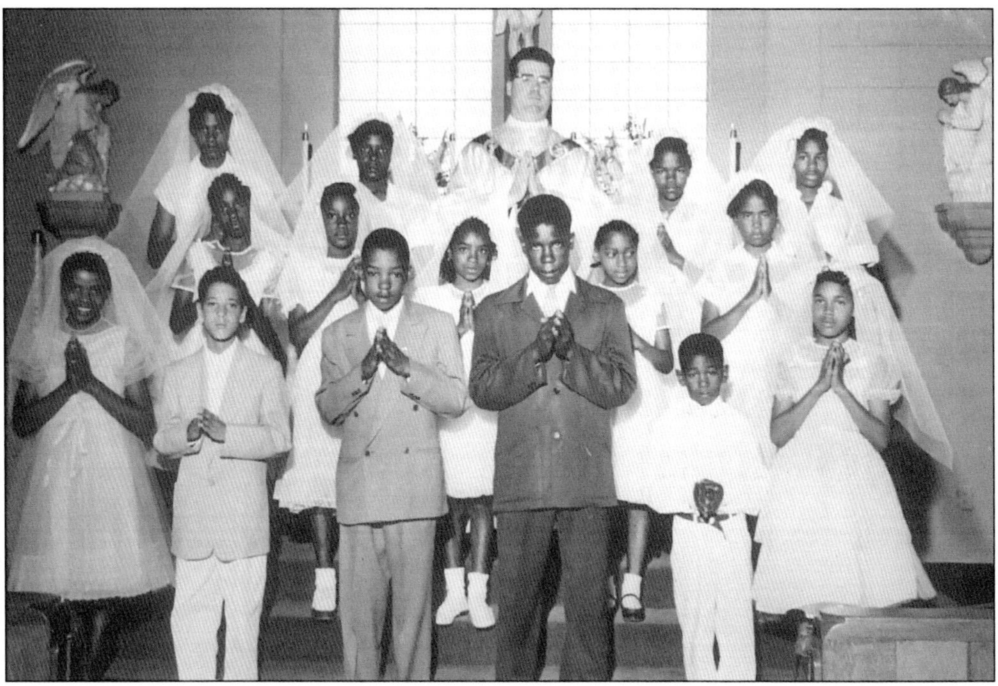

Fr. Patrick J. Malloy was appointed pastor of Holy Angels when Fr. Otto Moorman retired. He is seen here after a First Communion ceremony in the 1960s. Fr. Malloy was responsible for constructing a new rectory and school. He also established a credit union and helped promote urban renewal in Kinloch with the development of Rushmore Park. (Photo Courtesy Holy Angels Church.)

During the 1960s civil rights movement, black awareness became an important aspect of life for black Americans. to honor this awareness, this 7-foot statue of a black Virgin Mary was placed in the Holy Angles Church sanctuary. (Photo Courtesy of Holy Angels Church.)

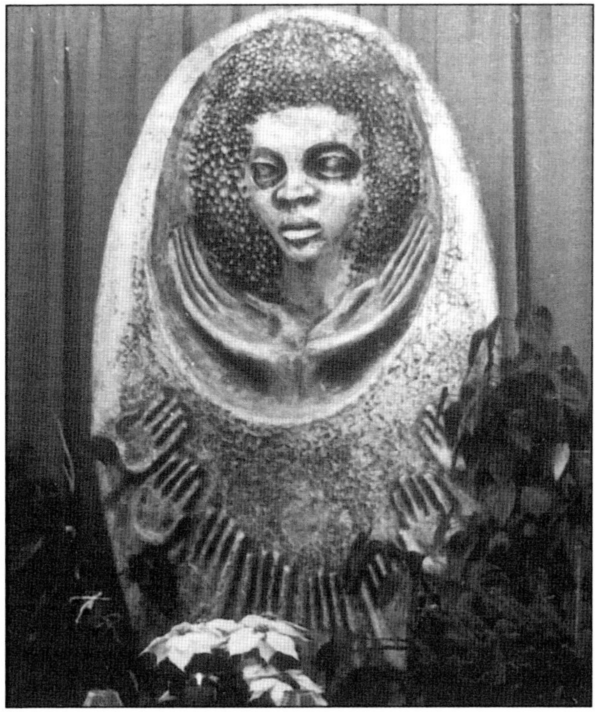

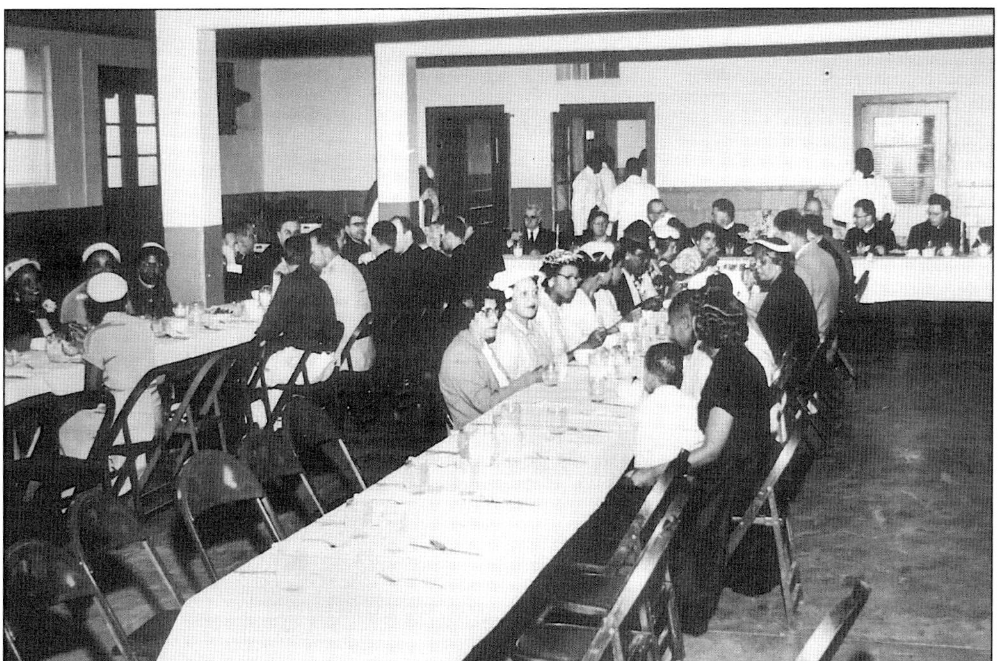

Some members of Holy Angels Church are pictured here preparing to take part in a church dinner. The church hall was the site of many church, school, and community activities such as dances, fund-raisers, and card parties. (Photo Courtesy of Holy Angels Church.)

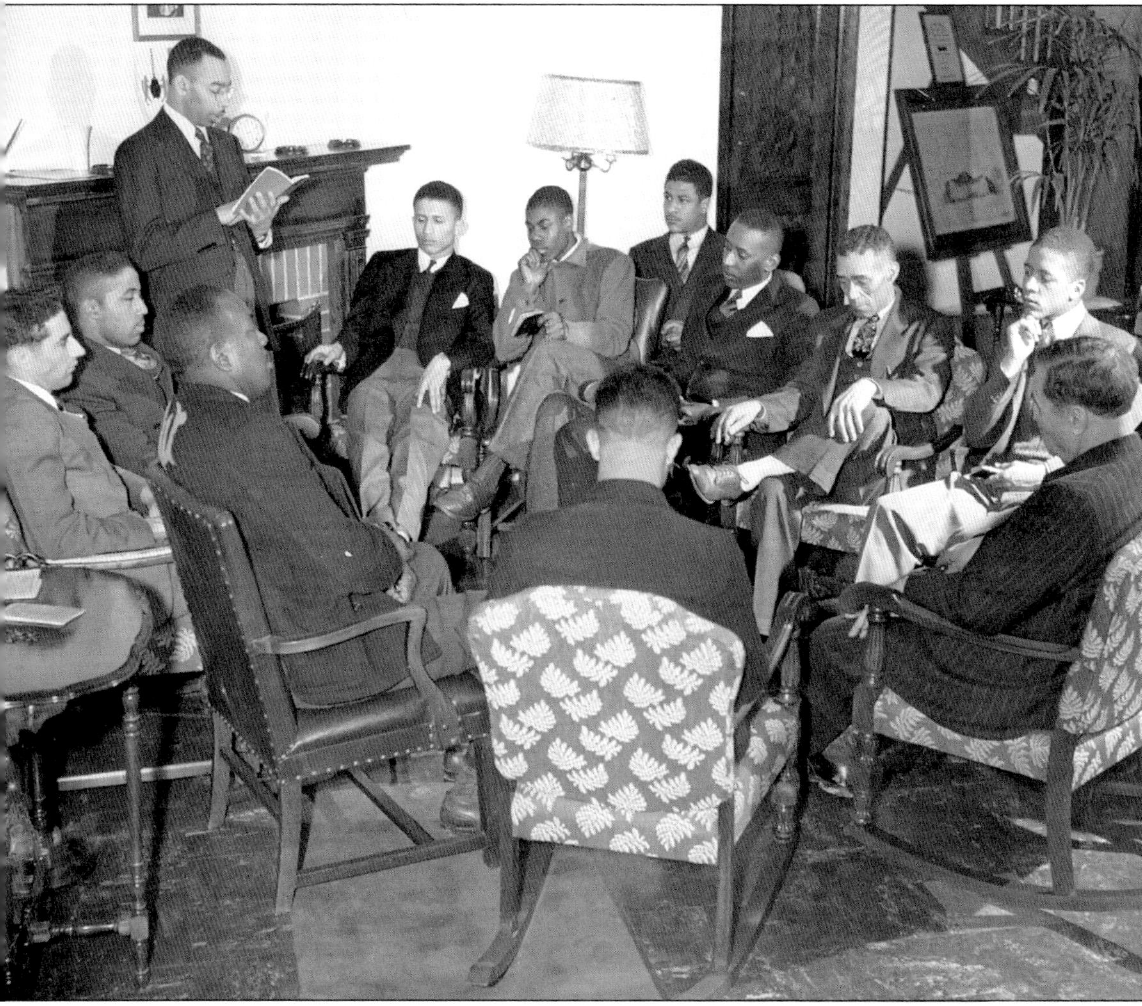

Floyd Brown (standing) is leading a scriptural reading here in 1941 at Manresa, on the Holy Angels Church grounds. Manresa was the first retreat house in the world for black Catholic laymen. It was used by men throughout the St. Louis area. These men were from East St. Louis. (Photo Courtesy of *St. Louis Post-Dispatch.*)

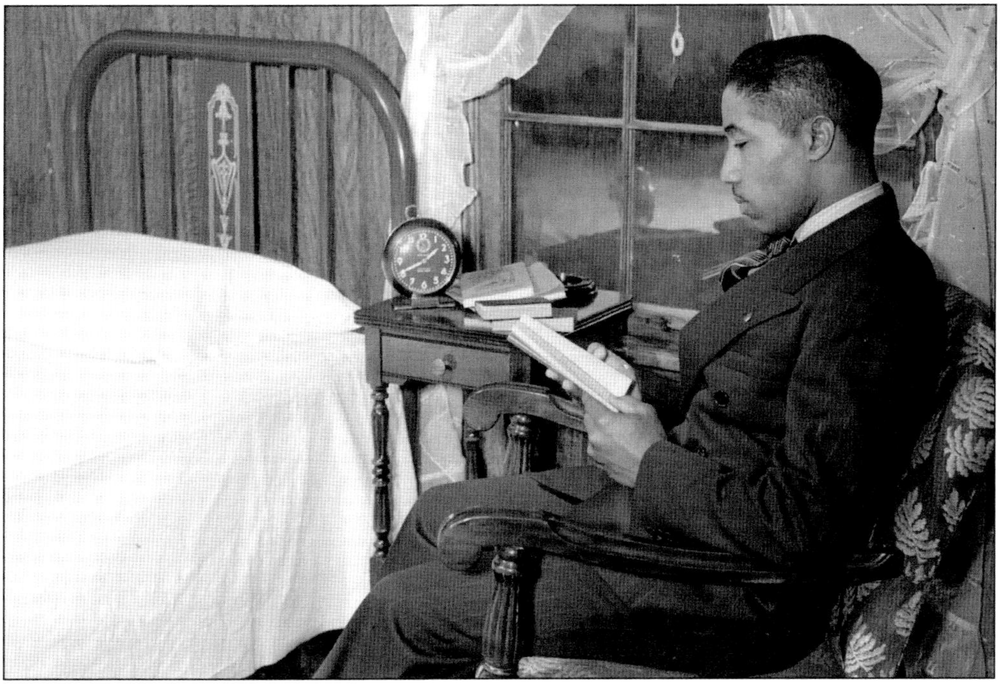

Kenneth Hall, a retreat captain, is shown here reading inspirational literature in his room at the Manresa Retreat House. (Photo Courtesy of *St. Louis Post-Dispatch.*)

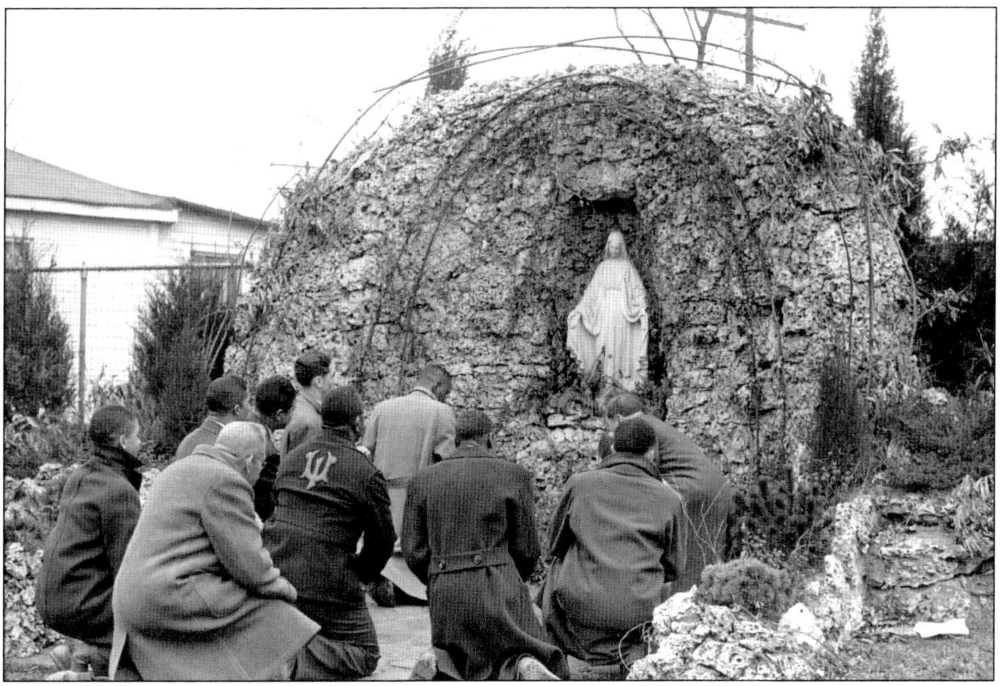

These Catholic men were participating in a retreat in the 1940s, when they were photographed on a visit to the Blessed Mother's shrine, which was located in the Manresa Retreat House garden. (Photo Courtesy of *St. Louis Post-Dispatch.*)

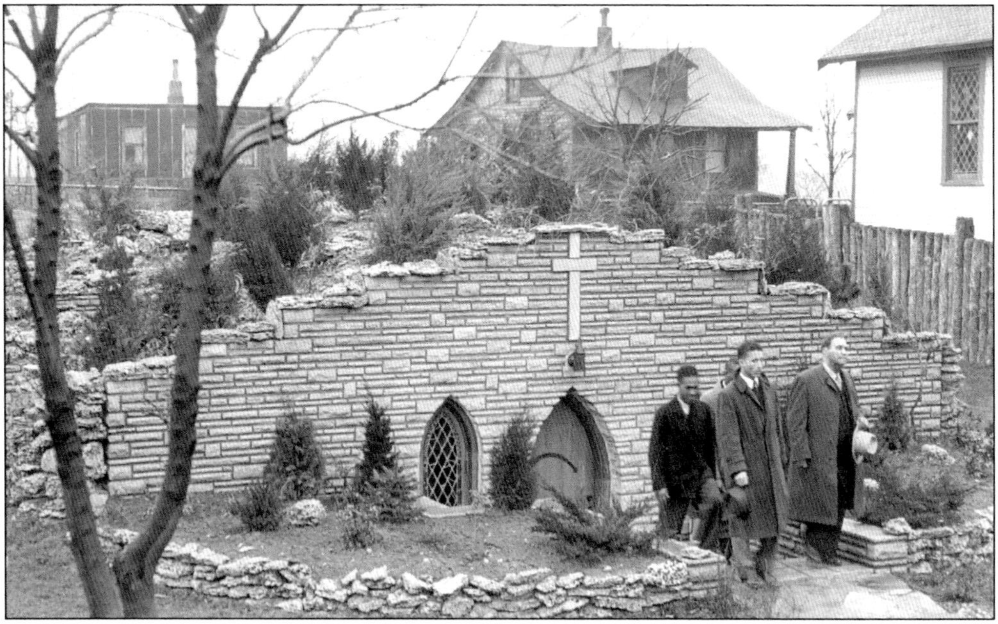

This photograph of the Manresa Retreat House for men was taken as the participants were leaving the cave chapel. The chapel is a replica of one found in Manresa, Spain, where St. Ignatius of Loyola founded the Society of Jesus. The cave was built partly below ground and covered with large sponge rocks, earth, shrubs, and flowers. (Photo Courtesy of *St. Louis Post-Dispatch*.)

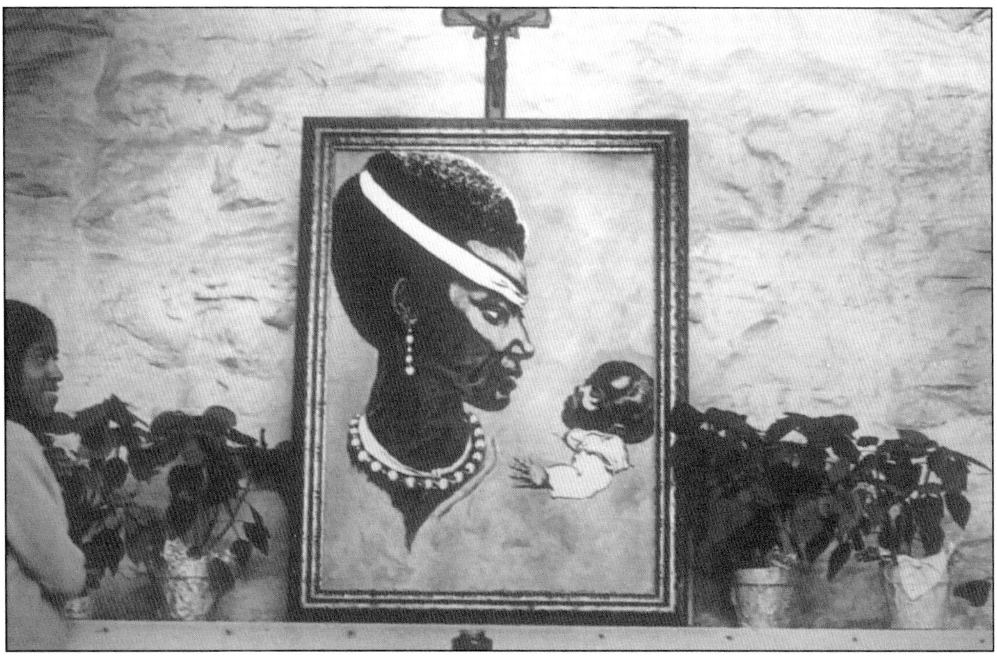

This young lady was admiring an African depiction of Mary and Jesus when she was photographed in the 1960s. The painting was located in the Manresa Chapel. (Photo Courtesy of Holy Angels Church.)

Four

BIRTH OF A CITY

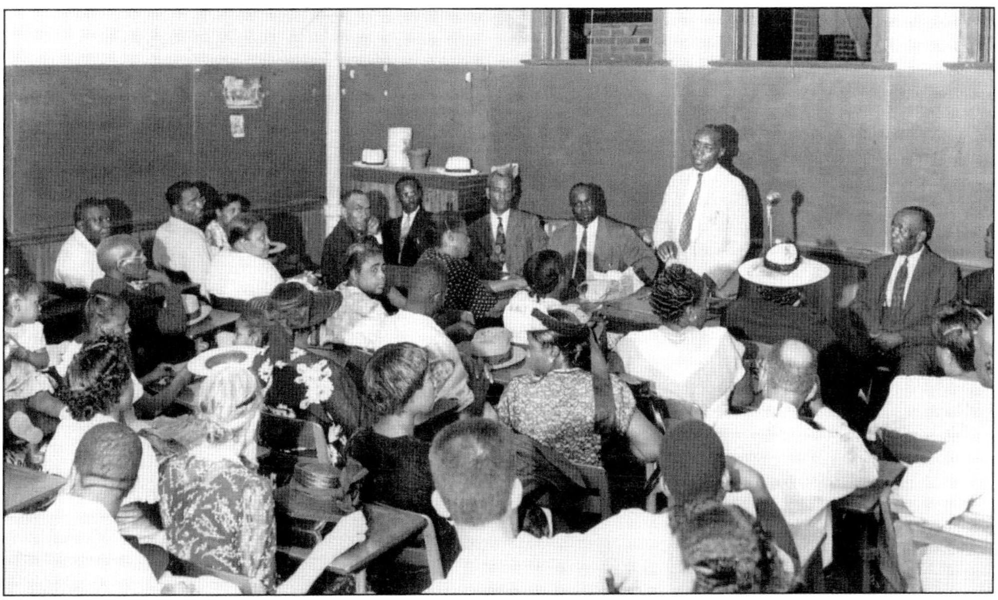

Members of the community, shown here, are celebrating after they received word that the county court on August 20, 1948, had approved their petition to become a fourth-class city. In 1941, after the incorporation of Berkeley, a petition had been filed by Kinloch residents to incorporate, but it was denied as was the one filed in 1947. The population at the time of incorporation was approximately 2,400. The assessed value of property in Kinloch, on which a city tax of up to 75¢ on each $100 could have been levied, was about $1 million. (Photo Courtesy of *St. Louis Post-Dispatch.*)

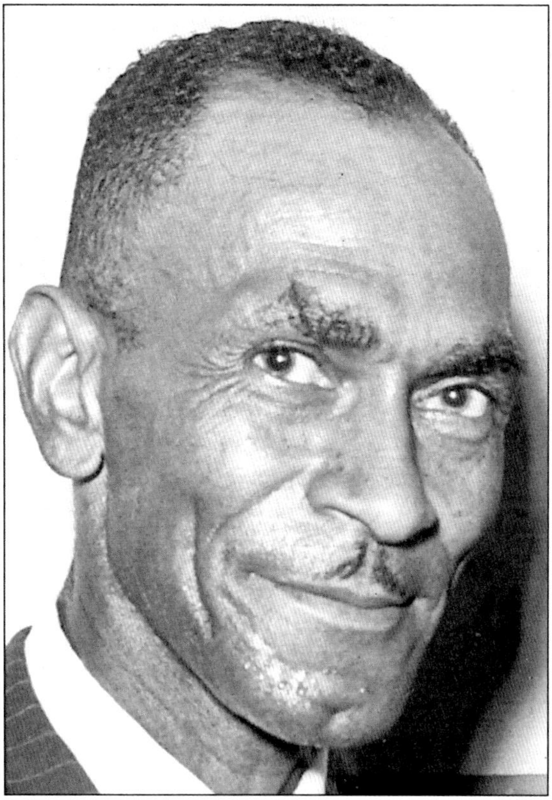

Willie Head, pictured here, was sworn in as the new city's mayor at a ceremony in the county courthouse in Clayton. Head was 55 years old at the time and worked as a general foreman of a construction company. He had moved to Kinloch from Aliceville, Alabama, in 1916. (Photo Courtesy of *St. Louis Post Dispatch*.)

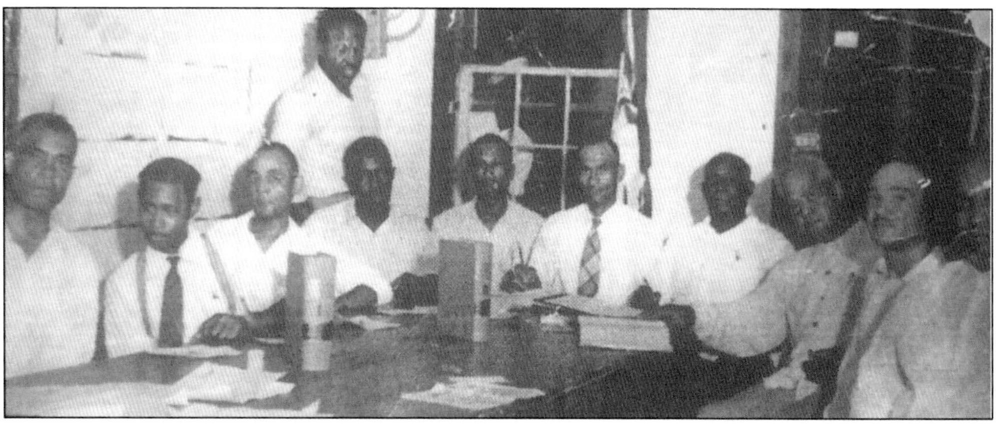

Mayor Willie Head along with the Board of Aldermen who had been appointed by the court, are shown here at one of their first meetings in the fire station at Lix and Scott Avenues. They are, from left to right: Atkis Boyd, Robert Payne, Charles Folwell, Moses Williams, Talmadege Alexander, Willie Head, Leslie Swaizey, Burton Dortch, Theodore Ferry, and Rev. Wash Yates. Napoleon Williams is standing. Not in the picture are Henry Chambers and William Phiefer. These officials served until the following April when an election could be held. (Photo Courtesy of Ruby Herndon.)

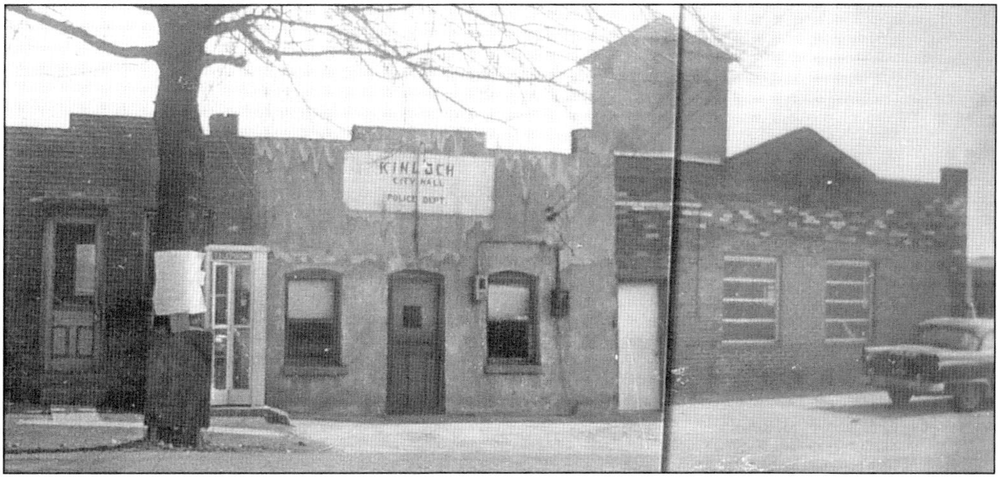

This is a picture of Kinloch's first city hall on Lix Street. (Photo Courtesy of the 1983 Kinloch History Committee.)

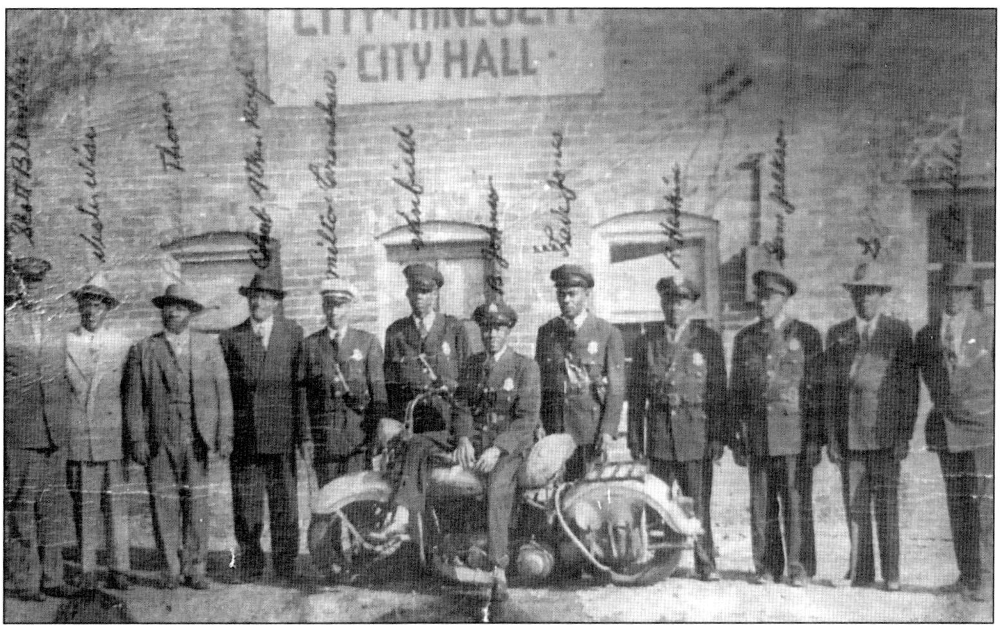

Kinloch's early police department is pictured here with Atkis Boyd, the appointed chief of police (fourth from the left). The first group of officers was comprised of ten men and two women, who worked part-time without pay until the city had funds to pay full-time officers. (Photo Courtesy of John A. Wright.)

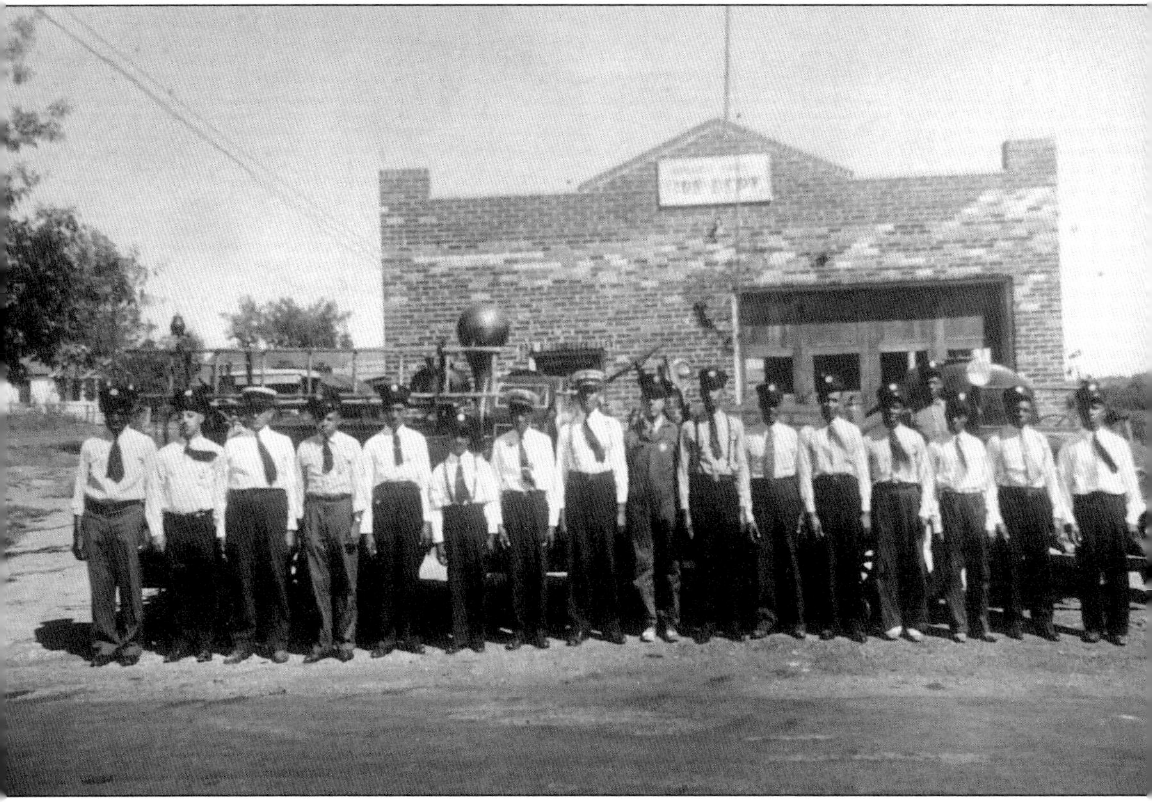

Pictured here is Kinloch's first volunteer fire department, organized in January 1936. The officers selected were: Atkis Boyd, chief; William Hughes, assistant chief; J.C. Godbold, fire marshall; Lon Leigh and Hurlon Teetes, captains; and William R. Shores and Johnny B. Hughes, lieutenants. Serving as firemen were Charles Clay, Earley Wilson, Moses Williams, A.J. Williams, James Howard, Charles Eldridge, Tribble McGregory, John Adams, Everette Robinson Sr., Lacey Lee, Milton Holmes, Clarence Hunter, Monroe English, Bryant Flemming, Joseph Bryant, Med Daugherty, John Clayburn, and Azell Williams.

During the early years, volunteers had a difficult task working regular jobs and serving as firemen in their spare time. Even though the department became tax-supported in April of 1944, it still remained volunteer-operated and continued to have fund-raising activities. Originally, only those residents who purchased fire tags were provided fire protection. (Photo Courtesy of Ann Boyd.)

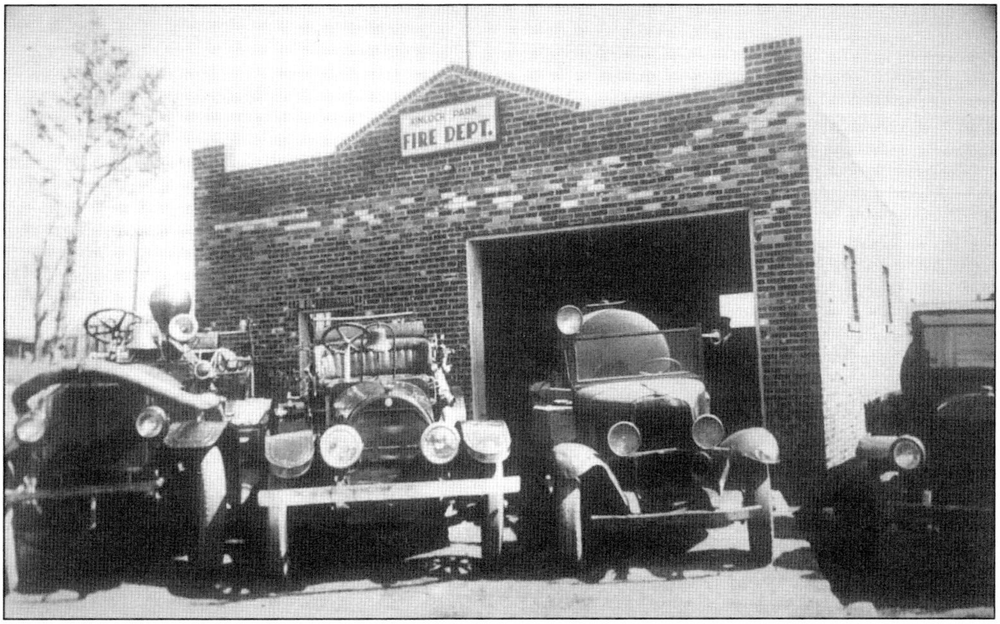

Shown here is some of the fire department's first equipment. Chief Atkis Boyd negotiated the acquisition of the first piece of equipment, an American La France 1000 GPM pumper. It was purchased from St. Louis with funds donated by local residents, but many times the firemen wondered if there would be enough gasoline to operate it. Other equipment was purchased over the years with funds raised through benefit picnics, dances, fire tag sales, donations and bond issues. (Photo Courtesy Ann Boyd.)

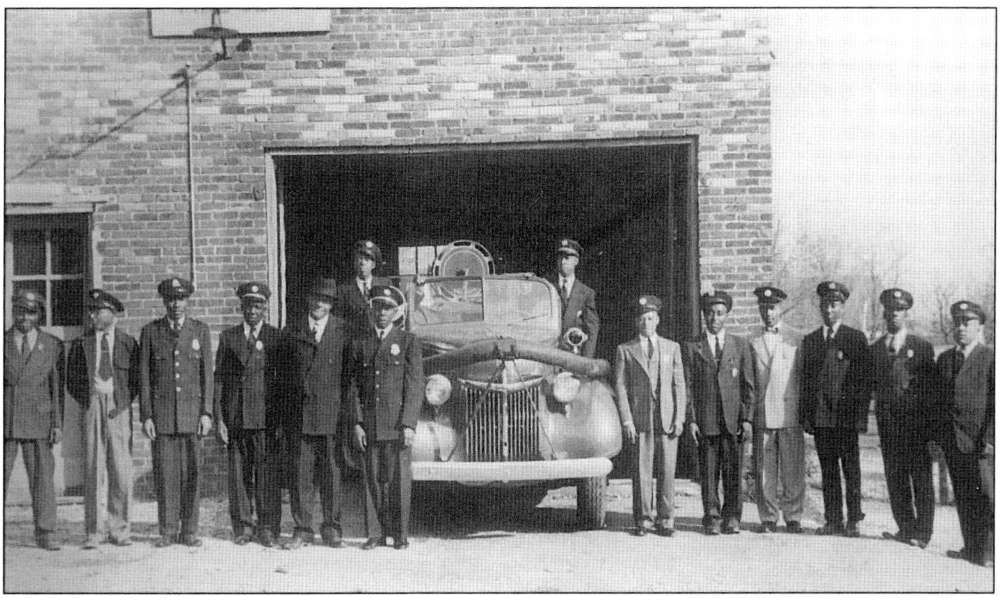

Officers of the fire department are shown here from left: James Wells, Arthur Tilman, Bluitt Johnson, Mose Williams, Atkis Boyd, Johnny B. Hughes, Med Daugherty, Ed Robinson, Earl Taylor, unidentified, unidentified, James Robinson, Willie Wells, and unidentified. (Photo Courtesy of Howard Whitener.)

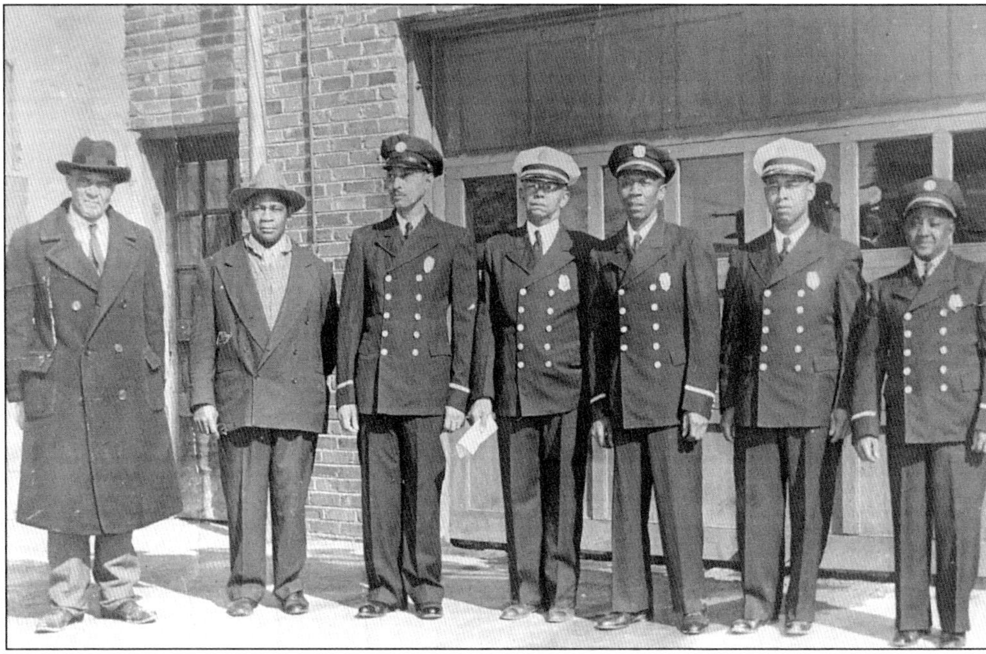

Early trustees and officers of the Kinloch Fire Department are pictured here outside of the old Fire Station. They are, from left: Atkis Boyd, president; Trustees Al J. Williams and Early Wilson; Doc Howard, building inspector; Edward Robinson, assistant chief; Johnny B. Hughes, chief; and Roger Shores, secretary. (Photo Courtesy of the 1983 Kinloch History Committee.)

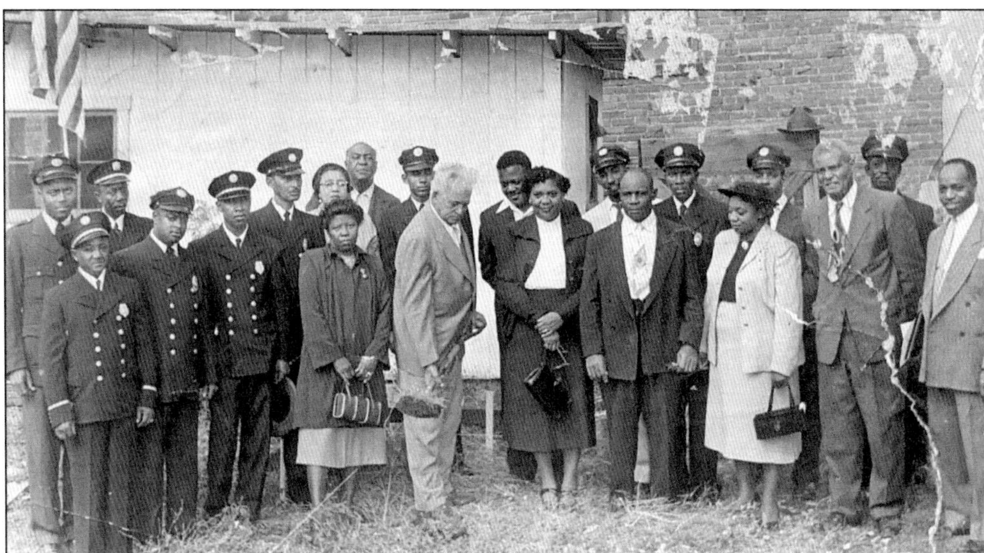

City and fire department officials and other Kinloch residents are pictured here in 1955, taking part in a groundbreaking ceremony for the new fire station. The citizens raised over $4,000 one weekend through a fireman's picnic to purchase the lots because the owner refused to let the department purchase the property in installment payments. (Photo Courtesy of the 1983 Kinloch History Committee.)

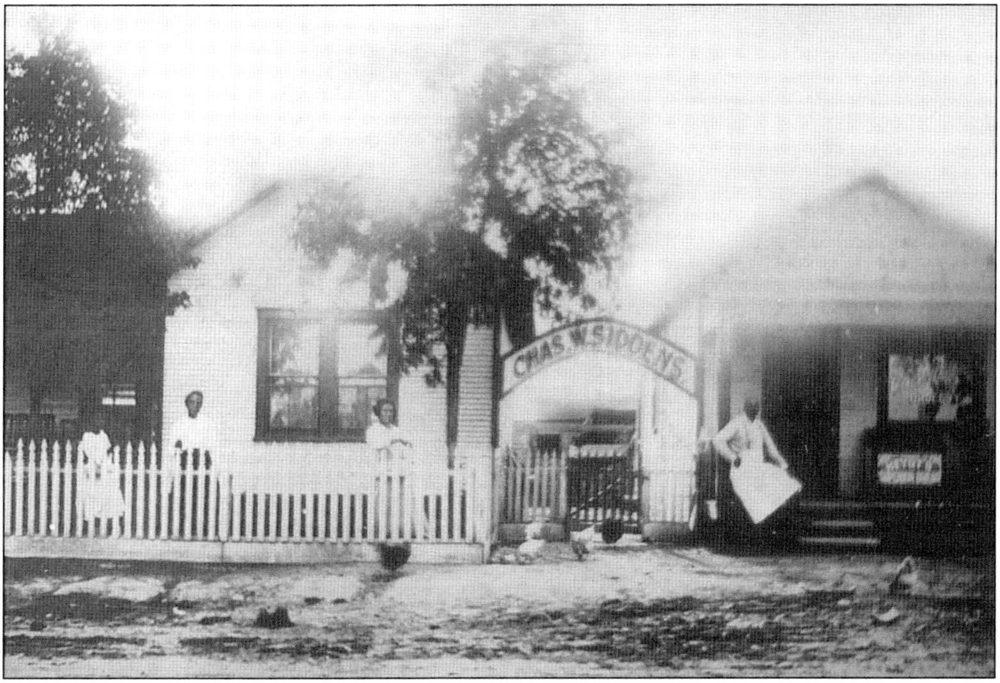

As the community grew, so did its businesses. What started as a few scattered establishments at the turn of the century, such as Charles Siddens' restaurant on Bangert and Smith (shown here), blossomed to over 80 places of business by the 1950s. (Photo Courtesy of Carlson Oliver.)

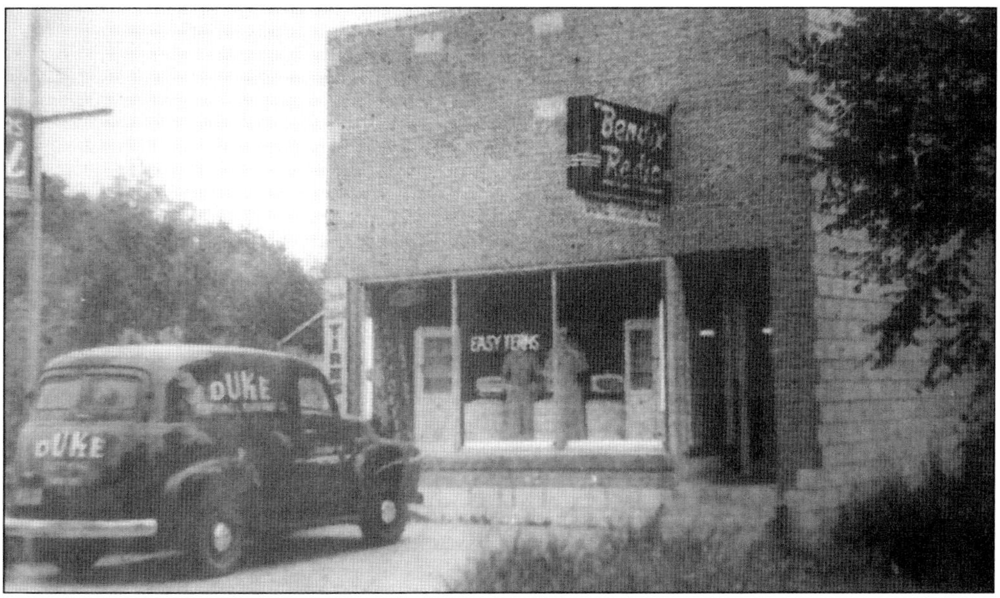

Sol Deutch, the town's only white merchant, came to Kinloch in the early 1940s selling goods door-to-door from his car. Deutch offered a variety of merchandise on easy terms. After finding success in the community, he opened this small business, which he named Duke, on Lix Avenue. (Photo Courtesy of Ruby Herndon.)

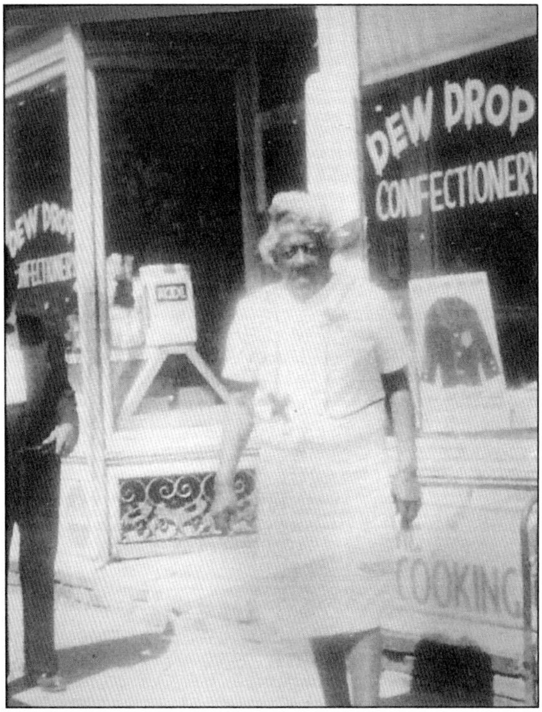

Mrs. Edna Roberts owned the confectionery in this photograph. She conducted business there from the 1930s to the 1950s. The confectionery was located on Lix Street. (Photo Courtesy of Kinloch City Hall.)

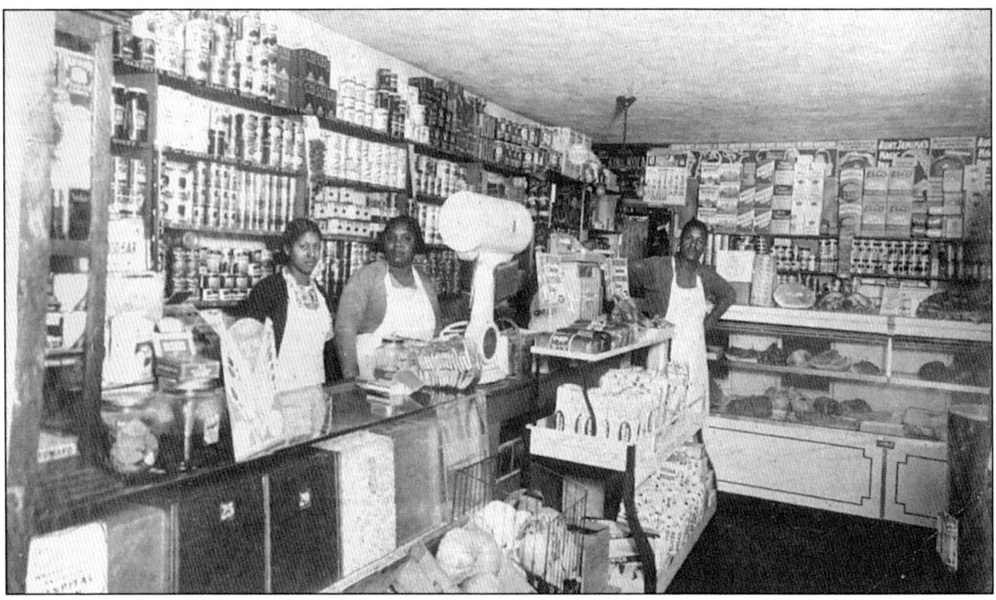

English's Grocery, in this photograph, started out as an S&B Coffee Company. They conducted business from their truck and traveled throughout Kinloch, Brentwood, Elmwood, and St. Louis making door-to-door sales of their roasted coffee beans as well as sugar and rice. The business grew, and the Englishes relocated the operation to the basement of their home. After a few years, the demand for their goods became so great they were forced to rent larger facilities and to eventually build their own store, which the family operated until 1967. (Photo Courtesy of Jewell English Reynolds.)

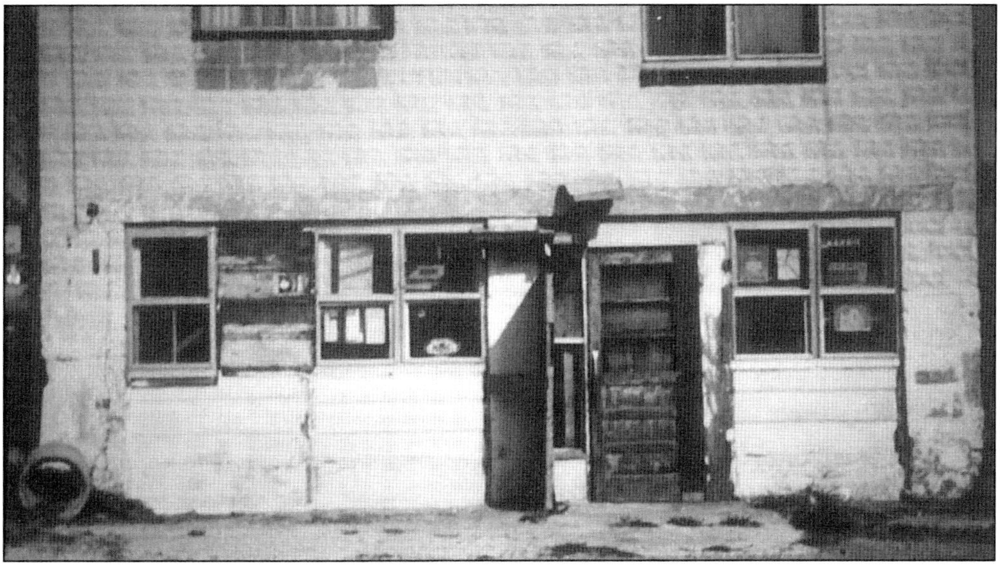

Marion Smith and his wife Rosie opened a confectionery at 8345 Scudder Road in 1944. They were fondly known as Uncle Dick and Aunt Rosie. Although the confectionery is gone, many Kinlochians fondly remember "Uncle Dick's" as a favorite place to purchase soft drinks and hamburgers, and where they spent many hours dancing and socializing as teenagers. (Photo Courtesy of Kinloch City Hall.)

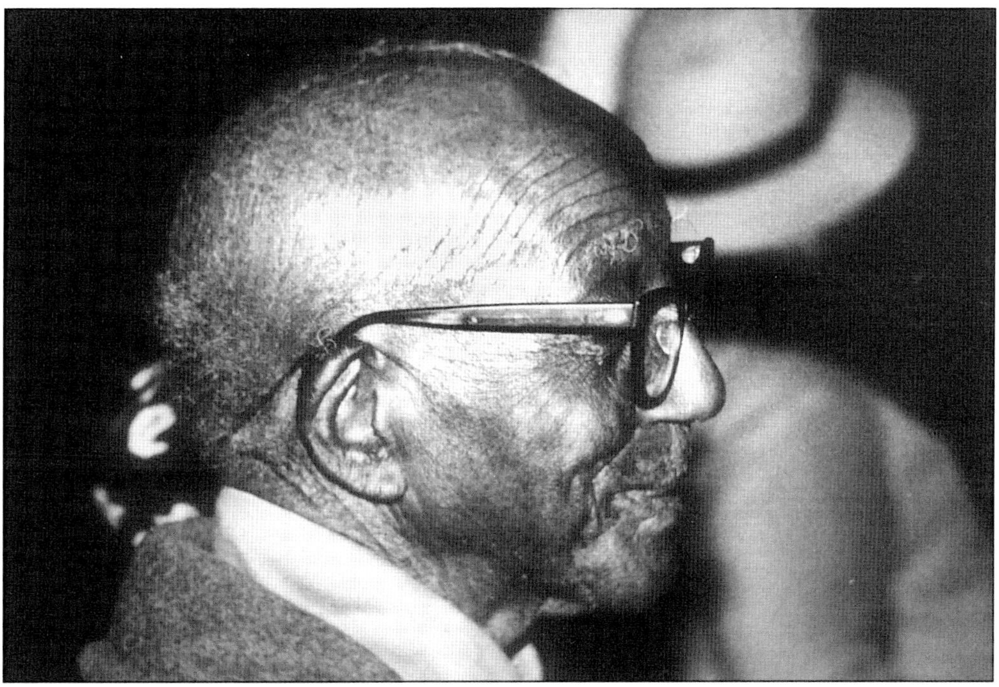

"Uncle Dick" (Marion Smith), pictured here, was one of the pillars of the community. As well as being a successful businessman who provided a place for teenagers to hang out, he was also superintendent of the Sunday school at First Baptist Church in Kinloch. (Photo Courtesy of Kinloch City Hall.)

ATwater 785 — Office Hours 9 to 11 a. m. and 6 to 7 p. m. Sundays by Appointment

Dr. J. S. Dorsey

Physician and Surgeon

Secretary of School Board

25 Carson Road — **South Kinloch, Mo.**

Visit the

REGULAR FELLOWS CLUB

Lix and Stanza

COLD DRINKS OF ALL KINDS AND SANDWICHES

Admission by Associate Membership Cards
See a Member and Get One

B. Dortch (Pres.) — V. R. B. Hadnot (Sec.)
G. Michell (Treas.) — T. Alexander (Bus.)

South Kinloch

- - Visit - -

KINLOCH CHICKEN SHACK

Bengert and Carson — **Bar-B-Q**

COMPLIMENTS OF THE

Kinloch Y. M. C. A. Office

Compliments of

KINLOCK CAFE

Chinese and American Foods

LIX AND HUGO — Vera Tucker, Prop.

Compliments of

KINLOCH PHARMACY

Hugo and Lix

Compliments of

TAYLOR'S CONFECTIONERY

Scudder and Carson

Free Delivery — ATwater 704

FOLWELL'S CONFECTIONERY

We Make and Bake Good Things to Eat

Lix and Warwick — **ATwater 576**

. . Compliments of . .

HALL'S BEAUTY SHOP

Carson Road — **South Kinloch**

FANNIE WELLS - - Beautician

SERVICE WITH SATISFACTION

1826 Winton — **South Kinloch**

Nelson Field Grocery Co.

QUALITY MEATS AND GROCERIES

•

Cheapest Prices in Town

5th and Lix — **South Kinloch, Mo.**

ATwater 9674

J. C. DAVIS & SON

CLOTHES ALTERED AND REPAIRED

N. E. Cor. Carson and Lix — **South Kinloch**

ATwater 768

Dortch Service Station

BATTERIES AND ACCESSORIES

Garage Service

Touring from 6 a. m. till 11 p. m.

J. J. BOYD

GROCER - - GENERAL HAWLING

Carson Road
ATwater 331 — **South Kinloch, Mo.**

This advertisement by Kinloch businesses was taken from the 1945–46 copy of *The Paragon*. (Photo Courtesy of Samuel and Bernice Boyd.)

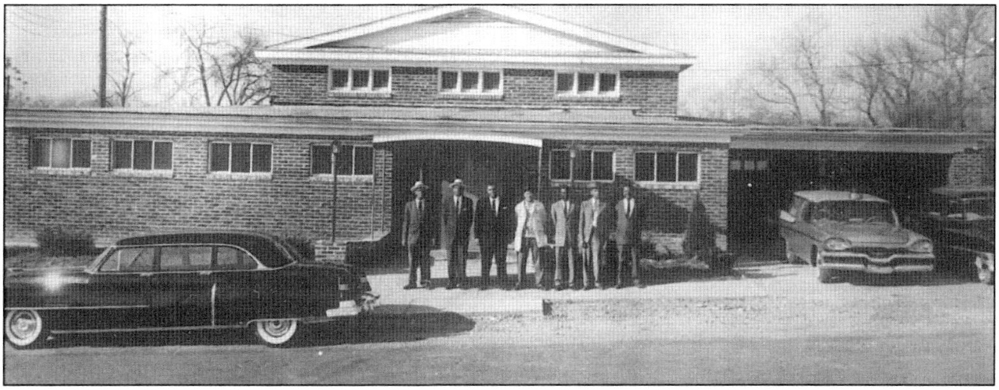

Boyd's Funeral Home on Lix Avenue (renamed Martin Luther King Boulevard) prior to becoming Kinloch City Hall, provided a meeting place for many community activities. It often served as a church when a congregation was in need of a place to conduct services. Pictured in front of the funeral home, from left to right, are: Atkis and Ed Boyd, co-owners; Donald and Samuel Boyd, directors; Robert Noland, driver; Early Wilson, building designer; and Henry Dowitt Jennings, funeral manager and director. (Photo Courtesy of Sam and Bernice Boyd.)

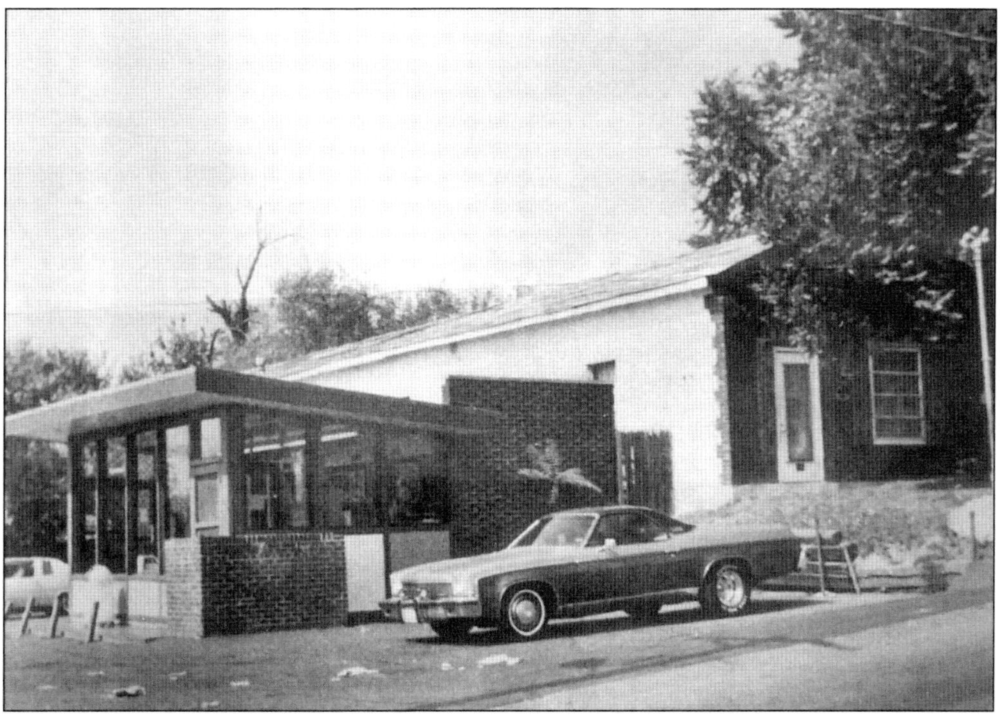

Pictured here is Hal's Drive-In Diner, a well-known spot and hangout for community teenagers during the 1960s and '70s. Owner Harold Gaskin served as president of the Kinloch Merchants Association during the 1980s. (Photo Courtesy of Harold Gaskin)

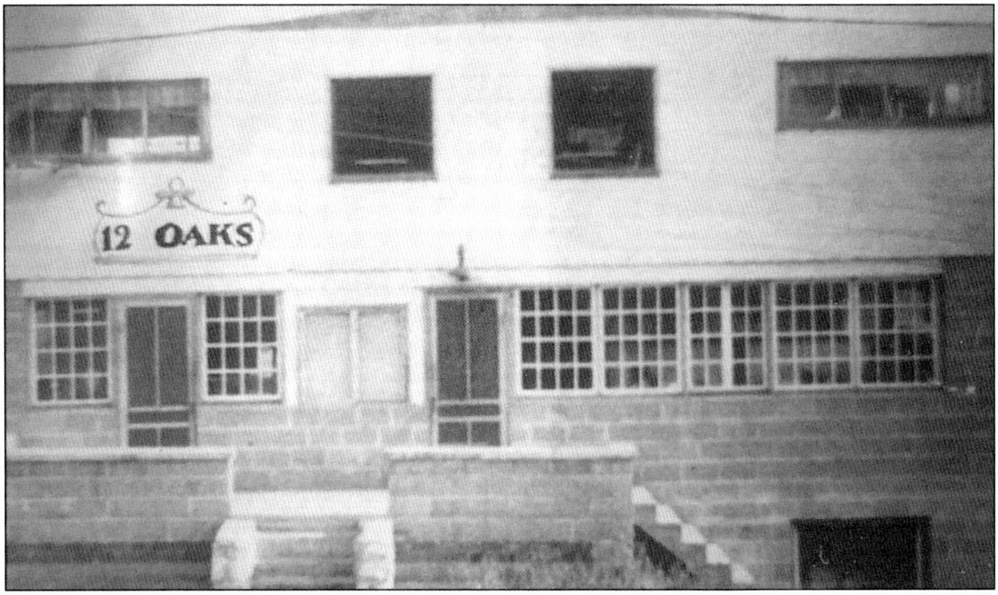

The 12 Oaks Club, pictured here, was opened in the early 1940s at what is now Fifth and Martin Luther King Avenues. The business was operated by Cordell, Hazie, and Richard Herndon. The club was part of the "Chitterlings Circuit" and attracted such entertainers as B.B. King and Lionel Hampton before it closed in the 1950s. (Photo Courtesy of Ruby Herndon.)

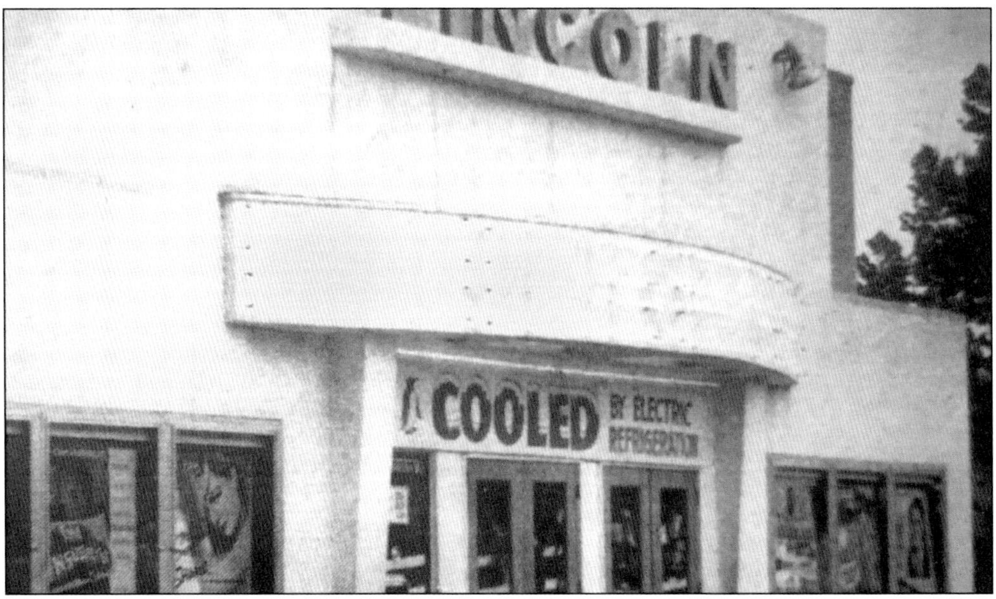

The air conditioned Lincoln Movie Theater, shown here, provided entertainment for Kinlochians during the early 1940s and '50s. Before Lincoln, however, silent movies were shown on the second floor of Miller's Hall on Scudder Road. Movies such as *Tom Mix* and *Charlie Chaplin* were accompanied by music from the town's only electric player piano. For thirsty movie-goers, there were two buckets of free, cold, well water and two long-handled dippers. (Photo Courtesy of Ruby Herndon.)

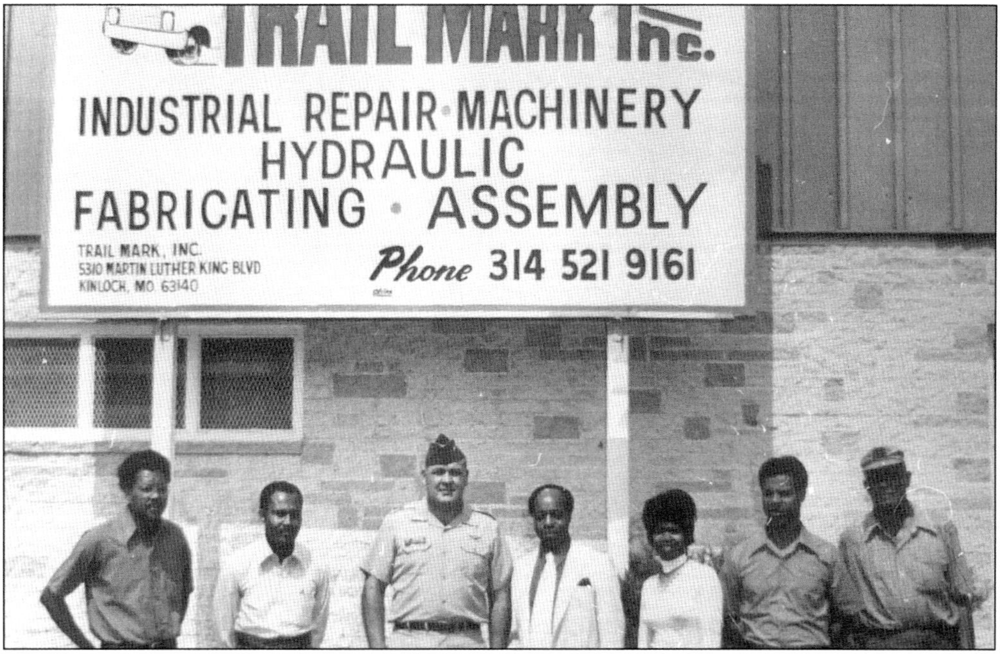

Kinloch residents saw a welcome addition to the business community in 1973 when Trail Mark came to the town. Trail Mark was a joint venture of the Small Business Administration and locally-concerned citizens. It was the first manufacturing facility in the city. The company opened with two contracts from Aviation Systems Command. One contract was for overhauling and repairing ground support equipment, and the other was for the manufacture and assembly of helicopter lifting slings. Present outside the company, from left to right, are: Isaiah Thomas, Kermit Robinson, B.G. Mackmull, Sylvester Smith, Alexandra Roberts, Douglass Simmons, and Atkis Boyd. (Photo Courtesy of Sylvester Smith.)

WALLS BARBER SHOP
Two Barbers To Serve You
L. Brown—1st Chair J. Walls—2nd Chair
Open Daily
Carson Rd. at Scott St. S. Kinloch, Mo.

ROSENA P. ENGLISH
Dealer in General Merchandise
Feed & All Grades of Coal
Lix & Scott So. Kinloch, Mo.
Phone Atw. 1319

Liberty Tailoring & Cleaning Co.
Cleaning, Pressing and Repairing
Alterations of all Kinds
Carson & McArthur
So. Kinloch Park, Missouri
S. H. Chambers, Prop. Yorktown 0016

ANNE THOMPSON
Dealer in Dry Goods, Hats, Hose
Dresses and Childrens Clothing, Mens' Wear
LIX & WILMORE STREETS
So. Kinloch, Missouri

Edward (Bus) Gunnell
Cleaning and Tailoring Company
12 Carson Road
Delivery Service
So. Kinloch Park, Missouri

Wells and William Jackson
KINLOICH CAB CO.
Ready to Serve You
Atw. 2165W

This advertisement for Kinloch businesses was taken from the 1940–41 issue of *The Paragon*. (Copy Courtesy of Victoria Cothran.)

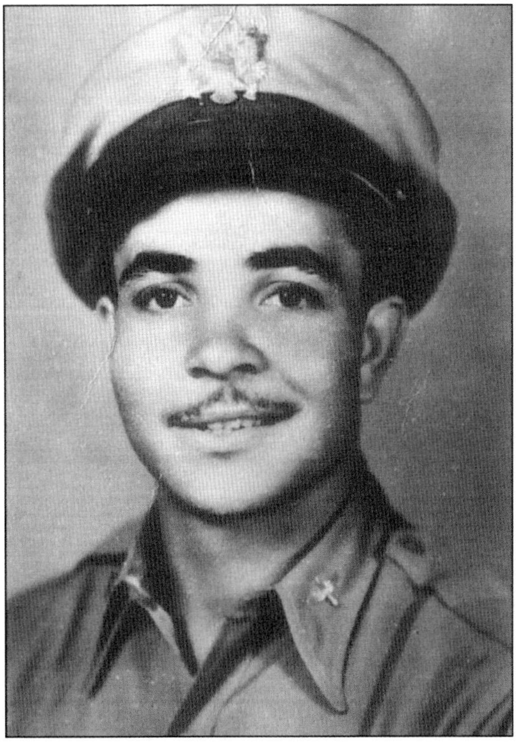

Pictured here is John Wilbur Squires, son of Mr. and Mrs. William Squires. John was one of the famous Tuskegee Airmen. After he graduated from high school, the family moved to Kinloch. In 1943, he joined the Aviation Corps and received his coveted wings in 1944. Unlike many who came home after the war, Squires died in a plane crash in Italy in 1945, while flying with the famous 332 Fighter Group. His picture can be seen in the aviation history mural at Lambert International Airport. (Photo Courtesy of Edmond and Dorothy Squires.)

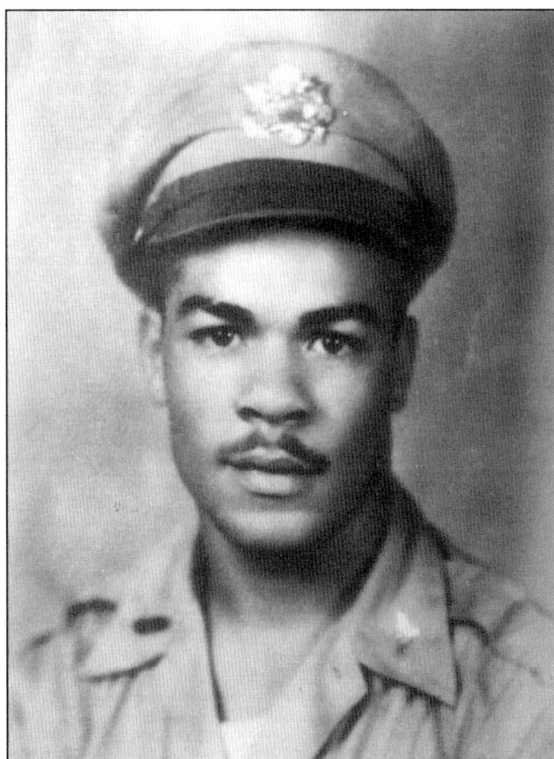

Charles A. Lane, pictured here, moved to Kinloch after World War II. After graduating from Tuskegee Institute, he joined the 99th Pursuit Squadron and flew 36 combat missions and fought in three aerial engagements. While a member of the 99th, he witnessed one of the first downings of an ME 262 jet aircraft by a P-51 Mustang. Lane later became director of the Greater Omaha Community Action Program. His picture can be seen in the aviation history mural at Lambert International Airport. (Photo Courtesy of Edmond and Dorothy Squires.)

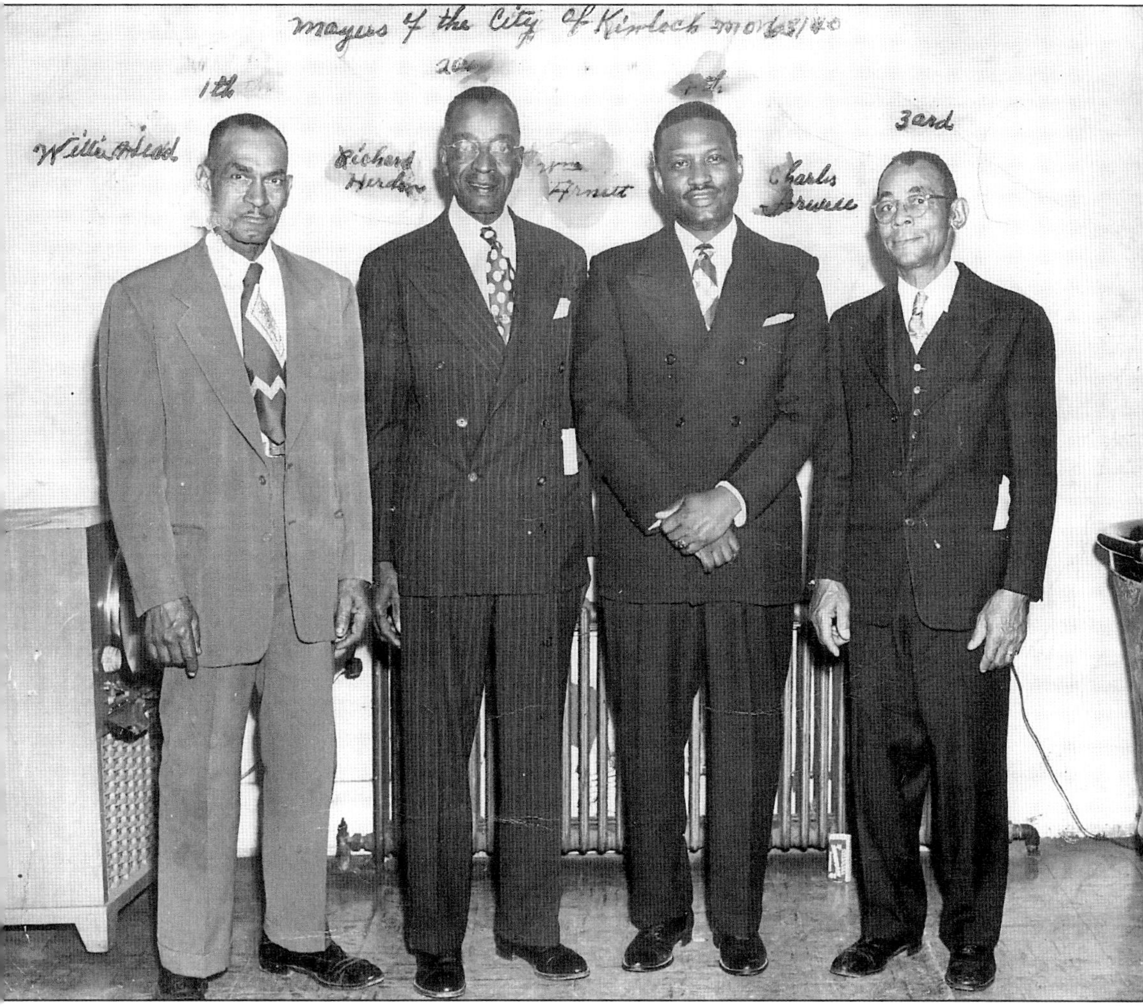

A rare moment was captured on film when the first four mayors of Kinloch came together. They are, from left to right: Willie Head, Richard Herndon, William Arnett, and Charles Folwell. Head, Herndon, and Folwell each served only one term. They were followed by William Arnett, who served three terms as mayor. Arnett took a leadership role in the redevelopment of the southeastern section of Kinloch. (Photo Courtesy of John A. Wright.)

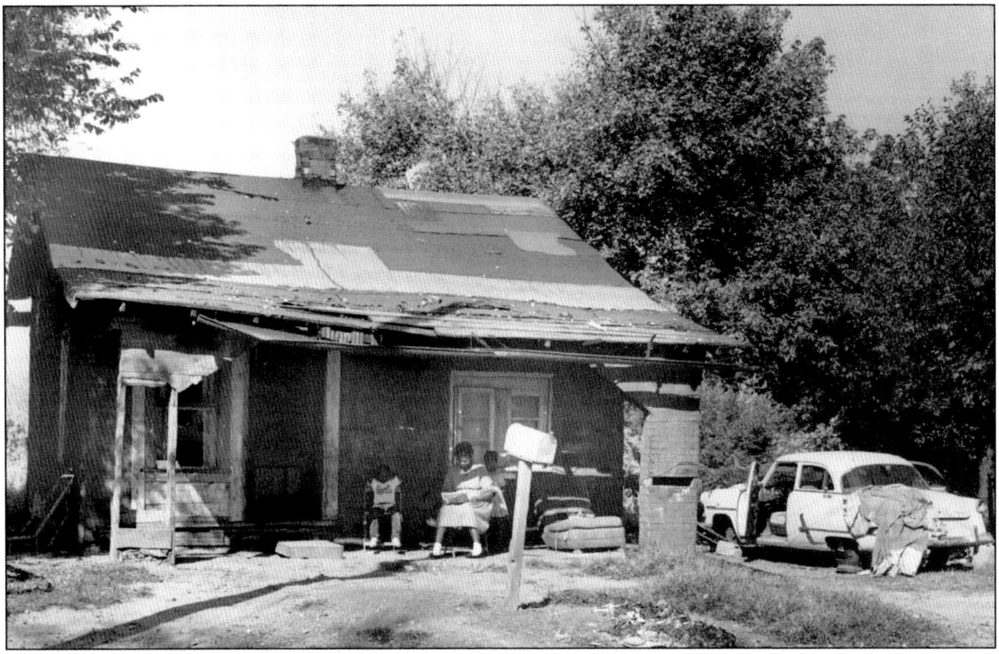

After less than a year in office, Mayor William Arnett convinced citizens to go to the polls in February 1956. By a margin of 454 to 15, voters approved an urban redevelopment plan, which called for the complete modernization of the city. An architectural team survey had revealed that 564 of the 1,700 structures like those on this page needed to be demolished. Residents were willing to do this to ensure a better future for the city. (Top photo Courtesy of *St. Louis Post-Dispatch*, and bottom photo Courtesy of John A. Wright.)

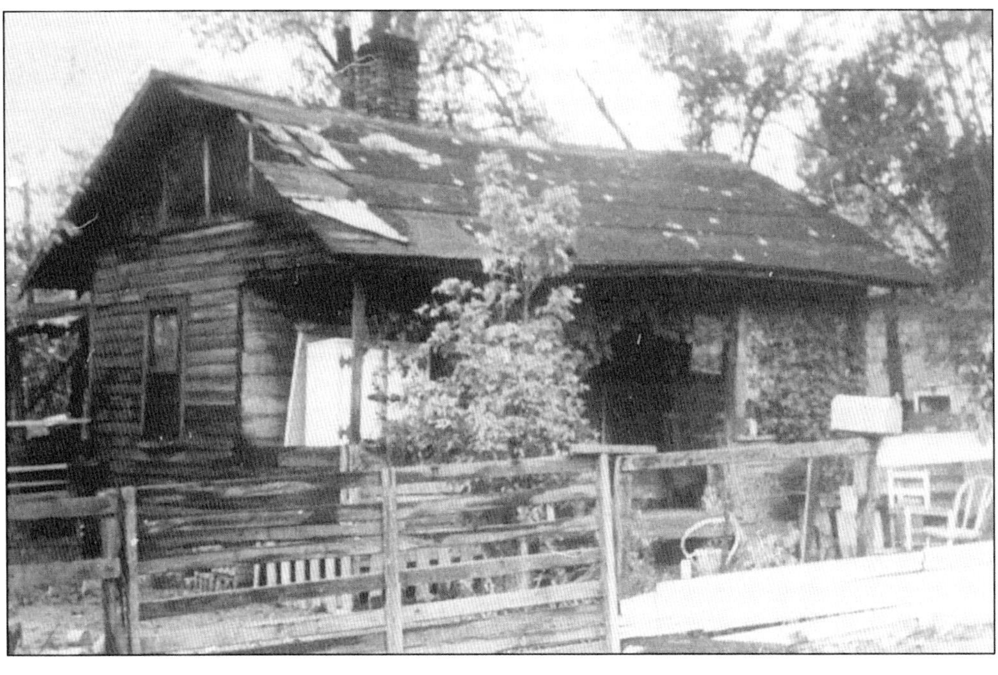

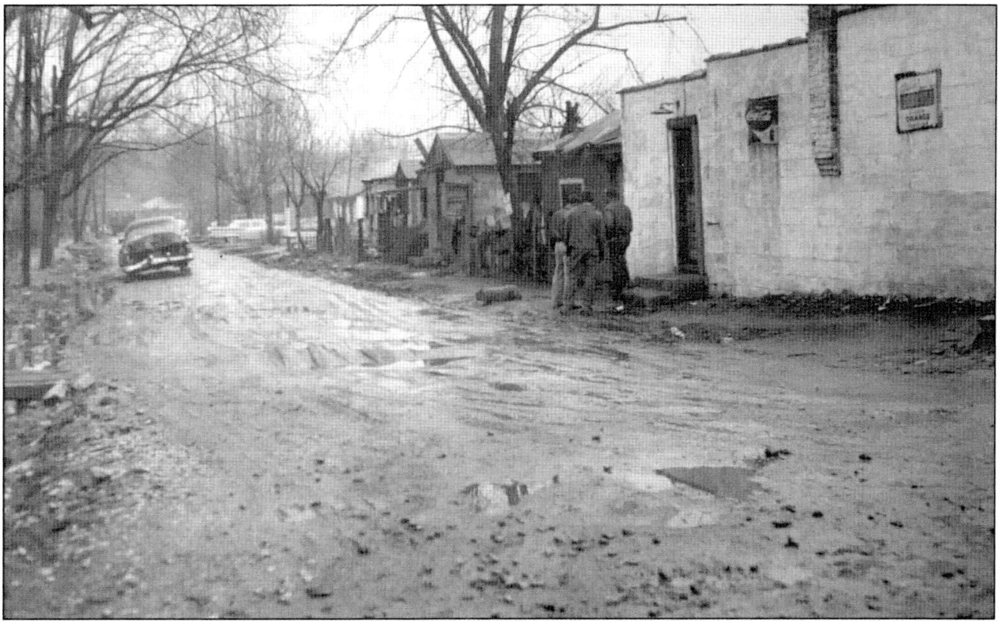

Prior to redevelopment by the Arnett administration, many of the streets in the southeastern section of the city were unpaved like the one in this picture. (Photo Courtesy of Holy Angels Church.)

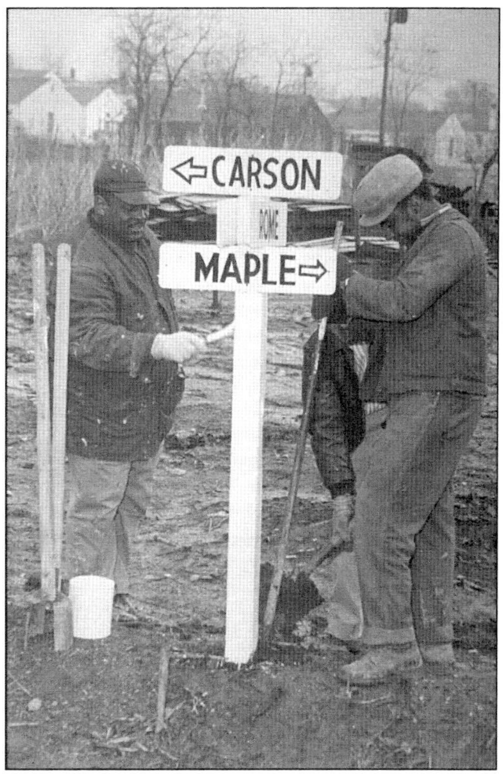

These men were photographed while installing some of the first street signs. For years, many the streets went unmarked due to the city's lack of funds. (Photo Courtesy of Holy Angels Church.)

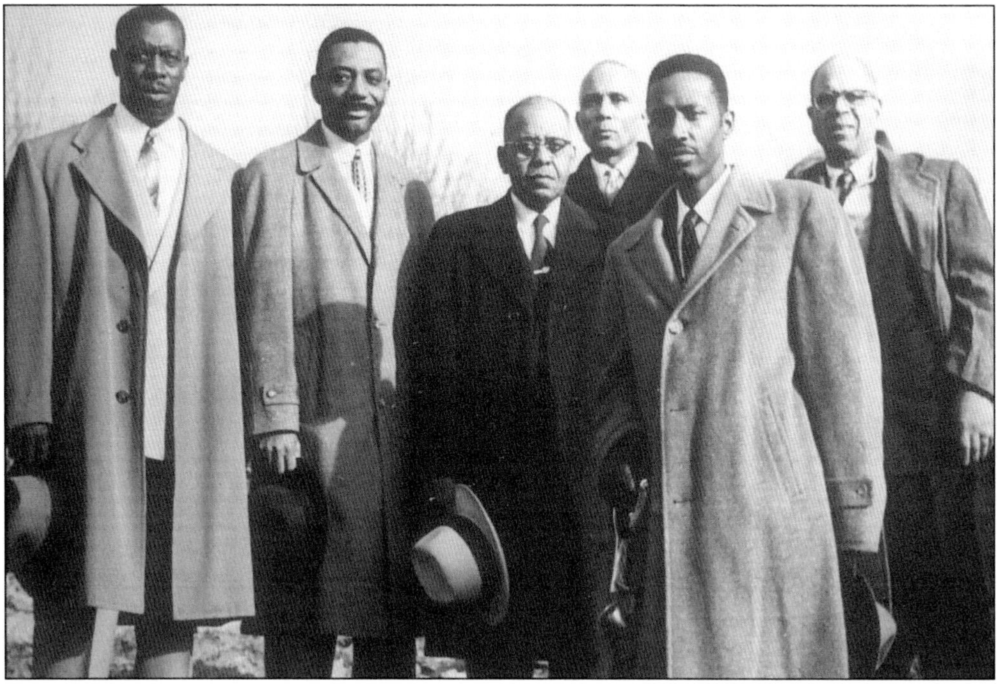

Mayor William Arnett is shown here with members of the Land Clearance and Redevelopment Authority. They are, from left: Ruben Walker, Woodrow Hughes, Henry Woods, John O'Guinn Sr., William Arnett, and Otto Belue. With the establishment of the Land Clearance Board, Kinloch became eligible for federal aid and funds for its program. (Photo Courtesy of William Arnett.)

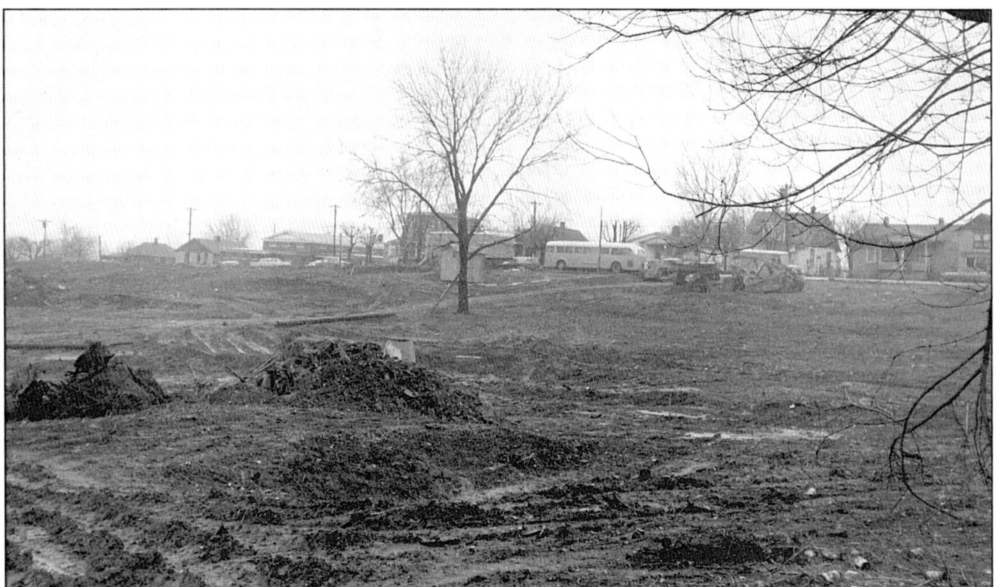

This picture shows the cleared land in the redevelopment area prior to development. (Photo Courtesy of Holy Angels Church.)

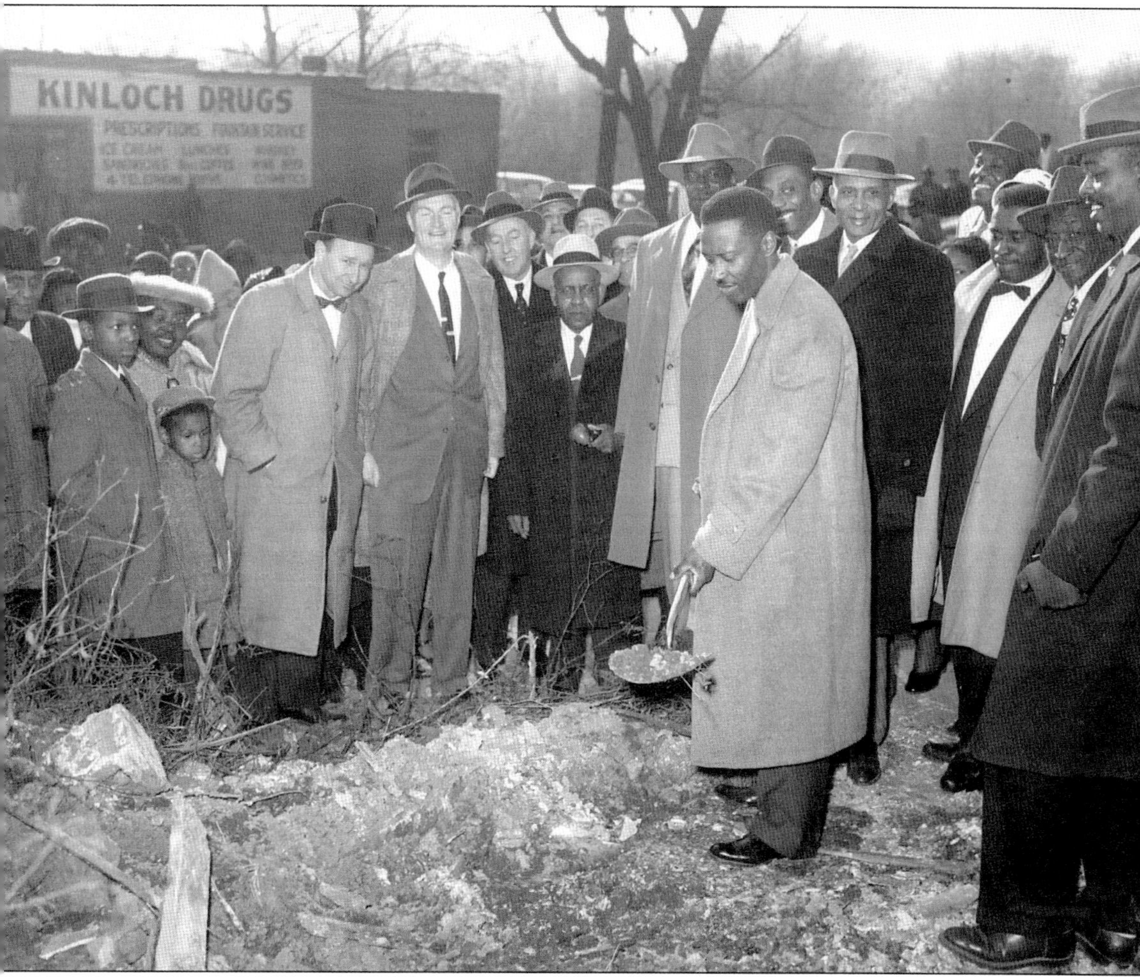

In 1959, Mayor William Arnett, shown here, broke ground for a $1.5 million housing project which was to be located at Scott and Lix Avenues. The St. Louis County Supervisor, James H.J. McNary (center with open overcoat) is shown while officiating at the ceremony. After completion of the housing project, Arnett cooperated with the school system in the construction of Smith Elementary School in the redevelopment area and in securing a large part of its non-cash credit for federal funding. (Photo Courtesy of *St. Louis Post-Dispatch.*)

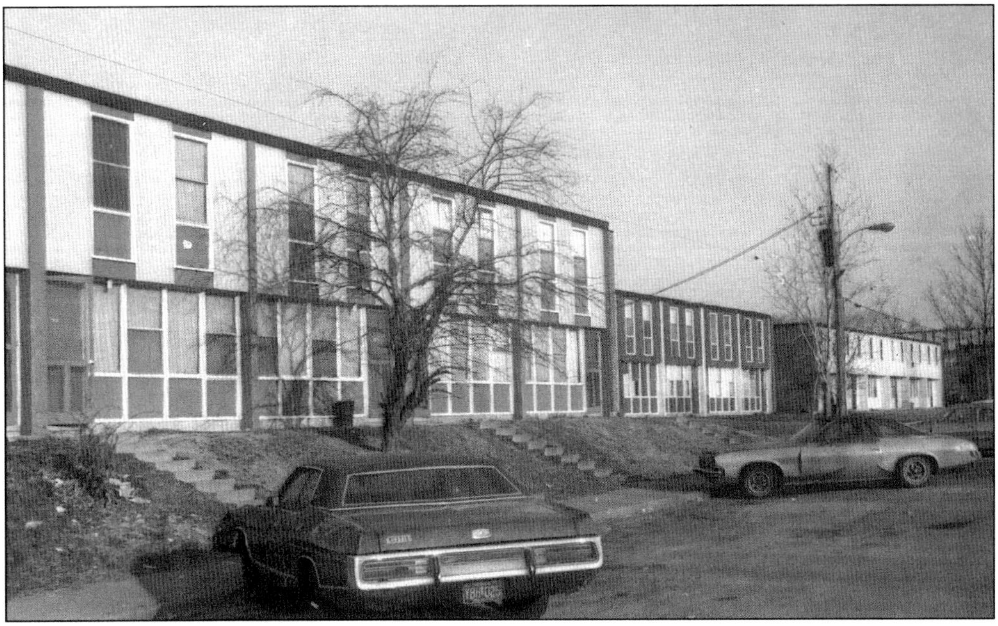

These low-rent units were part of the $1.5 million housing development project begun during the Arnett administration. They were named Belue-Hadnot to honor two former Kinloch educators—Harold Belue, a teacher and principal, and Myrtle Hadnot, a teacher. Housing units shown at the bottom of the page were for senior citizens. (Photos by John A. Wright.)

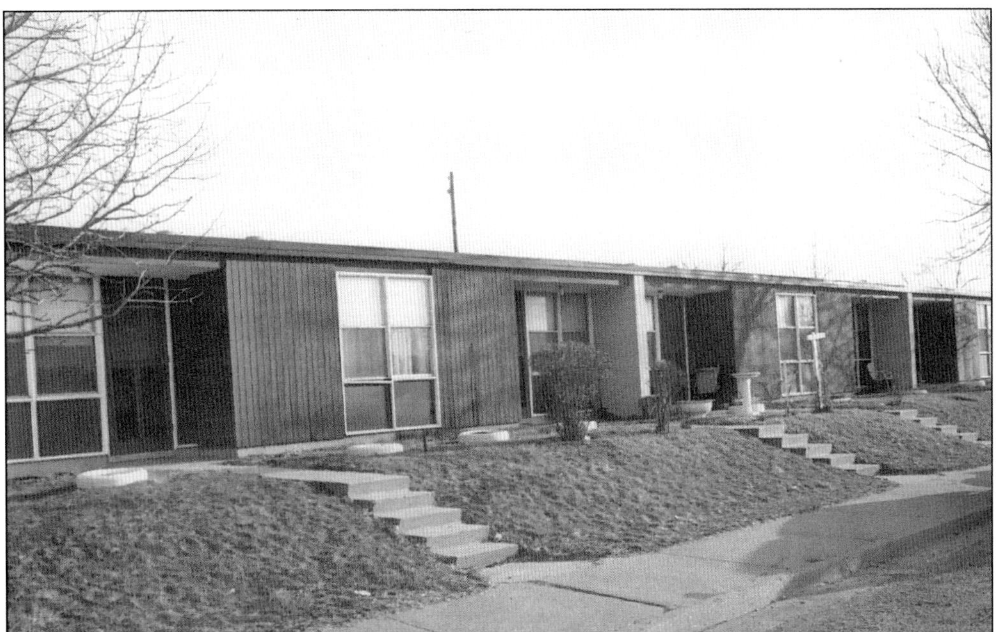

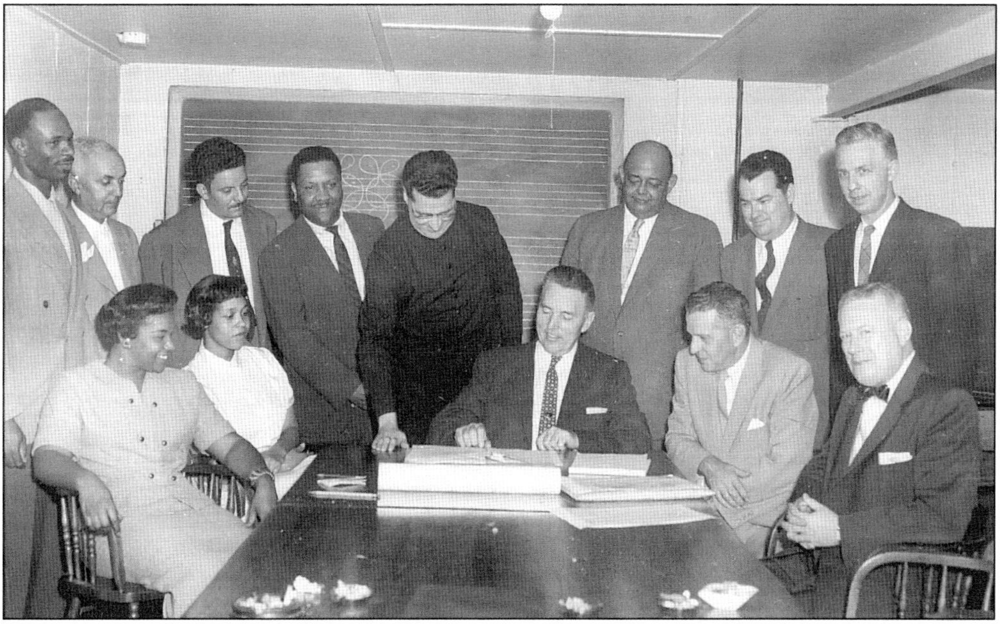

Father Patrick J. Malloy and members of Holy Angels Parish are pictured here with HUD officials discussing terms for the purchase of land for Marydale, a subdivision for black Catholics. This land was purchased through a "straw partner" arrangement, because the executors for the Cooper S. Hammond estate had refused to sell the property to blacks. The $10,000 that Fr. Malloy received to purchase the land was advanced to him by Archbishop Joseph E. Ritter. (Photo Courtesy of Holy Angels Church.)

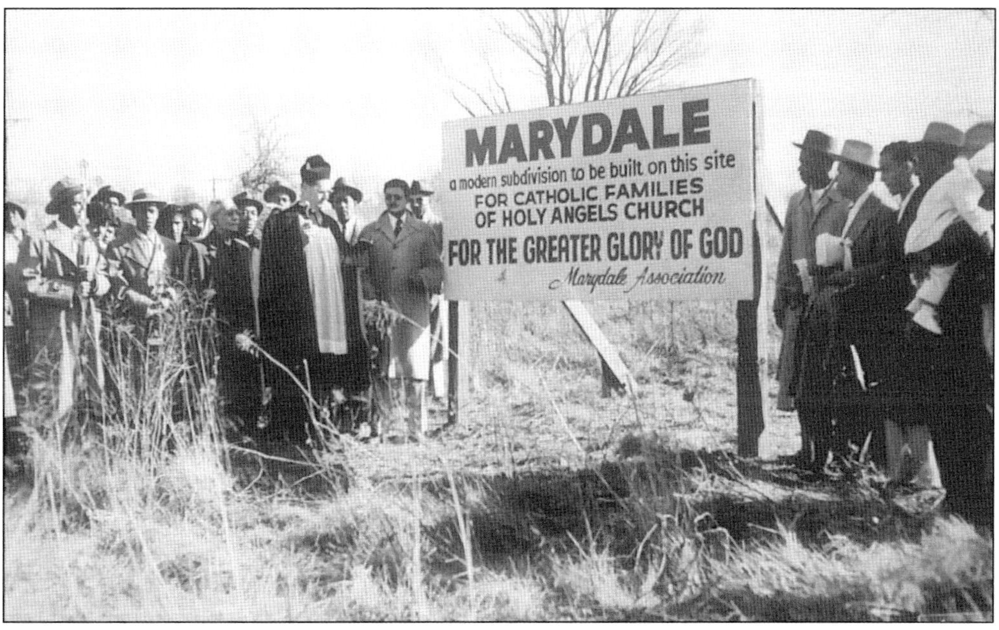

Father Patrick J. Malloy is shown here during the groundbreaking ceremony for the Marydale Subdivision in the northwest section of the city. (Photo Courtesy of Holy Angels Church.)

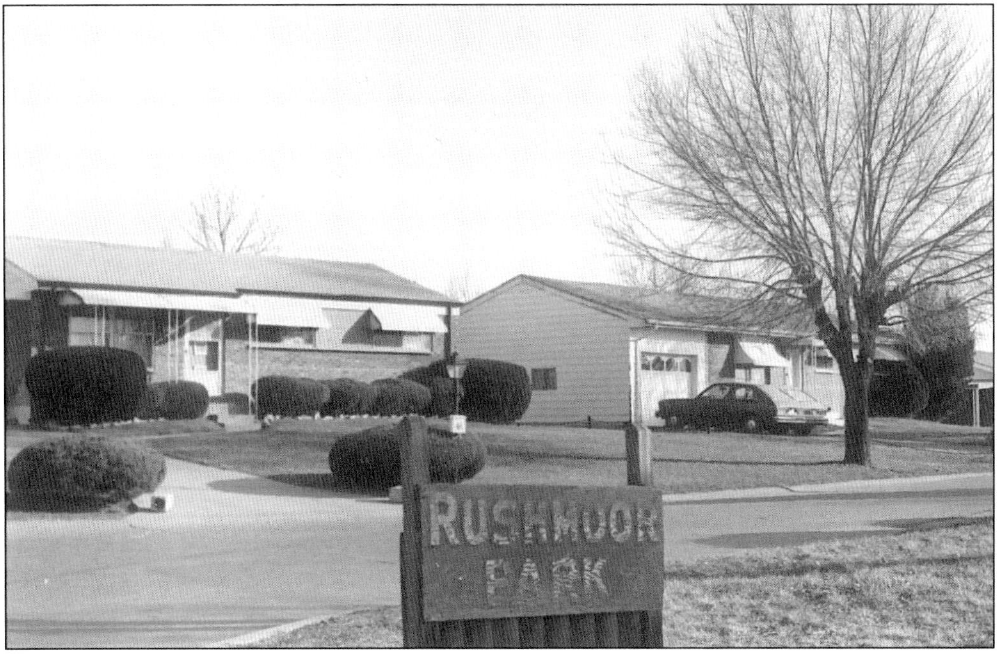

Father Malloy, pastor of Holy Angels Parish and one of the prime influential forces in Kinloch's redevelopment program, turned over the parish's Marydale Subdivision property to the city after the parish was unable to attract enough buyers. This property later became Rushmore Park, shown here. It was one of the finest neighborhoods in the community. (Photo by John A. Wright.)

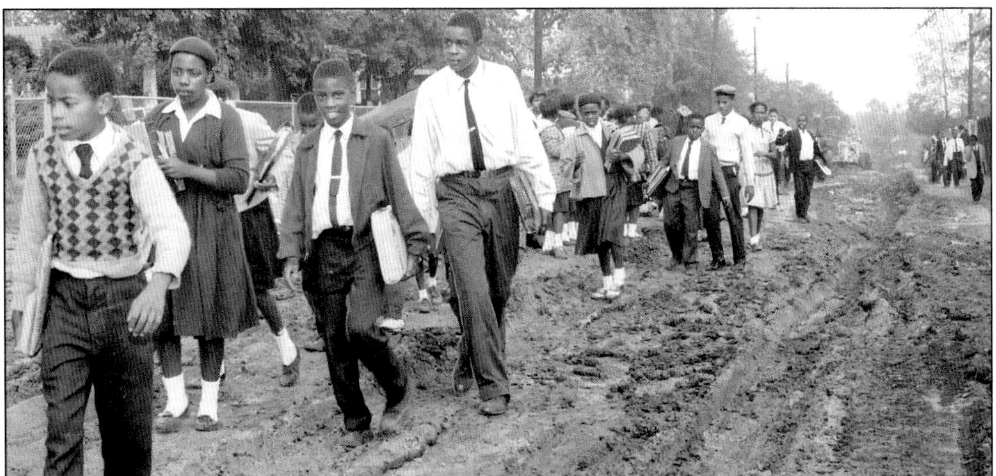

These neatly dressed Holy Angel School students are shown on their way home from school as they are trudging through mud produced by construction of sanitary sewers. The sewers were the result of the "Kinloch Amendment" to the Federal Housing Act of 1965. That amendment provided for 90 percent of federal grants for sewer construction in cities with a population less than 100,000, located in metropolitan areas and suffering unemployment rates of 100 percent above the national average. (Photo Courtesy of *St. Louis Post-Dispatch.*)

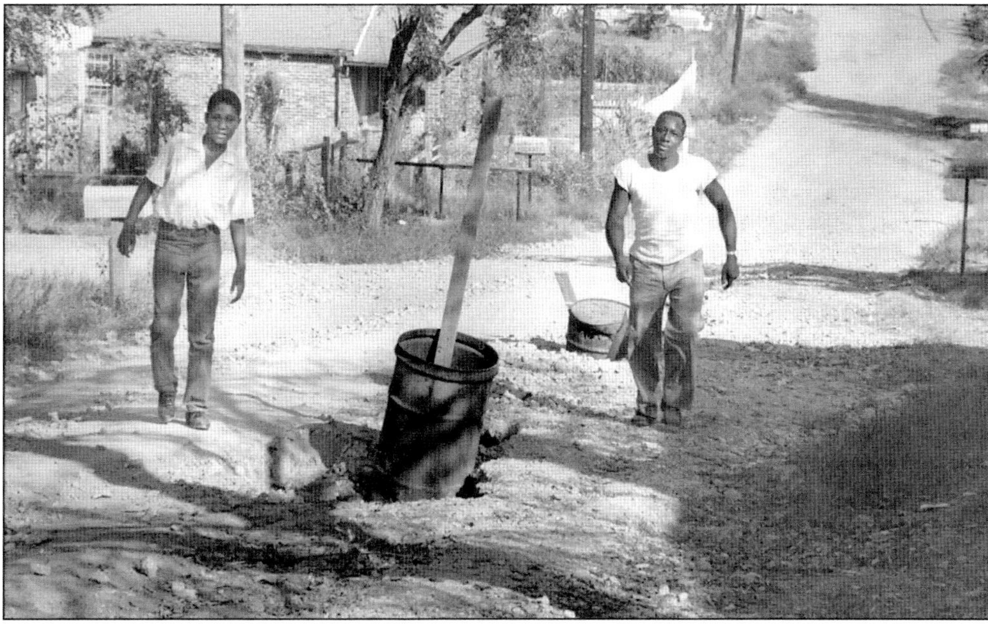

Shortly after the city's sewer construction was completed, the streets began to cave in. Leotis Kimbrough and Curtis Williams are shown here walking up Scott Street in the 8000 block. Barrels and boards had been stuck in sections of the street to keep cars and people from falling in. The lowest bidder, D.J. Fisher, submitted a bid $155,000 below the MSD engineering estimate. (Photo Courtesy of *St. Louis Post-Dispatch.*)

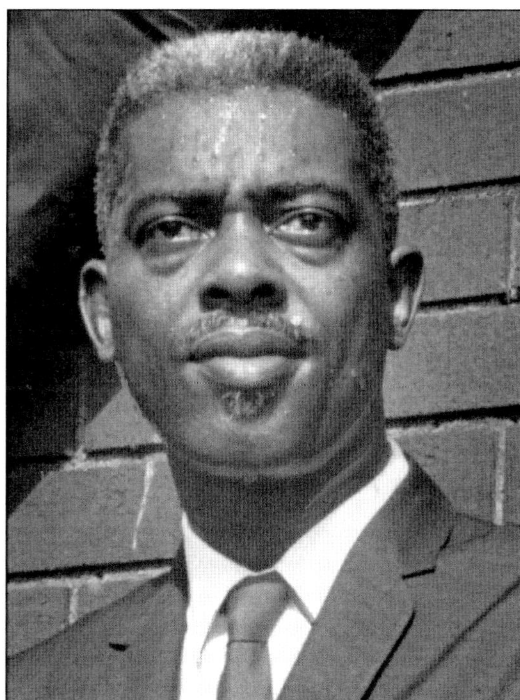

In 1961, Clarence Lee, a spray painter for McDonnell Douglas Aircraft (pictured here) defeated William Arnett in his bid for a fourth term as mayor. Many residents voted against Arnett because they feared he would start additional projects which would cause an increase in their taxes. (Photo Courtesy of *St. Louis Post-Dispatch.*)

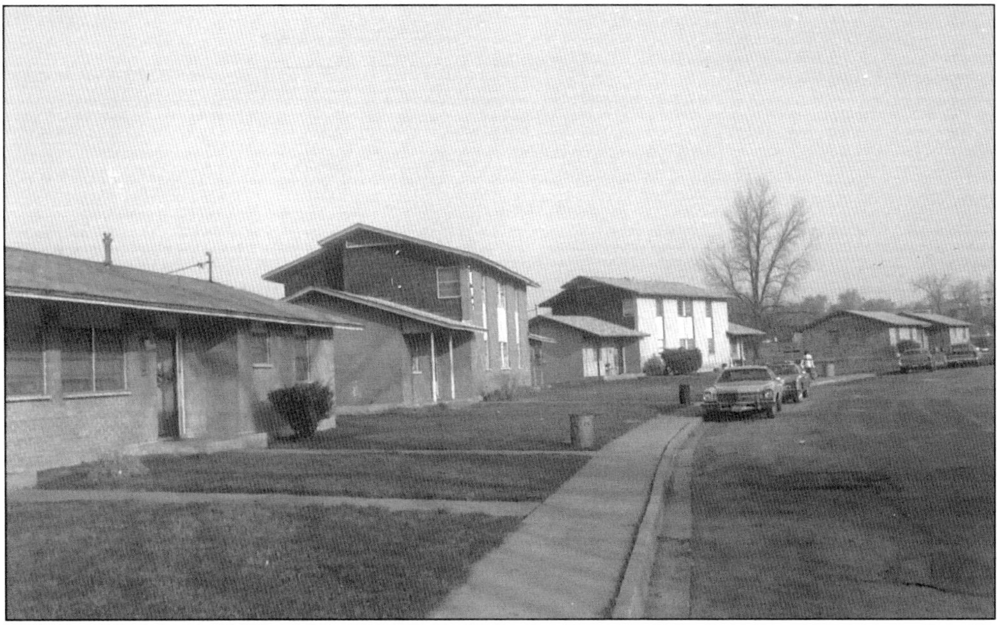

Groundbreaking for this $711,000 Folwell Public Housing Project was held in 1966. Among those present at the ceremony was Corrine Folwell Cannon, daughter of former Mayor Folwell, for whom the housing development was named. Also in attendance were Mayor Clarence Lee, County Supervisor Lawrence K. Roos, and Land Clearance and Redevelopment members Otto Belue, Woodrow Hughes, and H. Woods. (Photo by John A. Wright.)

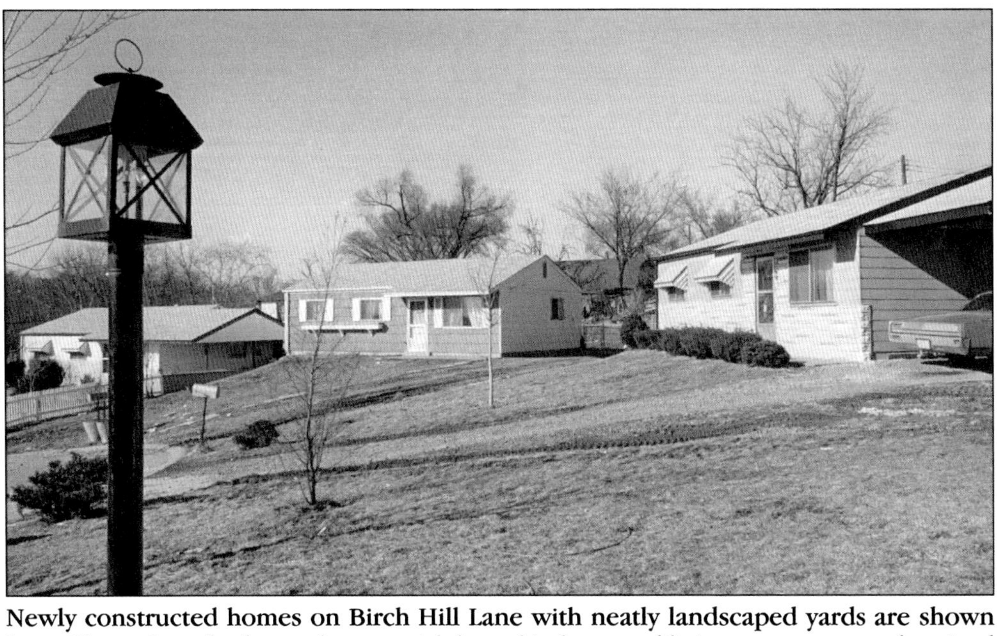

Newly constructed homes on Birch Hill Lane with neatly landscaped yards are shown here. These three-bedroom homes with large kitchens and living rooms were advertised at a starting price of $9,450 when they were completed in the late 1960s. (Photo Courtesy of *St. Louis Post-Dispatch.*)

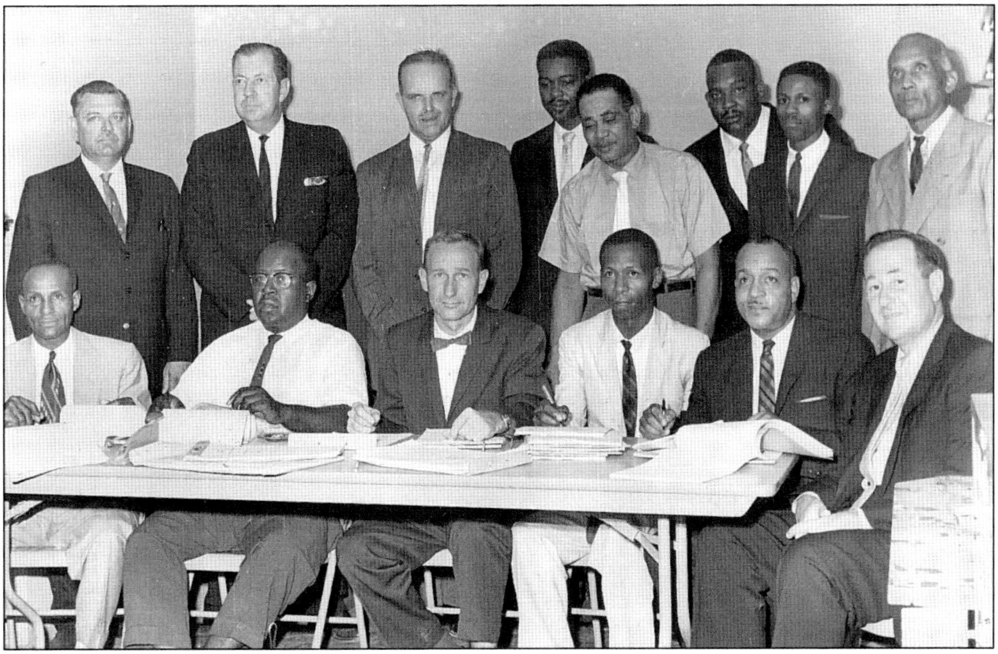

Members of the Kinloch Urban Renewal Agency are shown here with government officials working on the final plans for the development of the Boaz Apartments and St. Louis County's first rent supplement program. Napoleon Williams, executive director, is seated second from the left along with Benny Gordon, the project contractor who was St. Louis County's first black realtor, and standing fourth from the left is Mayor Clarence Lee. (Photo Courtesy of John A. Wright.)

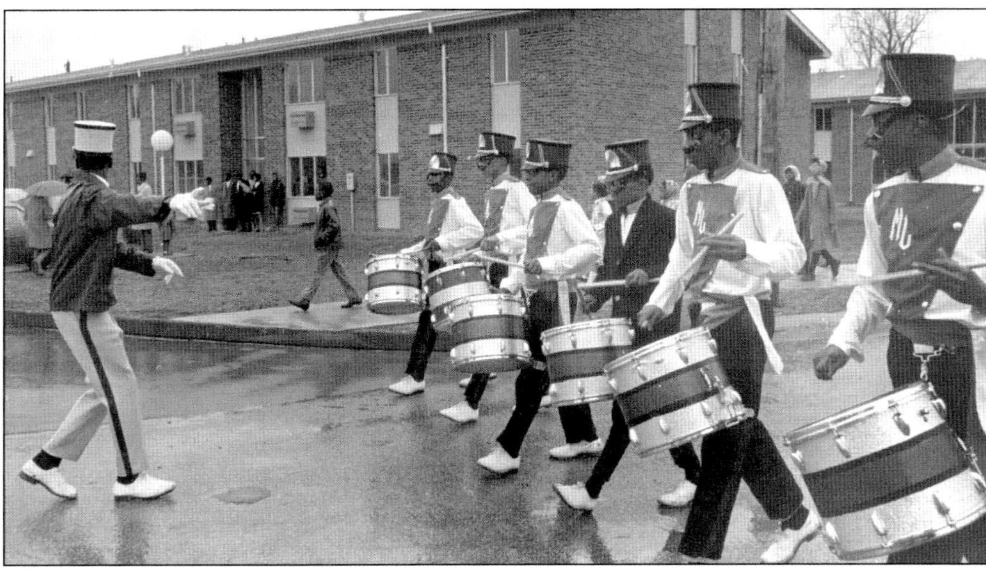

The Boaz Apartments on Mable Avenue, developed by the Boaz Masonic Lodge, was one of Mayor Clarence Lee's administration's major projects. On hand for the opening ceremony were the Memorial Lancers Drum and Bugle Corps, shown here along with federal and county officials. (Photo Courtesy of *St. Louis Post-Dispatch.)*

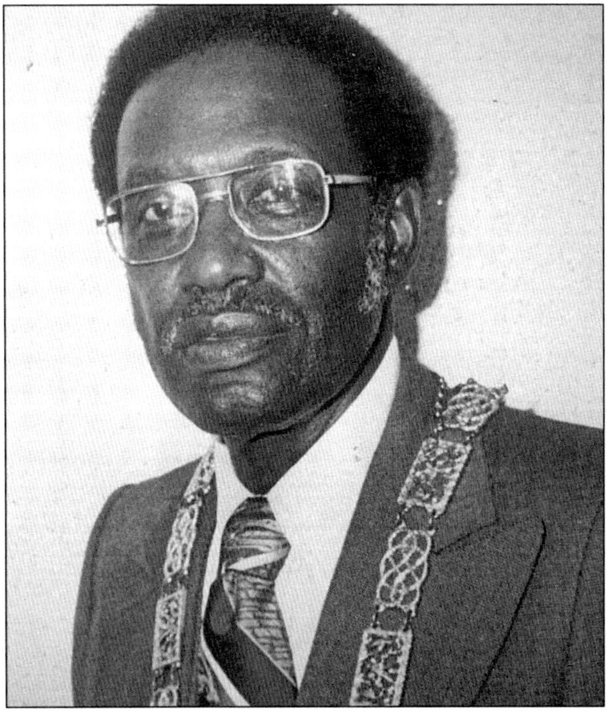

Through the years the Masonic lodges have provided valuable services to the community. Mayor William Arnett, the former Progressive Lodge's Worshipful Master, pictured here, served as the Grandmaster of the Masonic Lodges for the State of Missouri. (Photo Courtesy of William Arnett.)

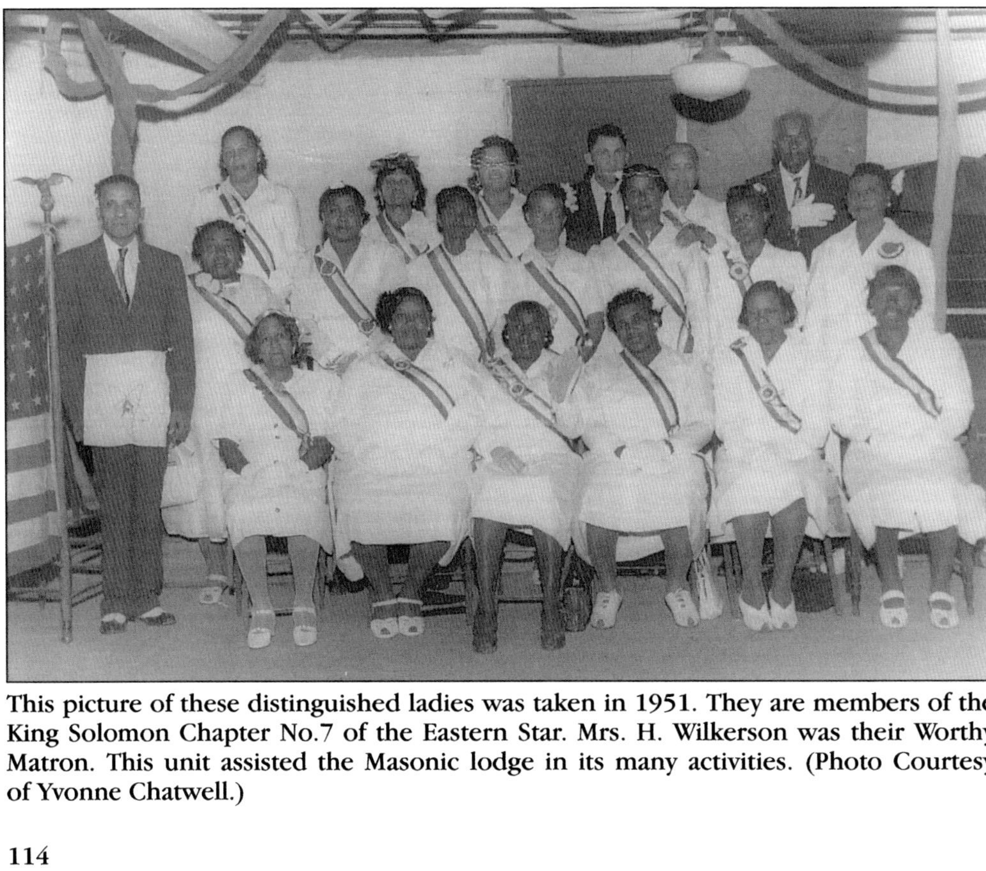

This picture of these distinguished ladies was taken in 1951. They are members of the King Solomon Chapter No.7 of the Eastern Star. Mrs. H. Wilkerson was their Worthy Matron. This unit assisted the Masonic lodge in its many activities. (Photo Courtesy of Yvonne Chatwell.)

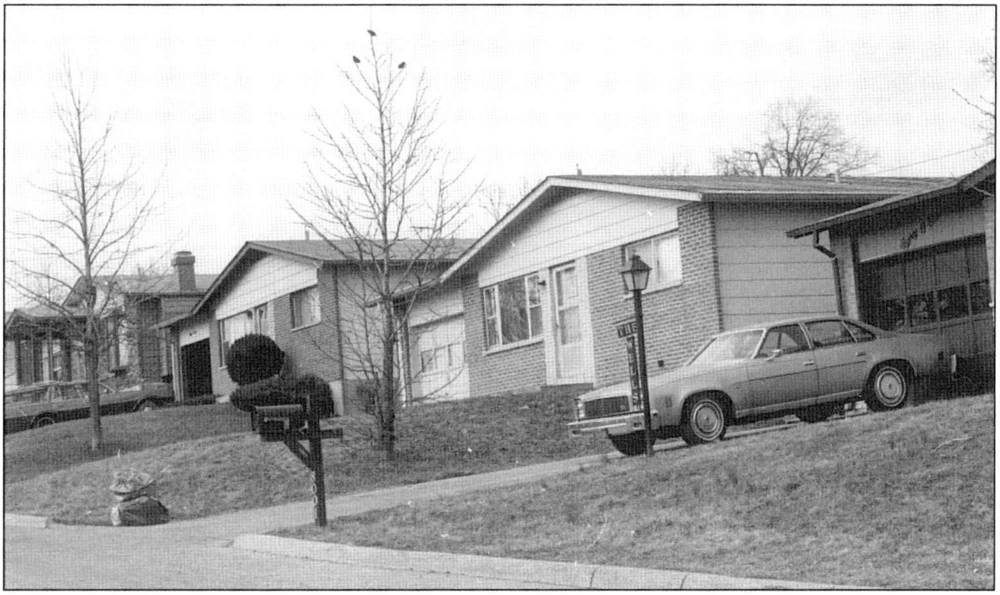

Pictured here are some of the homes developed in the northeast part of the city by developer William Petty. Petty, president of the Board of Aldermen, ran against Clarence Lee in the 1965 mayoral election and lost by a two-to-one vote. However, he remained on the board with a year left on his unexpired term. Not relying on the city's newspaper, *The Kinloch Word*, Petty produced his own mimeographed newsletter publicizing his positions. (Photo by John A. Wright.)

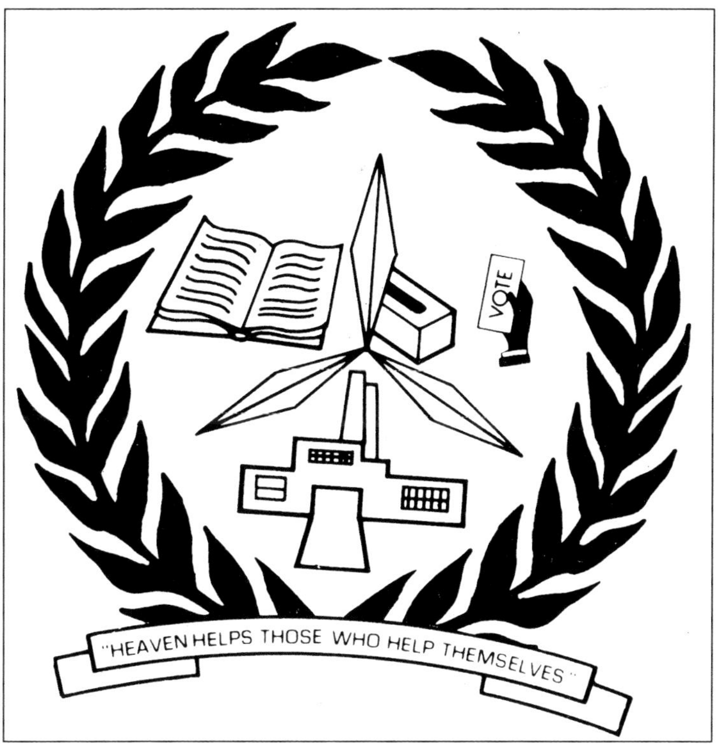

In 1966, the Kinloch Gateway Center, under its Director Norman Seay, conducted a citywide contest which produced the city's emblem, designed by 19-year-old Flemming Duke. The emblem depicts a ballot, open book, and factory enclosed in a wreath, which symbolized victory over poverty and ignorance. Under the wreath is the motto: "Heaven helps those who help themselves." (Photo Courtesy of Joseph Wells.)

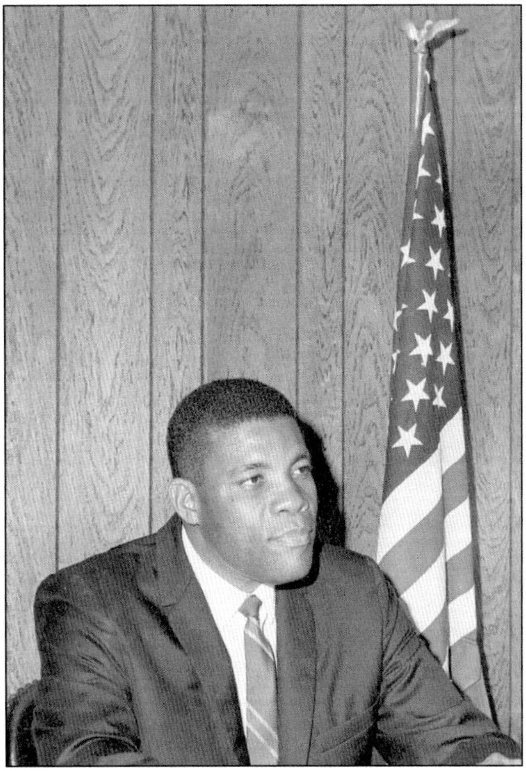

In 1969, Mayor Clarence Lee decided not to seek re-election, and Robert P. Metcalf (pictured here) was elected mayor. Metcalf, a Monsanto employee and former city judge, served two terms. (Photo Courtesy of *St. Louis Post-Dispatch.*)

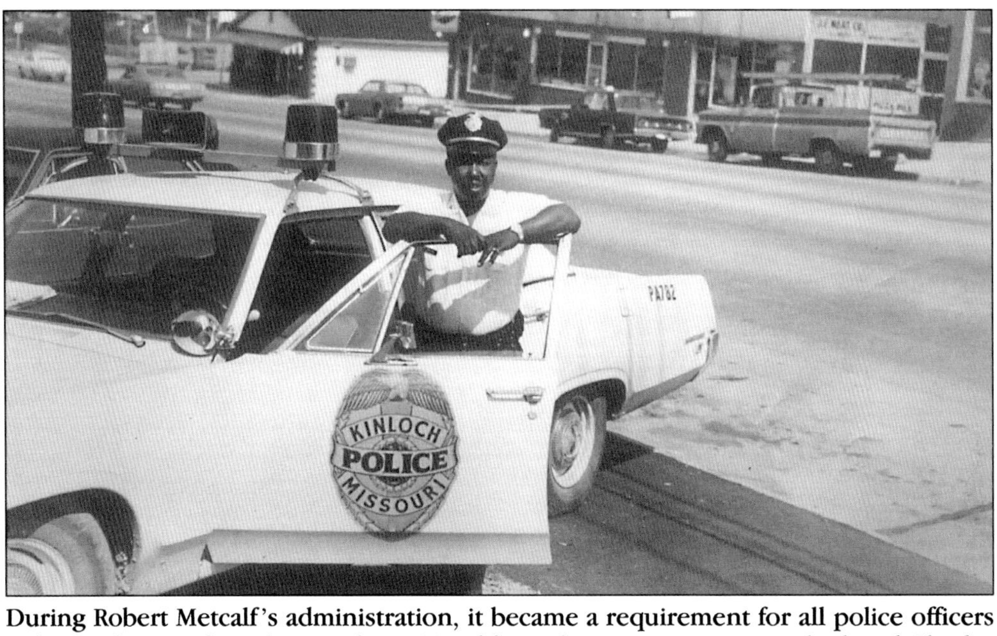

During Robert Metcalf's administration, it became a requirement for all police officers to be graduates of a police academy. To address this new requirement he hired Charles L. Whitener, the city's first trained police chief, in 1969. Whitener was a graduate of the Missouri Highway Patrol and the St. Louis Police Academy. (Photo Courtesy of Charles Whitener.)

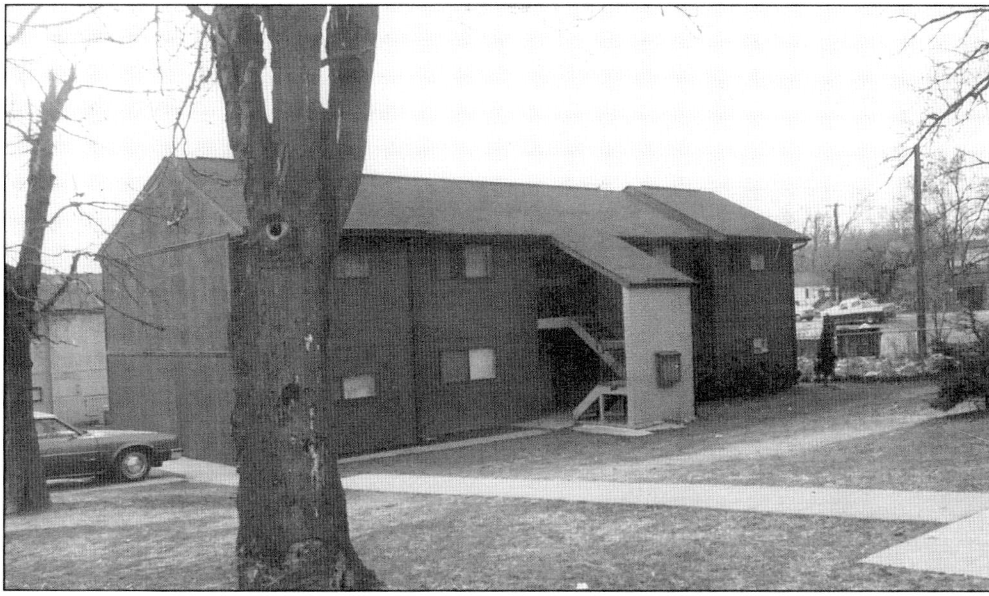

This building is one of the Kinloch Manor units developed with the assistance of the Urban League's Housing Corporation on the ten remaining scattered sites in the southeast part of the community. The funding application was prepared mainly by Mayor Metcalf's staff with assistance from the East-West Gateway Coordinating Council. This development enabled the city to fulfill its obligation to the federal government, and thus made it eligible to apply for federal grants. (Photo by John A. Wright.)

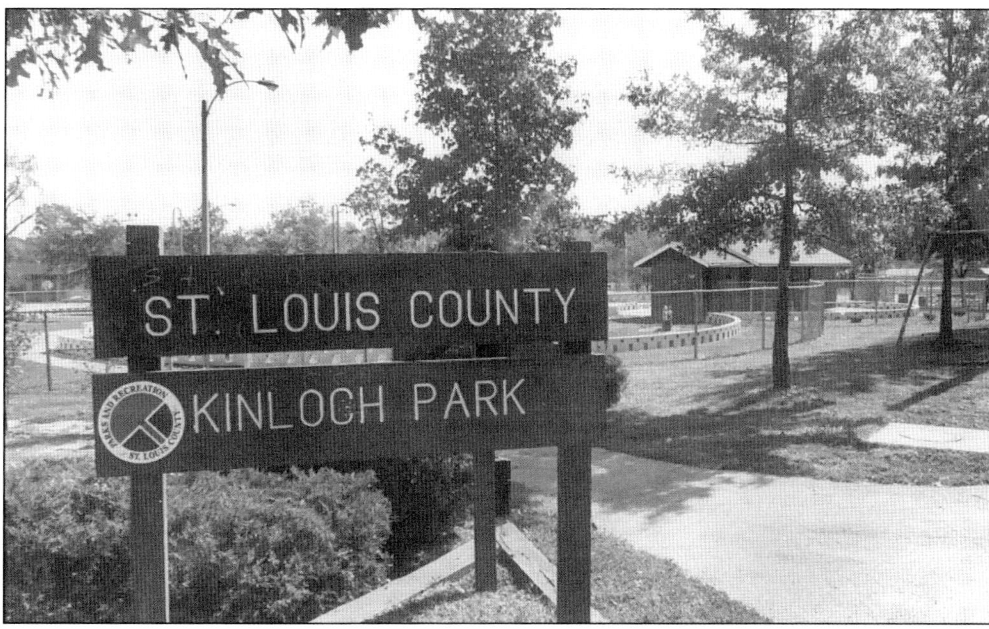

The Kinloch County Park at Hugo and Scott Streets opened in June of 1967. On hand for the dedication was Wayne Kennedy, director of county parks, and Mayor Clarence Lee. The park has a baseball diamond, a shelter, restrooms, and a lighted playground with swings, sand pit, spray pool, and a large wavy slide. (Photo by John A. Wright.)

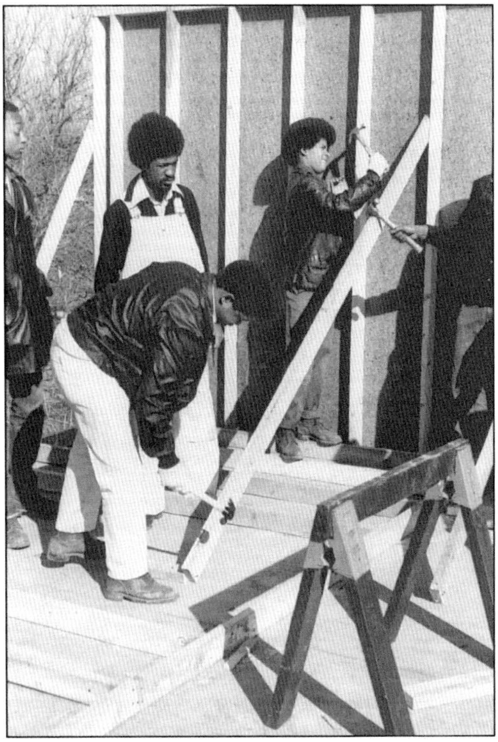

Kinloch High School students are shown here with their instructor, Robert McCain, constructing walls for the house they are building on 5th Street. (Photo Courtesy of John A. Wright.)

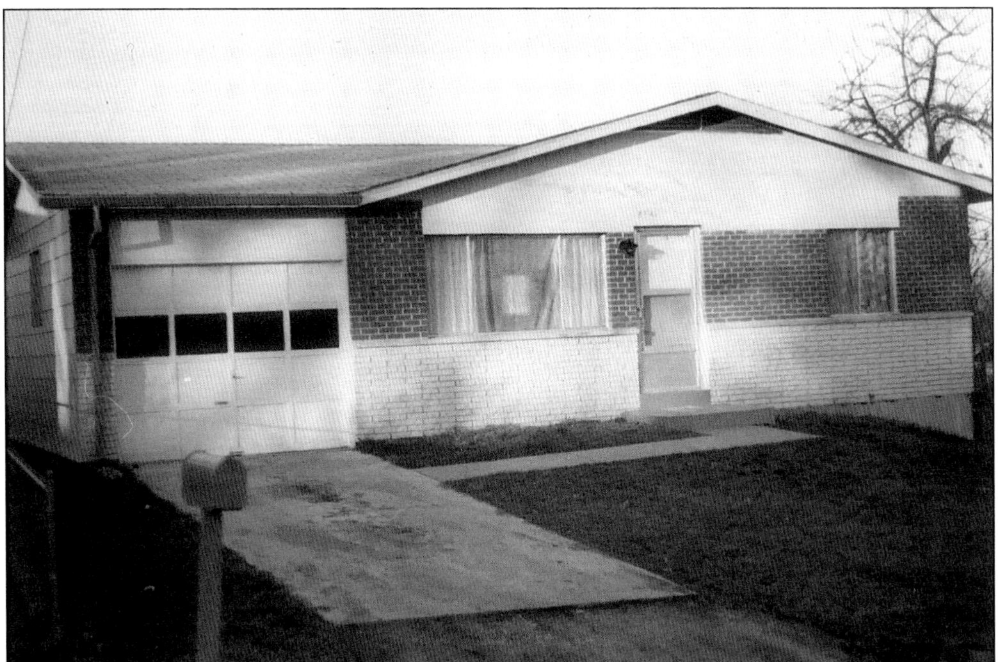

This frame and brick three-bedroom home on 5th Street is the finished product of a year's work by Kinloch High School students in 1972. (Photo Courtesy of John A. Wright.)

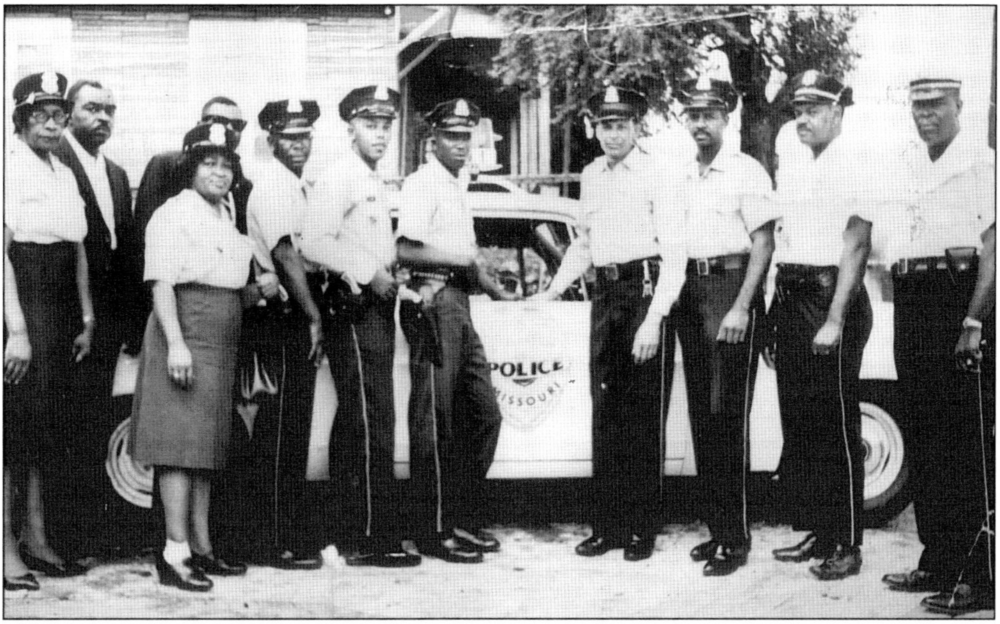

Shown in this picture are part of Kinloch's 13 full and part-time police officers, who served under Marshall Cornell McGee prior to the appointment of Charles L. Whitener as chief of police. From left to right, are: Officers Bradfield, Holbrook, Payne, unidentified, Wells, Jones, unidentified, Cockrell, Combs, Asst. Chief Orville Jones, and Cornell McGee, chief. (Photo Courtesy of Charles Whitener.)

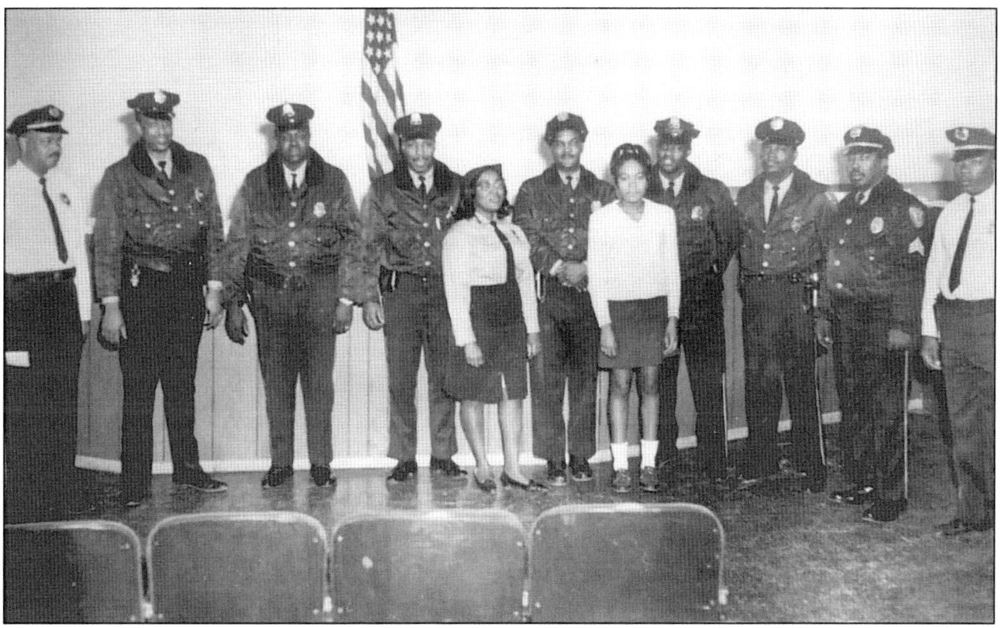

Shown here is the 1968 police force under Chief of Police Charles Whitener. From left to right, are: Orville Jones, Gwen Turner, John Bondus, Lewis Clark, Louise Robinson, Jerry Jones, unidentified young lady, Louis Steed, Stanford Belle, Charles Whitener, and Nathaniel Dunn. (Photo Courtesy of Charles Whitener.)

ST. STANISLAUS SEMINARY
FLORISSANT, MO.

March 16, 1929

Dear Professor,

As you are probably aware, I have organized the Claver Library and placed it at the service of the community. Already it has 700 volumes and more than a score of periodicals in use; and among its works are several of the English classics, some helpful books in other departments, and an extraordinary supply of juvenile literature, all of it wholesome and some of it highly literary. Now all of this has been put to the service of the community without one cent of cost to the people of South Kinloch,- but you can easily imagine at what a cost of time and trouble and some actual expense to myself; yet I shall be well repaid if the library be properly appreciated and properly used.

It is to ask your cooperation in this that I am now writing to you, and I feel assured that you will give it. More than anyone else in the community you realize the benefit of such a library, and even its assistance to you and your staff in your work. Please help the children and their parents to recognize the opportunity, and its favor, that is given to them; but that the service can be continued only on the condition that they observe the very simple library rules. They must return the books in due time, and they must take care of the books which they have borrowed on their cards. They should not write in them, or disfigure them; they should not let them lie about exposed to injury from any source. If they will not do this, I shall be obliged, of course, to withdraw the library from public service, or even altogether. I cannot duplicate some of these books, and I have little hope of getting others quickly. The present establishment under its conditions is, I think, phenomenal,- probably never so freely and quickly furnished,- and it would be a pity were it to prove a failure. Many persons are quite critical of me for having begun it, predict its disaster by the theft of the books ot their lack of care and are quite ready to give their "I told you so", expecially where they know that the Colored folk are involved. I am confident that you will help me to save the situation.

The Claver Library is not, as you may see, an exclusively Catholic library. Naturally enough there are many Catholic books, but these are scarcely one-tenth of the library's contents. And for the non-Catholic this should not be a disadvantage, especially for the Negro whom bigotry classes with ourselves, for Catholicity, its doctrine, history and practice, is the most misunderstood or falsely represented of the great subjects which engage thought. With this means of being rightly informed the people of South Kinloch can have no excuse for misrepresentation of the Catholic Church. This misrepretation would be not merely ignorance - sometimes excusable - but nasty bigotry; and the Negro has been so much the victim of prejudice, and its consequence bigotry, that he ought to hate it in every form.

Yours sincerely,

A.J. Garvey, S.J.

The Peter Claver Library was the first known library open to the public in Kinloch. It was established by Father A.J. Garvey and operated out of Holy Angels Church. This letter to a St. Louis University professor provides some information on the reasons for the library's establishment, its collection, and the philosophy behind its operation. (Letter Courtesy of Holy Angels Church.)

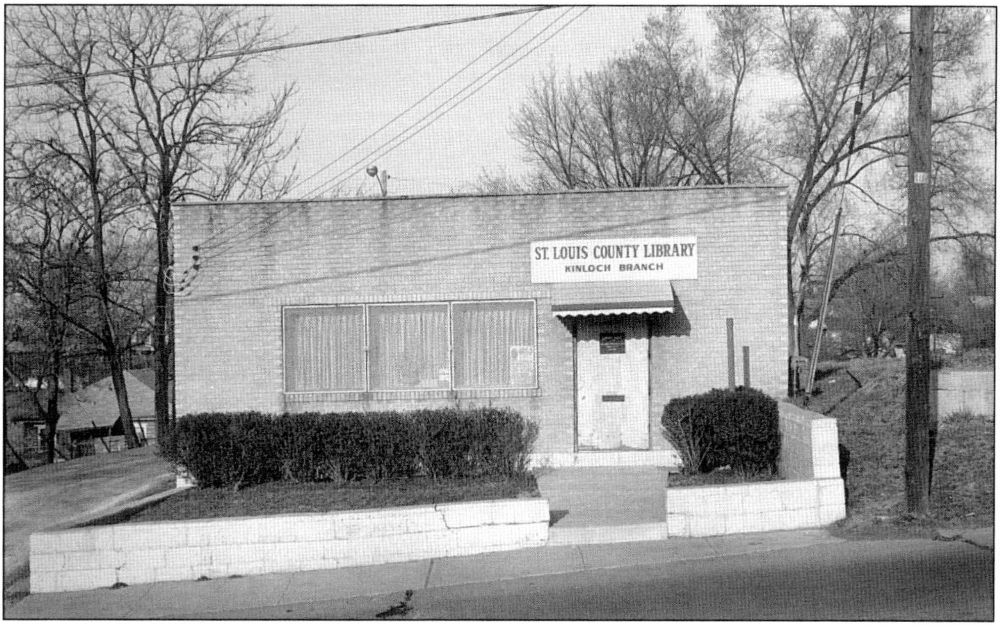

Kinloch's public library, shown here, grew considerably from its humble beginnings in 1947. Prior to coming under the county library district, the library operated in the Roberts Building for a few years and was the seventh public library in the country funded by the Works Progress Administration. The library was owned at that time by the community, managed by a library association composed of 126 members, and open to all residents of Kinloch and Robertson. (Photo Courtesy of the 1983 Kinloch History Committee.)

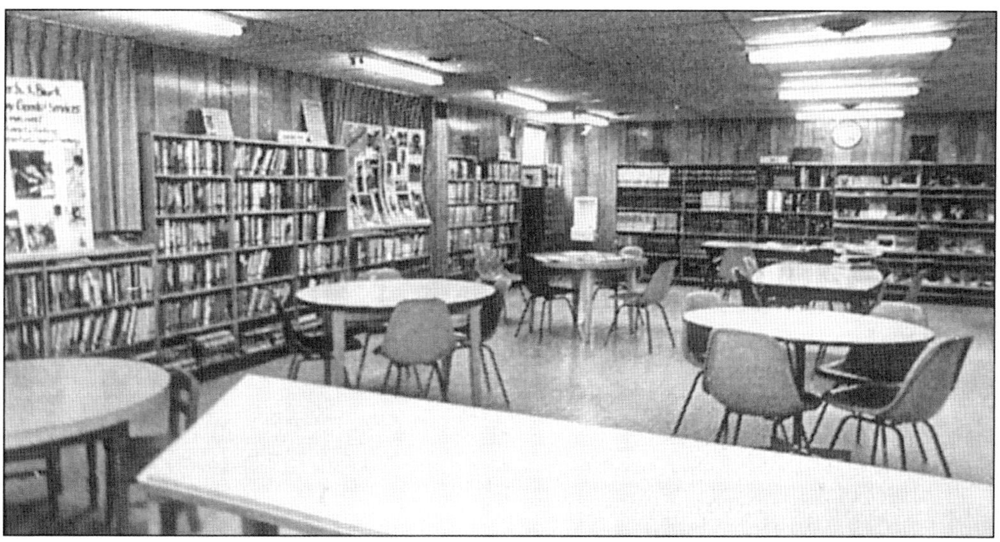

As it can be seen from this picture, the Kinloch library provided a pleasant and comfortable environment for the Kinloch patrons. Librarian Leola Shipp, who assumed her duties in 1961, offered movies, a reading program, storytelling, and summer activities for residents of all ages. (Photo Courtesy of the 1983 Kinloch History Committee.)

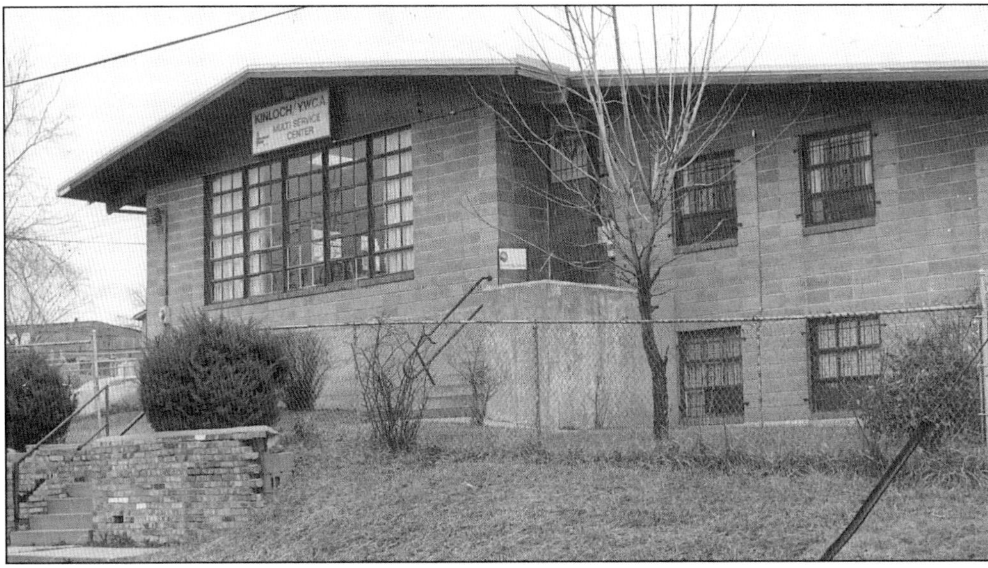

Through the determination and hard work of the women of Kinloch and assistance from the Metropolitan YWCA board, funds were raised to erect this building free of debt on January 18, 1953. The YWCA program started in 1947, when two Kinloch residents, Alice Scales and Geneva Cothran, began holding meetings in their homes. The group soon grew to 50 women and was called the "Home Group." (Photo Courtesy of the 1983 Kinloch History Committee.)

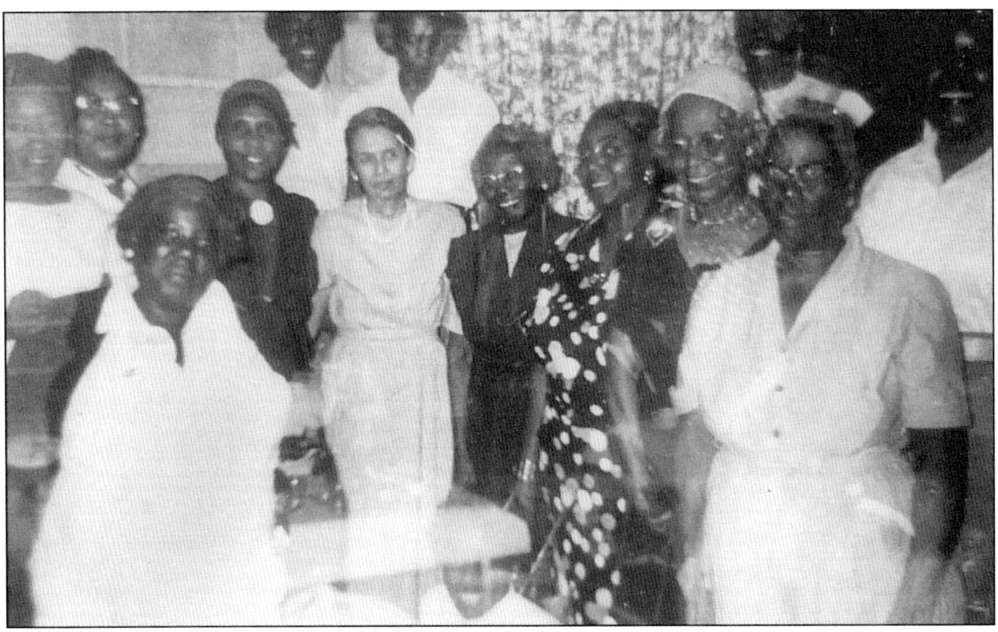

Shown here are some of the members of the Home Group who were responsible for the YWCA program being brought to Kinloch. The first elected officers were: Chairman Alice Scales, Vice Chairman Geneva Cothran, Secretary Federica Young, Assistant Secretary Larinda Grayson, Recording Secretary Imogene Dulaney, and Treasurer Rosena English. (Photo Courtesy of the 1983 Kinloch History Committee.)

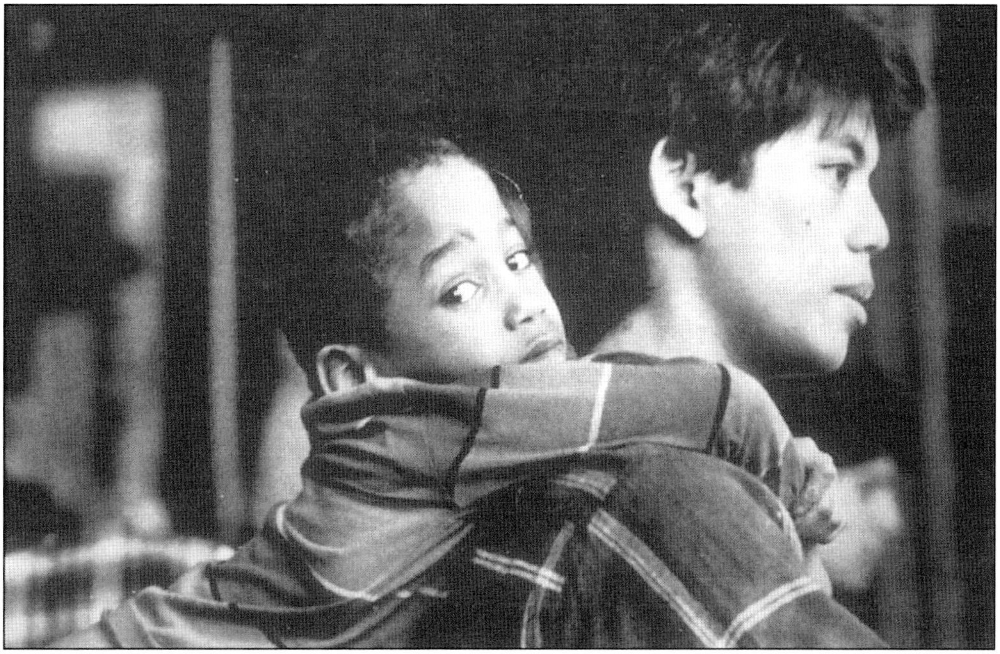

One of the successful ventures sponsored by the YWCA was its tutoring program with Washington University students. Pictured here is Sam Ramiriz, a student and Campus Y member who is taking time out from tutoring to have some fun with a student. (Photo Courtesy of the YWCA of Metropolitan St. Louis.)

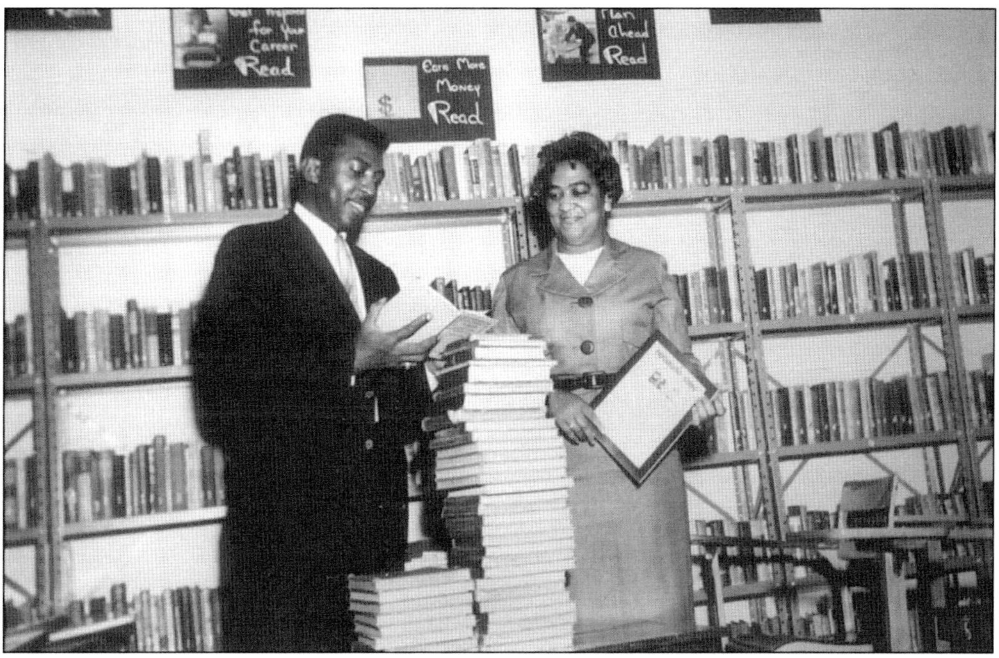

William Terrill, principal of John F. Kennedy Junior High School, and YWCA "Operation Challenge" Chairman Margarite Clay are pictured here reviewing some of the books purchased through the sales of surplus books. (Photo Courtesy of Margarite Clay.)

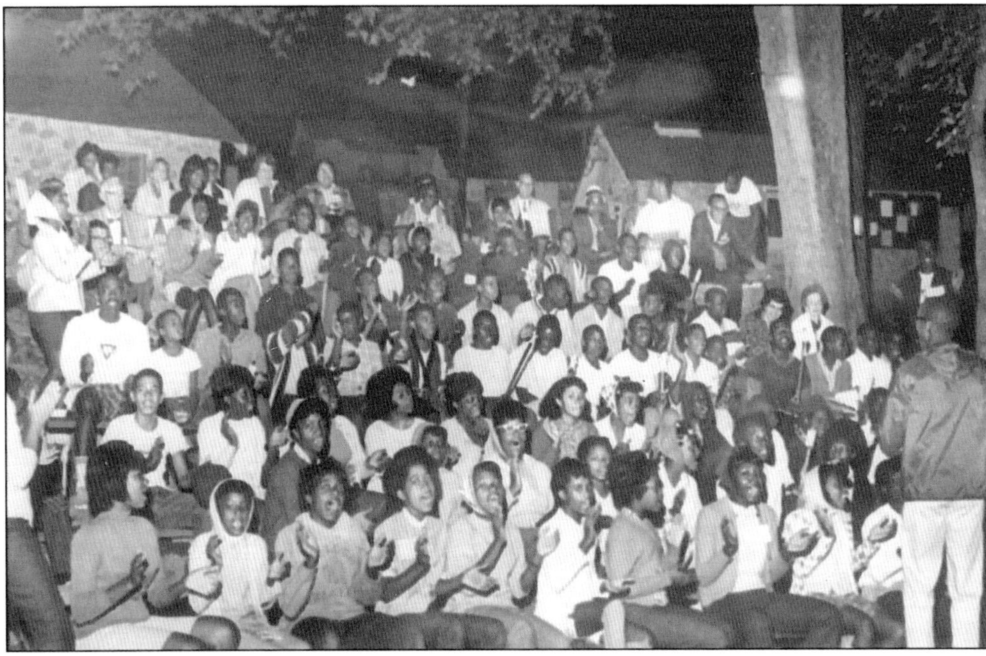

The YMCA came to the community in the 1940s and provided a variety of activities for community youth. Many young people participated in the YMCA's annual "Y Circus." The boys and girls in this picture are enjoying an old-fashioned singing session around a campfire during a summer outing. (Photo Courtesy of John A. Wright.)

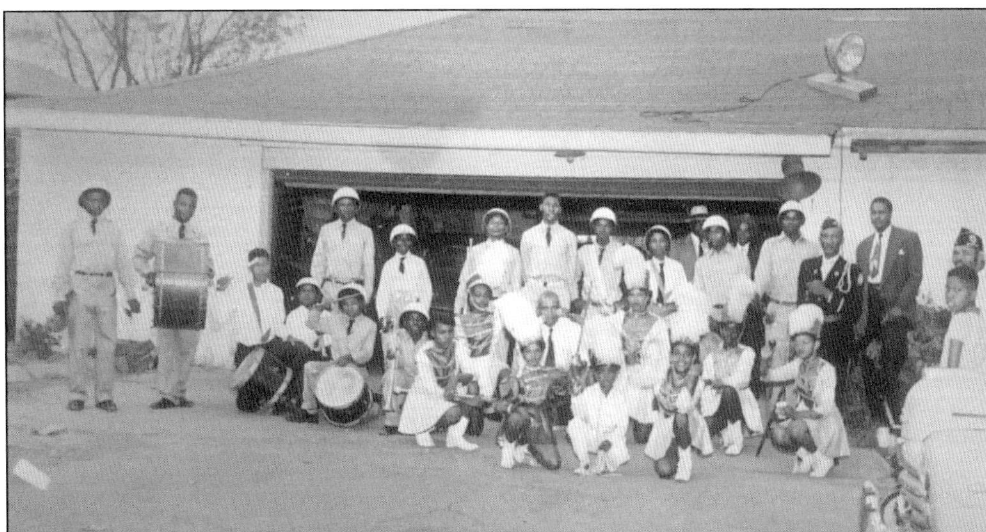

These boys and girls pictured here are part of a Drum and Bugle Corp organized by Victor Burton. Burton, on the far right dressed in the dark uniform, organized the corp in the 1940s. He is remembered by many as an energetic, civic-minded individual who devoted much of his time to service organizations and public affairs. Burton is given credit for starting the boy scout program in Kinloch. In 1961, he received the Silver Beaver Award, the highest award given to citizens. (Photo Courtesy of Ann Boyd.)

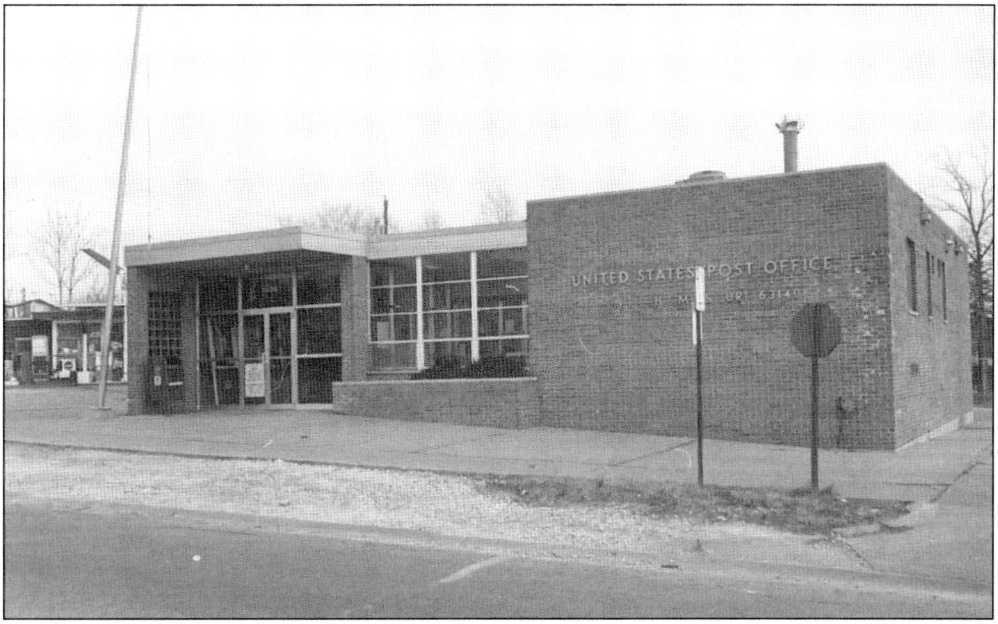

Kinloch postal services began at the train station next to the Wabash RR tracks, then to mailboxes on scattered sites along the road. Seeing a need for a more serviceable site, Vitula Author opened a station at her home. She then served as the community's first postmistress. This postal branch, located on Martin Luther King and Scott Avenues, operated under the Berkeley Post Office. (Photo by John A. Wright.)

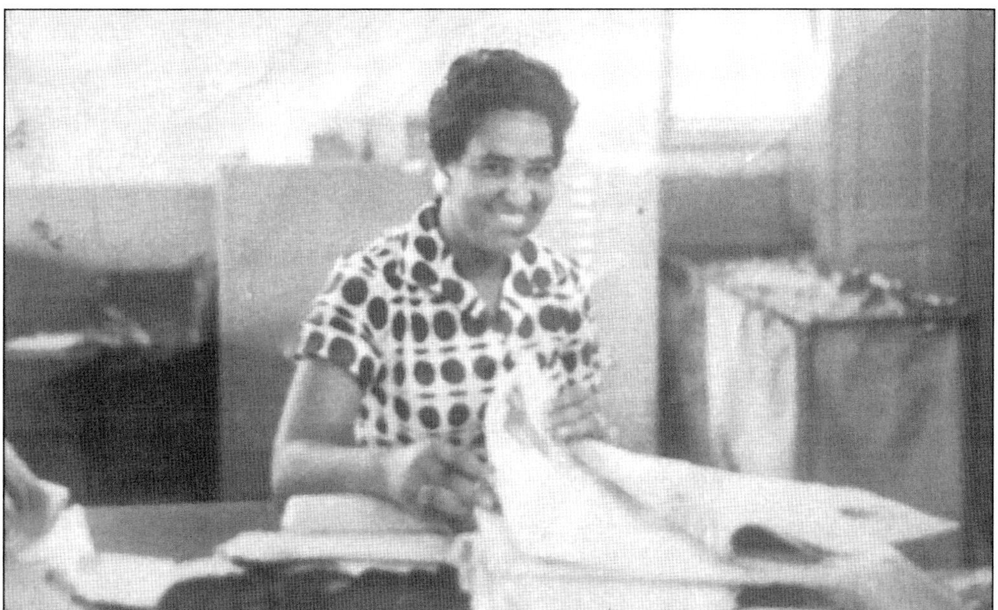

Margarite Clay is shown here working at her desk in the Kinloch Post Office. She served as postmistress from 1962 until her retirement in 1980. She followed her husband, Edward Clay, the first postmaster under civil service, who served from 1948–59. (Photo Courtesy of Margarite Clay.)

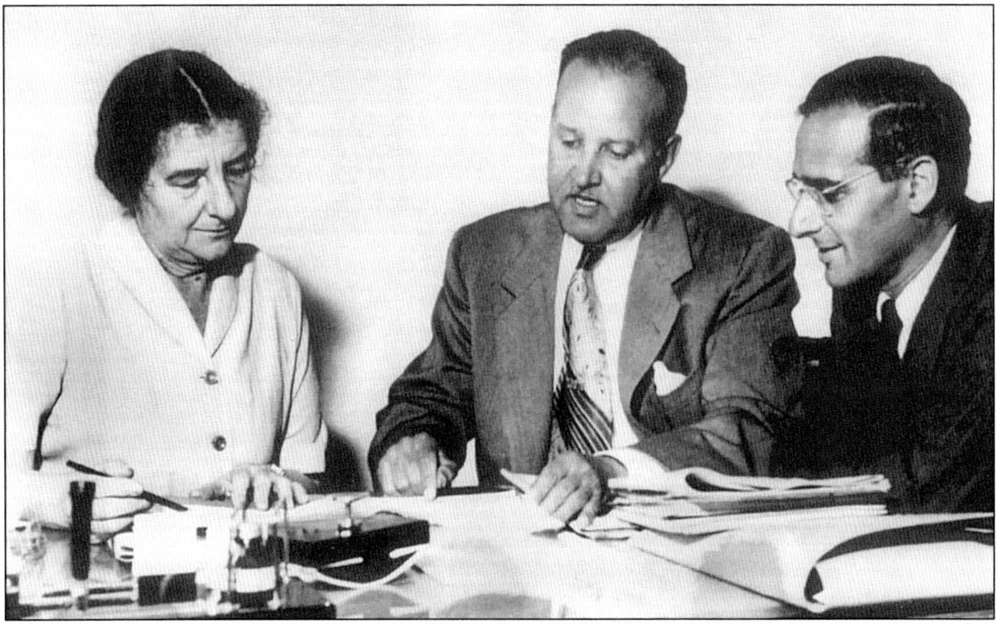

Kinloch residents can be found in every walk of life and have made contributions that have impacted the local, national, and international community. Shown here is John G. Turner from Stanza Street with Golda Meir. Turner was sent to Israel by the United Nations to provide technical training to labor relations officers in 1951. It is reported that Turner was recruited by Branch Rickey as a young man to play baseball. However, his mother would not let him accept the offer, because he would have had to play as a white player. (Photo Courtesy of Edmond and Dorothy Squires.)

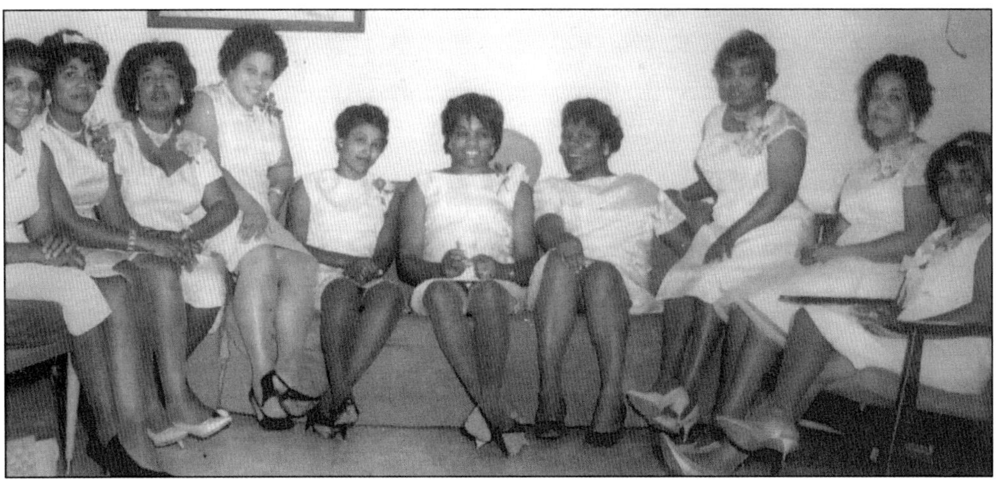

Early Kinloch residents seem to remain friends and stay in contact, no matter where they find themselves. These members of the Wild Rose Social Club, formed in May 1961, have remained friends through the years. In the early years they involved themselves in civic and humanitarian endeavors. Members from left are: Jean Gillard, Maize McNoltie, Louise Robinson, Bernice Robinson, Mary Hold, Zelma Pegus, Mary Lane, Mildred Williams, Alice Shelby, and Dorothy Lewis. (Photo Courtesy of Dorothy Lewis.)

POSTSCRIPT

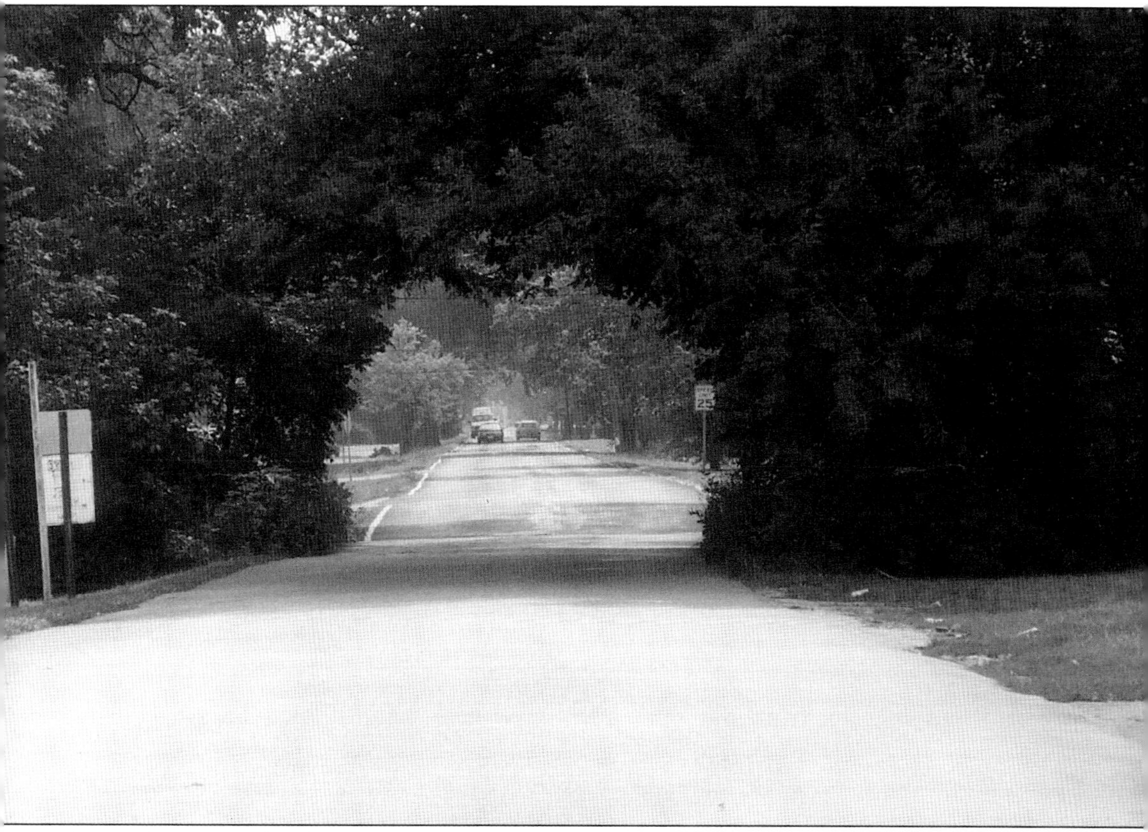

Shown here is Suburban Avenue. The chains that once blocked access to this road leading into Ferguson from Kinloch have long since been removed, and so have many other barriers which created Kinloch. Many Kinlochians now realize that the access many of them wanted came at a cost, including the loss of a community and institutions. One Kinloch administrator stated it best, "We got what we wanted but we lost what we had." (Photo by John A. Wright)

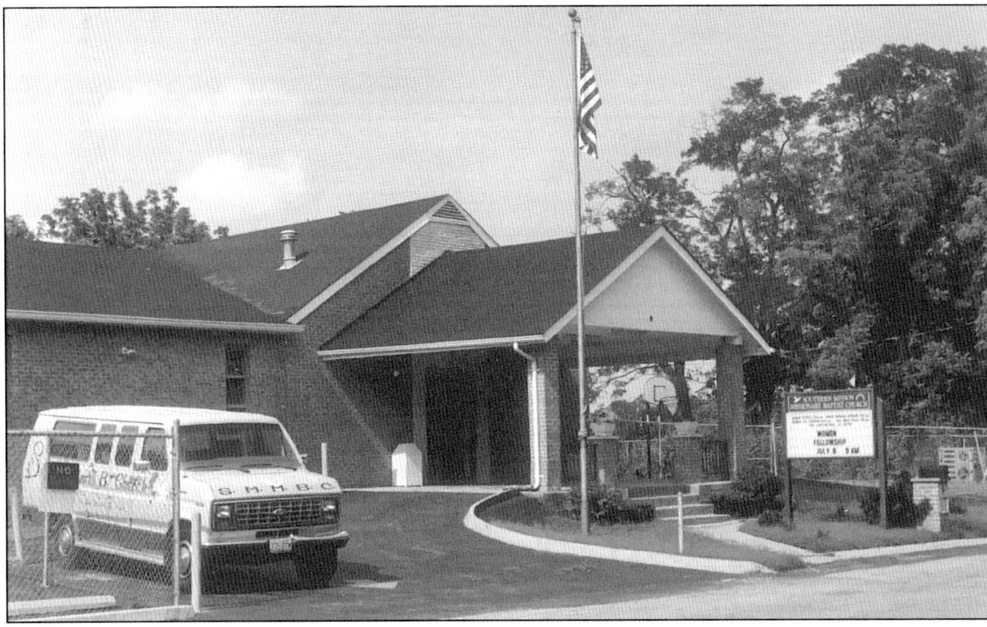

The recently-established Southern Missionary Baptist Church, pictured here, plans to remain in Kinloch along with a few other churches. In the early history of the community, it was the churches that provided leadership and stability which was so essential for the survival of the community. Today, that leadership is still vital and may mean the difference between the community's demise and survival, although on a limited scale. If it is true what a minister once said when asked about looking to God for help: "God may not come when you want him but he is always on time," then we will have to wait and see what the future holds for Kinloch. (Photo by John A. Wright)

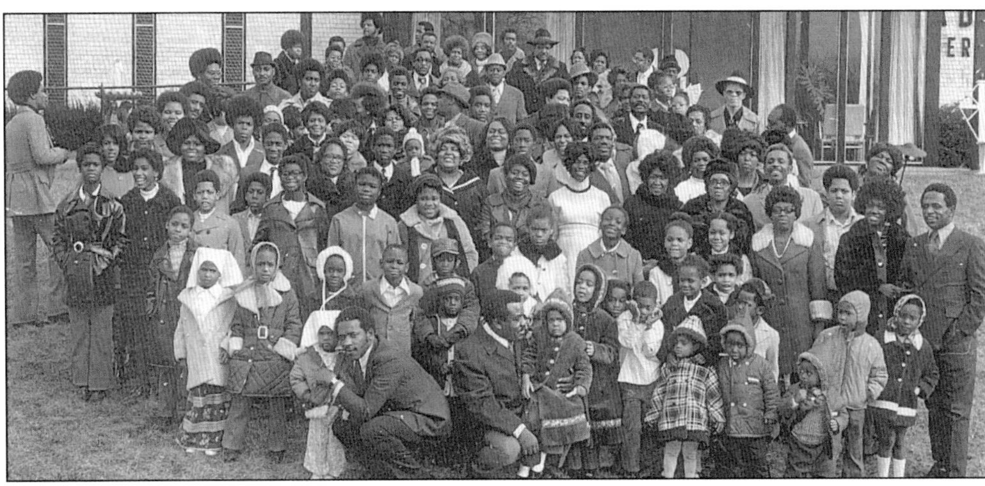

Although most Kinlochians have moved away to other communities, many gather every year to celebrate family, community, and a place in time where there was hope and an opportunity to dare to dream of unlimited possibilities. Pictured here are some of the descendants of Fred and Sally Davis, early Kinloch residents, gathered during a reunion in front of Wade's Funeral Home on Martin Luther King Boulevard in the 1960s. (Photo Courtesy of Lesie Oliver)